FASHION SHOW

SHOW

PARIS STYLE

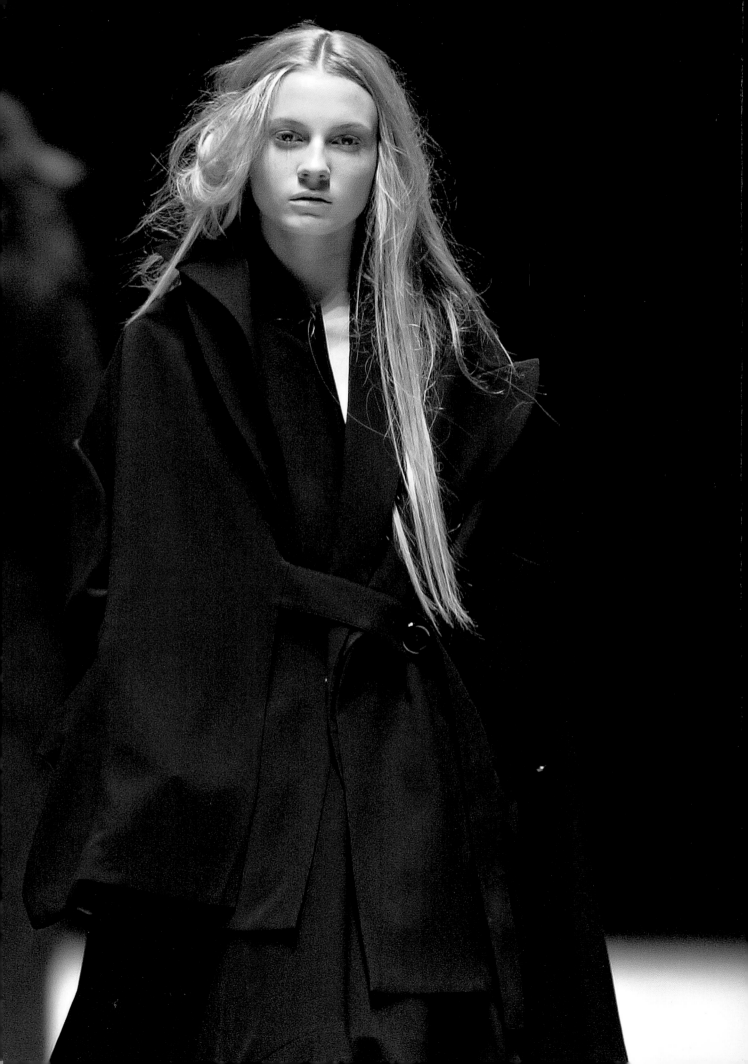

Essays by Pamela A. Parmal and Didier Grumbach   Profiles by Susan Ward and Lauren D. Whitley

FASHION SHOW

PARIS STYLE

 MFA PUBLICATIONS   *a division of the Museum of Fine Arts, Boston*

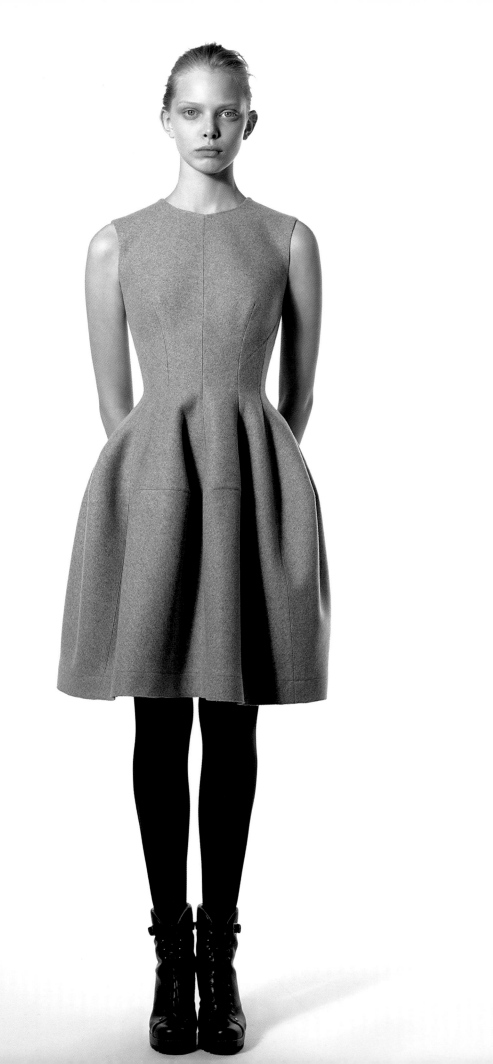

Contents

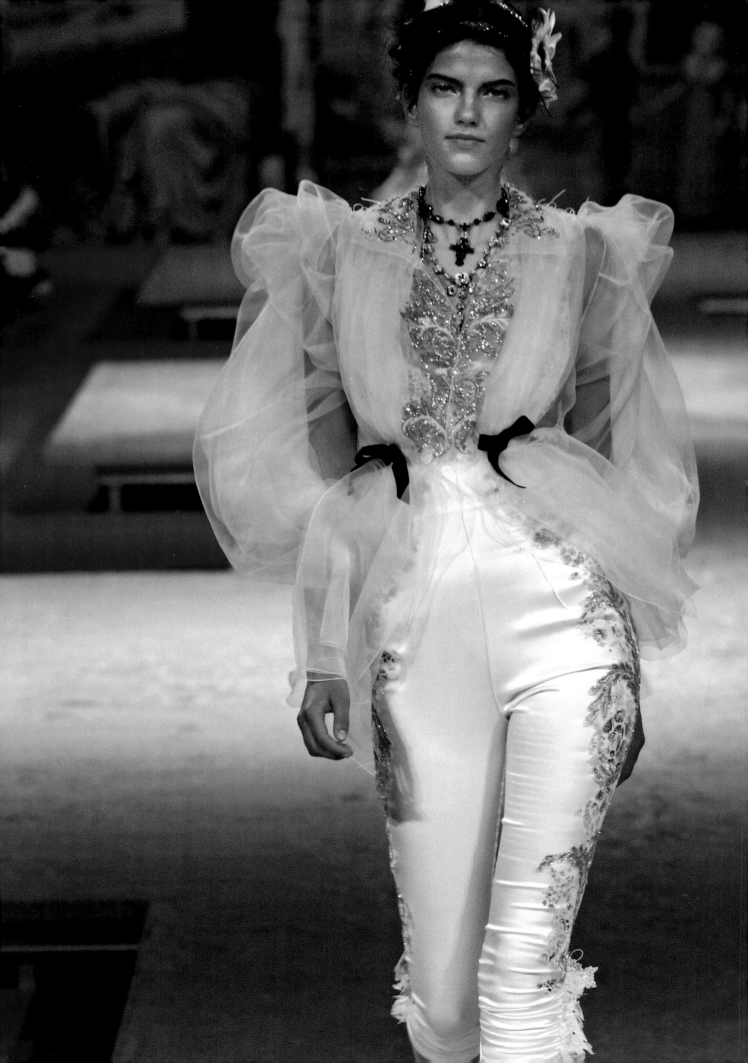

Director's Foreword

MALCOLM ROGERS

Ann and Graham Gund Director
Museum of Fine Arts, Boston

There are many definitions of art. The Museum of Fine Arts, Boston, has always adopted a broad definition and, from its earliest history, has collected textiles, costume, musical instruments, and the decorative arts, in addition to those media more traditionally accepted as fine art. In doing so, it recognizes the contributions made to our cultural heritage by those designers and craftsmen whose work enriches our lives on a daily basis.

As the boundaries between the arts blur — with contemporary painters and conceptual artists borrowing themes from fashion, and fashion designers trained in art schools creating collections that intersect with social commentary, resemble performance-art pieces more than fashion shows, or in other ways break with tradition — the time is ripe for an assessment of contemporary fashion. Has the rarified clothing sent down the runways evolved beyond simple garments to clothe the body and developed into a purer art form? Or are the extravagant runway shows of the late twentieth and early twenty-first centuries merely savvy marketing tools? *Fashion Show* profiles ten of the most talented and creative designers showing in Paris today and looks at the city's long history as the center of the fashion world. It discusses the many ideas and issues that have shaped contemporary fashion and examines why, in a modern, globalized economy, Paris has remained its focal point.

Neither the exhibition nor the publication would have been possible without the exceptional generosity of the ten participating houses: Azzedine Alaïa, Hussein Chalayan, Chanel Haute Couture, Dior Haute Couture, Christian Lacroix Haute Couture, Maison Martin Margiela, Rochas, Valentino Haute Couture, Viktor & Rolf, and Yohji Yamamoto. We are profoundly grateful to them for their collaboration and for lending us the works featured in the exhibition, which we are honored to bring to Boston and to the MFA.

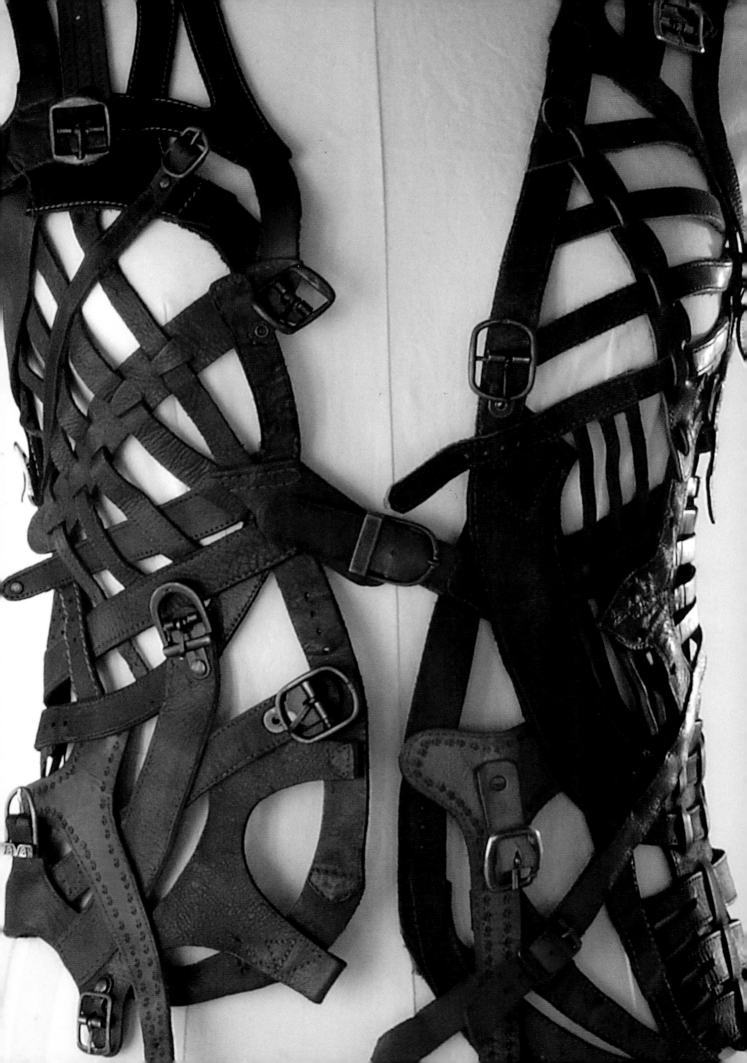

Introduction

PAMELA A. PARMAL

*David and Roberta Logie Curator
of Textile and Fashion Arts*

Fashion is a business, but a business fueled by creativity. In recent years, executives in the fashion industry have placed the cultivation of creativity at the center of their business plans. The revival in the 1990s of the Givenchy and Christian Dior labels by Bernard Arnault, chairman of LVMH Moët Hennessey Louis Vuitton, along with the continued success of Karl Lagerfeld at Chanel, have shown what a strong creative identity can do for a house's sales. This increased appreciation for imagination and talent has brought to Paris some of the most challenging and creative designs to hit the runway in years.

While some designers continue to follow the tradition of haute couture and focus their attention on making beautifully crafted, wearable clothes, others push its boundaries in order to reevaluate long-held traditions of how clothing is made and worn. Still other designers treat fashion as social commentary, using the runway as a tool of artistic expression to explore world events, environmental issues, or the status of women. The breadth of designers working today and the varied approaches they take to their craft make the late twentieth and early twenty-first centuries an especially exciting period in the history of fashion.

Fashion Show: Paris Style is an exploration of contemporary fashion in Paris — both its aesthetic diversity and the intellectual approaches taken by today's designers — as well as a look at why Paris has remained the center of such creativity for more than three hundred years. It features ten of the most creative and talented designers showing in Paris today: Azzedine Alaïa, Hussein Chalayan, Karl Lagerfeld for Chanel, John Galliano for Christian Dior, Christian Lacroix, Martin Margiela, Olivier

Theyskens for Rochas, Valentino, Viktor & Rolf, and Yohji Yamamoto. They hail from Germany, France, Italy, the United Kingdom, Belgium, the Netherlands, Japan, Cyprus, Gibraltar, and Tunisia, and their work is as varied as their backgrounds.

These designers provide an overview of the diversity, talent, and creativity that marks contemporary Paris fashion. John Galliano and Hussein Chalayan graduated from Central Saint Martin's College of Art and Design (known as St. Martin's School of Art until 1989) in London, where, according to the college, "the students are encouraged to challenge the prevailing ethic" and "push the boundaries." They, along with Viktor & Rolf and Martin Margiela (graduates of similar programs in Arnhem and Antwerp), bring to their work a concept-oriented approach, and their shows often function as social commentary or a wry look at their own profession. Galliano and Christian Lacroix give their creative energies free reign, bringing to their designs a melding of cultures and history, while Yohji Yamamoto and Azzedine Alaïa are consummate artisans who redefine both traditional methods of construction and assumptions of how clothing should be worn. While many of these designers challenge our concepts of what clothing can and should be, Valentino, Karl Lagerfeld, Christian Lacroix, and now Olivier Theyskens glory in the haute couture traditions of the past and make skillfully cut and crafted designs that are well suited to their discriminating clientele.

What unites the designers represented here is that they all show in Paris, and this book aims to take a close look at the history of why Paris has been, and remains, such an important place in the fashion world. That history began in the seventeenth century, when Louis XIV's finance minister Jean-Baptiste Colbert identified fashion and the luxury trades as key elements in the French economy. Colbert made Versailles the center of the fashionable world and Paris the place to acquire the latest luxury apparel and furnishings. Succeeding French governments have continued to support the industry, and apparel goods have been among the leading French exports throughout the eighteenth, nineteenth, and twentieth centuries. Both the Chambre Syndicale de la Couture, first established in 1868, and the Comité Colbert, established in 1954, consider it their mission to promote French luxury fashions to the global marketplace.

Paris's history as the center of the luxury trades is key to understanding the city's enduring importance. That history continues to resonate with today's designers, as can be seen in the 2006 collections. Galliano's Spring–Summer 2006 couture collection for Dior is full of references to the eighteenth century, with corsets, evocations of Marie

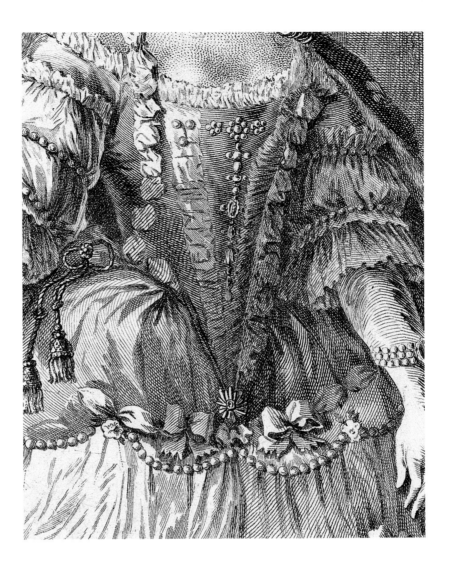

Antoinette, and designs recalling the terror of the French Revolution. Lacroix, for his part, has always incorporated eighteenth-century and other historical references into his work. Others, such as Viktor & Rolf and Lagerfeld, look back only a few years, to the 1950s and 1960s. Lagerfeld's 2006 designs pay homage to Chanel's history and to many of the most important designers of the 1960s, while Viktor & Rolf's meticulous collection brings to mind the perfectly groomed woman of the 1950s trapped behind the "feminine mystique."

Like the work of today's designers, this book is concerned with both the present and the past. It attempts to provide a historic context within which to appreciate Paris's role in the history of fashion and its ability to sustain that role over the centuries. Its second half is devoted to the work of the ten fashion houses participating in the exhibition it accompanies. These influential designers' presence on the Paris runways is proof of the city's continued role as the center of fashion.

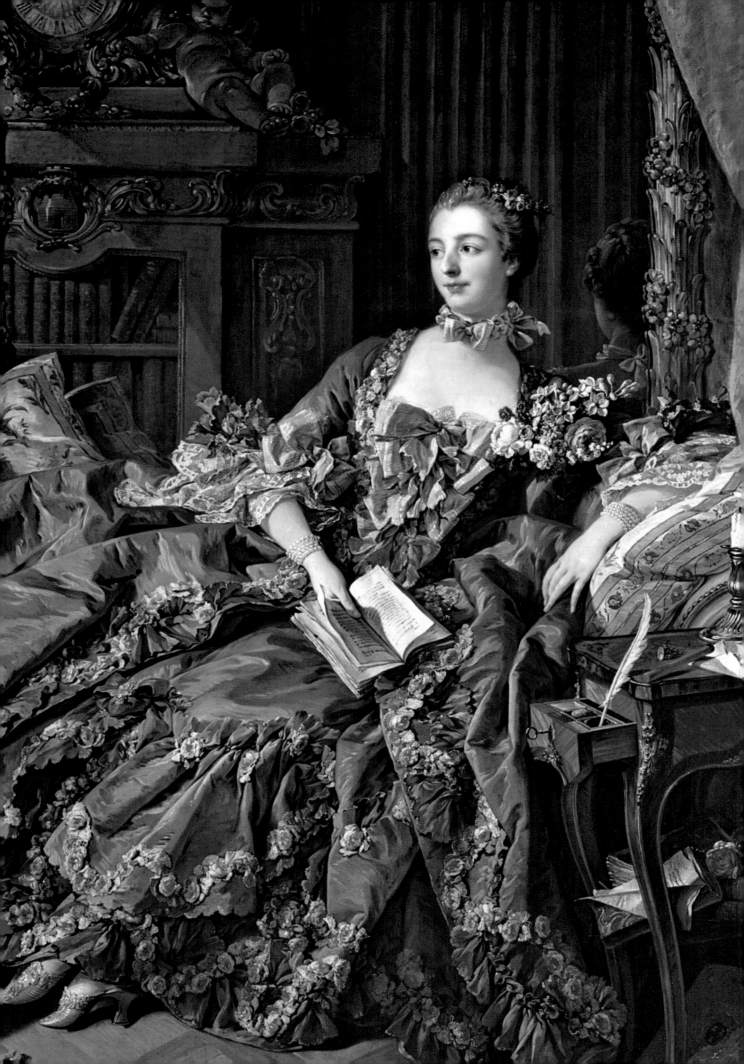

La Mode: Paris and the Development of the French Fashion Industry

PAMELA A. PARMAL

"To be in Paris without seeing fashion is to have one's eyes closed."

— MARQUIS DE CARACCIOLI, *Voyage de la Raison*, 1772

Paris has been the capital of the fashionable world since the seventeenth century, when Louis XIV endeavored to create a luxury economy within France, with the city as its epicenter. Right from the start, fashion was a key motivator of this economy. The king (who reigned from 1643 to 1715) focused much of his attention on launching new modes of dress — choosing novel textile patterns, developing increasingly complex ribbon trims, and deciding on the most flattering placement of a feather in his hat. The constant evolution in style established his court's dominance in the sartorial realm and fueled the luxury economy by propelling others to reject perfectly usable goods in favor of the latest fashions worn at Versailles.

During the eighteenth century, new methods of production, marketing, and delivery made fashionable goods more widely available. Visitors to Paris found luxury stores, talented craftspeople, and an effective distribution system that met any desire and instilled many more. The basic elements of the Paris fashion economy had been established, and they flourished. As wealth spread throughout the social classes in the nineteenth and twentieth centuries, the fashion system evolved to meet new demands. Ready-to-wear and the couture took on the form we know today, and department stores, the fashion press, and an important export economy made apparel one of the leading industries in France. This essay explores the rich history of the fashion industry in Paris and investigates why the city has remained the focus of fashion to this day.

The Establishment of Paris as the Center of Fashion

Louis XIV and his finance minister from 1661 to 1683, Jean-Baptiste Colbert, deliberately set out to make Versailles the most fashionable court in Europe and Paris the center of the European luxury goods trade. Colbert's economic policies, generally categorized as mercantilism, emphasized the expansion of commerce and supported the establishment of luxury boutiques in the city — more than two hundred of which were already located on the Isle de la Cité near the Palais de Justice.[1] For the latest in fashion, Paris became the place to go. Nowhere could one find a higher concentration of luxurious and fashionable silks, fine wools, fans, laces, and ribbons, as well as furniture, porcelain, and metalwork.

Colbert's plan also called for developing the manufacture of luxury goods within the country, so that he could furnish the city's shops with French-made wares. One of the most important aspects of mercantilism was the retention of wealth by the state. Thus Colbert discouraged the importation of foreign manufactured goods and encouraged the exportation of French ones.[2] He believed the luxury market could be a vital sector of the French economy, and he was right: high fashion would be one of France's leading exports until the stock-market crash of 1929.

Because Colbert placed great value on retaining gold and silver bullion, he devoted much attention to establishing the production of luxury fabrics, especially cloth and lace made of gold and gilt-silver thread. The finance minister despaired of the large sums of money spent by the court on cloth of gold and silver from Genoa, needle laces from Venice and Flanders, fine wool from England, and leatherwork from Spain and Russia. Colbert took several steps to ensure that high-quality goods would be readily available in France. He improved existing textile- and fashion-related manufactures, as well as establishing new ones. And he regulated the guilds that controlled the manufacture and sale of goods to ensure their quality and to guarantee that merchants did not take advantage of their customers.

In his efforts to make the luxury goods industry thrive, Colbert had a very willing partner in Louis XIV. The king's attire was one of the most important and visually spectacular methods by which he expressed his power and that of France. His clothing habits followed a Christian moral tradition in which one's nature and place in society were expressed through dress; luxurious, expensive, and ostentatious clothing was reserved for those of appropriate rank.[3] At the top of the French social hierarchy, Louis dressed for effect. Textiles

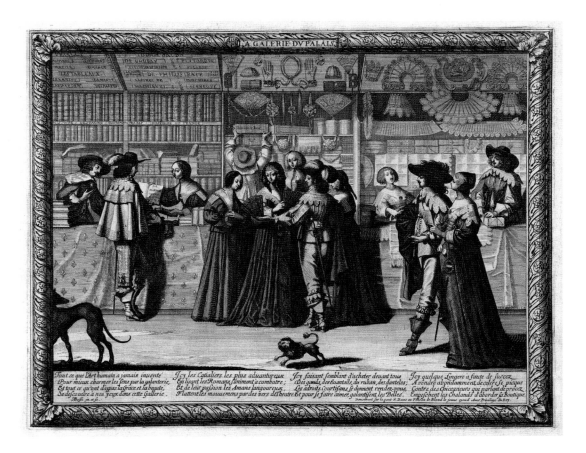

The shopping galleries near the Palais de Justice offered Parisians and visitors to the city the latest in luxury goods during the seventeenth century.

patterned with gold and silver threads, laces, ribbons, and elaborately embroidered cloth studded with diamonds created a luxurious and lavish symbol of the wealth, prosperity, and power of the Sun King.

Sebastiano Locatelli, an Italian abbot who visited Paris during the 1660s, witnessed Louis XIV as he reviewed his army at Saint Denis on April 6, 1665. Locatelli's description of the royal dress presents a picture of the Sun King shining brightly on the field of honor. He wrote that the king set himself apart from the dukes who accompanied him by wearing a brilliant red, or flame-colored, hat — one of Louis XIV's favorite colors, as it represented the flames of the sun. The king also wore a coat of blue wool densely embroidered with gold and silver threads that was left unbuttoned to reveal a cloth-of-gold vest, embellished with diamonds and fastened with large gold galloons (bands of trimming made of metallic thread). Around his neck, Louis wore a cravat of Venetian lace, and around his waist, a sash wrapped in the antique manner and fastened with two gold lilies, each with a diamond sparkling at the top. He wore woolen knee britches tied with flame-colored garters embroidered with gold thread, and stockings of tobacco color that matched his shoes made of English calfskin. He

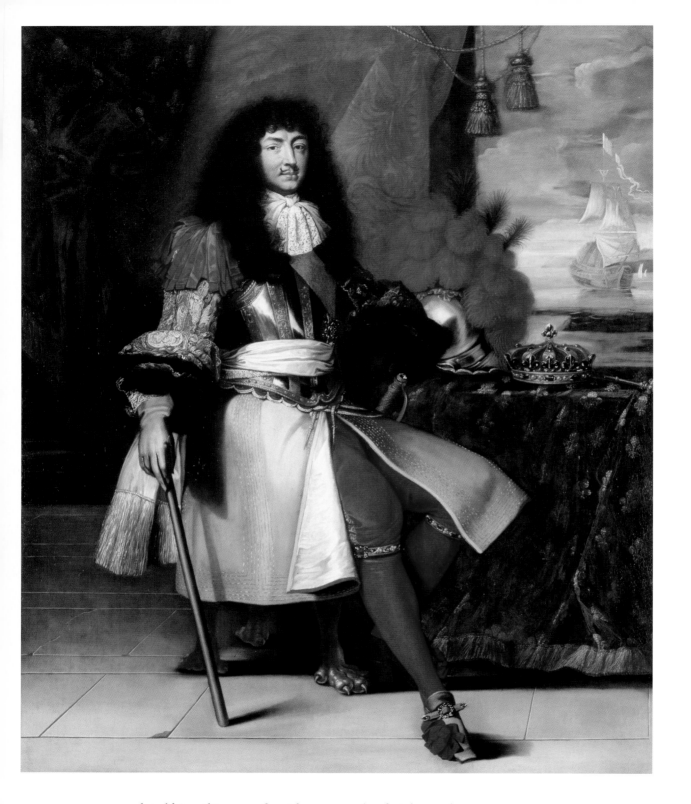

completed his military outfit with spurs made of violet steel, enameled and fastened with gold buckles encrusted with diamonds.[4]

Members of the court paid close attention to Louis's sartorial extravagances. Courtiers were expected to follow his lead, and they spent large sums of money doing so. The proper dress could provide access to the king for those who might not otherwise have it. In his 1636 etiquette manual, Nicolas Faret had stated that clothing was one of the most useful expenditures made at court. He explained that knowledge and exploitation of the correct attire could open doors that were often closed even to those of high rank and virtue.[5] Access to Louis was important, for the king dispensed royal sinecures — jobs that paid well for little work, a valuable source of income for many courtiers.

The importance of dressing fashionably at Versailles created a great demand for luxury textiles, ribbons, and lace not only among the French aristocracy and members of other European courts but among the increasingly wealthy members of France's growing merchant class. Word of mouth and correspondence quickly spread knowledge of the latest court fashions to Paris and farther afield. Other methods of dissemination also existed. In the early fifteenth century, Isabeau de Bavière, wife of Charles VI, had instructed the court embroiderer to create a doll's wardrobe in the latest French style to send to her sister, Isabelle, the queen of England. Similarly, in the sixteenth century Henri IV had sent fashionably dressed dolls to his fiancé, Marie de Medici, before she arrived in France.[6] The use of dolls, or *poupées de mode*, became common during the seventeenth century, and by the eighteenth, they were dispatched to fashionable dressmakers in the provinces. They not only showed off the most fashionable fabrics and trims but also offered a model for the dressmaker or tailor to follow in constructing the garments. The dolls were used until the nineteenth century, when fashion plates and paper patterns took their place.

While dolls represented an established means of transmitting fashion, newer, and eventually more important, methods of dissemination developed during Louis XIV's reign. These included the production of fashion plates and the introduction of fashion journalism. In 1672, Jean Donneau de Visé launched *Le Mercure Galant*, which ran from 1672 to 1674. The journal covered the current court styles, along with the latest news and fashionable songs. It was revived in 1677 as *Le Nouveau Mercure Galant*, and again in 1678 under its original title. At that time, a royal privilege protected the name and the illustrations, and the journal became a propaganda tool for the French court. Colbert made good use of it to spread French fashions outside the court and to create a demand for his country's new manufactures.

Donneau de Visé wrote in the January 1678 *Extraordinaire*, a special quarterly edition of *Le Mercure Galant*, that he would report on the latest fashions for the benefit of the provincial nobility and those in foreign courts, so they could remain knowledgeable of the latest trends.[7] This edition included a set of illustrations engraved by Jean Lepautre after designs by Jean Berain. Both artists already worked for the court. Berain served as a court designer and

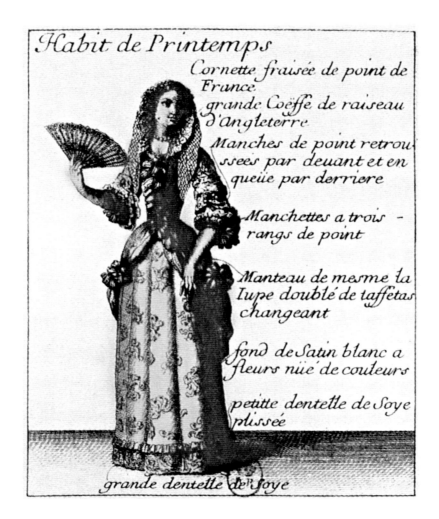

Le Mercure Galant, the first journal to cover fashion in the French court, illustrated this plate and described the textiles and trims in great detail, even indicating where they could be bought in Paris.

developed costumes for theatrical performances and masques, as well as ornamental designs for furniture, gardens, and the boats that floated in the canals of Versailles; Lepautre, one of the most successful etchers of the period, also created decorative designs for the court. Among the *Mercure Galant* illustrations were three plates of women and two of men in fashionable dress. The sixth plate included an aristocratic couple inside a fashionable Paris shop, probably that of a merchant mercer who supplied the most stylish fabrics and trims.

In the text that accompanied the plates, de Visé detailed the textiles and trims used to make the garments. For instance, he described the woman's costume in the plate reproduced here, especially the lace, at great length. He related how the most fashionable lace was densely patterned with flowerettes with raised centers, and how small stems and flowerettes were attached to the larger flowers in place of the usual bars. His thorough, technical description of the fabric reflects lace's importance; members of the court spent huge sums of money on the fashionable trim and valued it highly as a luxurious accessory. In fact, lace was the first item in de Visé's list of the top thirteen pieces of women's fashionable dress. The other articles he enumerated included petticoats and aprons of white satin trimmed with a wide range of lace styles, and gloves adorned with ribbons. These textiles, trims, and accessories were all sold by mercers, and their inclusion in the list acknowledges the significance of these wares to fashionable dress.

De Visé also provided information on where the fabrics could be acquired in Paris. At the end of his essay, he recommended several Paris merchants whose relationships with members of the court would ensure that readers found the latest fashions at their shops. For the most up-to-date ribbons, for instance, he recommended le Sieur le Gras at the Palais, who, as the furnisher of the king's ribbons, always had the most beautiful and fashionable examples.[8] Although *Le Mercure Galant*'s in-depth fashion coverage was short-lived, the journal was significant as the first serial publication to cover changing fashions and to exploit them to encourage readers to frequent the mercers, tailors, and hairdressers it advertised.

Developing the Luxury Trades

Because the primary focus of fashion was on textiles, Colbert lavished particular attention on the development of a strong textile industry in France. Tapestry weaving was one of his focuses, and the Gobelins tapestry manufactory in Paris came under the direction of Charles LeBrun, Louis XIV's court artist. Under LeBrun's guidance and Colbert's financial support, the factory diversified and became the source for the furniture and decorative arts that so magnificently furnished Versailles, Fontainebleau, and the rest of the king's palaces. The Gobelins was named the Royal Manufactory of the Crown's Furnishings in 1664, employing painters, sculptors, goldsmiths, cabinetmakers, embroiderers, and tapestry weavers, as well as the engraver Jean Lepautre and the designer Jean Berain. With LeBrun's direction, all of these artists used their talents to glorify the king and France and to create the most envied court in Europe.

Colbert realized that in addition to supporting the manufacture of luxury goods, he needed to establish procedures for maintaining the quality of the wares produced and ensuring that they were sold honestly to the public. To accomplish this, he addressed the guild structure. Guilds had been organized in France as early as the eighth century to associate individuals of the same community or profession for mutual support, protection, and economic advantage.

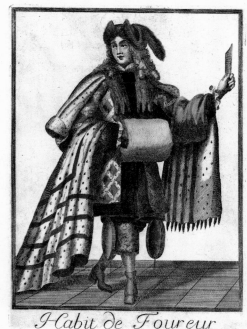

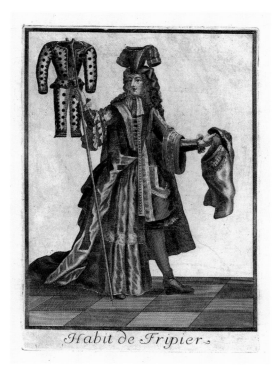

Habit de Foureur

Habit de Fripier

Merchant guilds developed by the tenth century, and craft guilds developed by the twelfth. The craft guilds, in particular, concerned themselves with training new members of the profession and regulating the quality of their products; the three levels of membership were apprentice, journeyman, and master. In 1673, Colbert issued the *Code du Commerce*, which set rules of conduct for guild members. Colbert also incorporated all unincorporated trades, believing that without the supervision and quality control provided by the guild officers, he could not ensure that his standards were met.

The corporations associated with the clothing trades made up the largest group of guilds in Paris. At this time, all clothing was custom-made, except for a few ready-made garments such as work clothes and unfitted men's and women's leisure garments. Those who could not afford custom-made clothes bought their clothing secondhand. Savary de Bruslon's *Dictionnaire Universel de Commerce* of 1726 lists 126 guilds associated with dress, comprising three categories: the manufacturers who provided the raw materials, the merchants who sold them, and the craftsmen and women who actually produced the garments and accessories. The trades involved with creating the textiles and trims included the weavers, dyers, finishers, metal-thread makers, ribbon makers, lace makers, passementerie or trim makers, artificial flower makers, furriers, and feather dressers. Various merchants such as mercers, drapers, and linen merchants sold these goods, and

Nicolas de Larmessin II's series *Costumes Grotesques* caricatured the many tradesman of Paris, including the furrier, the secondhand-clothing seller, the tailor, and the stocking merchant.

PAMELA A. PARMAL

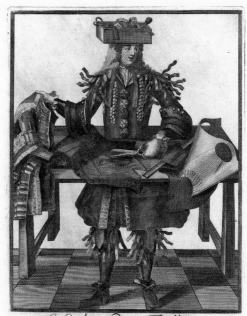

Habit de Tailleur

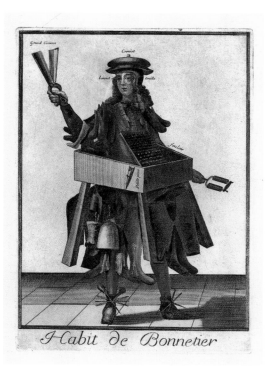

Habit de Bonnetier

their shops provided an intersection between the manufacturers,
the customers, and those who produced the finished garments.
A customer might visit several merchants to select fabrics and
trims, and then would take the materials to a craftsperson to have
them made into clothing. Tailors, dressmakers, linen makers, and
others such as glove makers, hat makers, fan makers, jewelers,
and embroiderers turned the materials into fashionable attire.

In developing the manufacture of the raw materials, Colbert
concentrated not only on luxury textiles such as silk and cloth of
gold but also on fabrics at various price points. He established
weaving manufactures of fine wool stuffs, which had primarily been imported from England, Holland, and Spain, and also
supported the manufacture of cheaper grades of wool for those
of less means and for export outside of France. Colbert brought
weavers from Italy, Flanders, and Spain to France and encouraged them to open manufactories, hoping to improve the quality
of French products. He gave the foreign craftsmen and the
towns where the businesses were established government subsi-
dies, relief from taxes, and royal privileges as incentives. In
addition, he lent his support to the creation of a silk-stocking
industry in which silk hose were made on the newly invented
knitting frame and to the formation of lace industries in Alençon,
Aurillac, Quesnoy, Sedan, Loudun, and Arras, where he brought
Venetian and Flemish lace makers to teach the local women.

The merchants who sold the fashion-related goods each specialized in particular wares. In addition to dealing in patterned silks and the more expensive textiles woven with metallic yarns, the mercers retailed many of the fashionable trims used in clothing, as well as jewels and lace. The drapers specialized in wool cloth, while the linen merchants sold linen and cotton fabric and had the right to supply white goods such as bed sheets, tablecloths, towels, and accessories such as caps, aprons, shirts, and chemises. Furriers sold fur garments and accessories, and hosiers sold knit stockings and other wares.

Together with the spice merchants and merchant goldsmiths, the mercers, drapers, furriers, and hosiers were the primary merchant guilds in France during the seventeenth and eighteenth centuries. These guilds were known as the Six Corps and held the highest status among French corporations. They participated in ceremonial and symbolic events, and it was from their ranks that a number of top appointments were made to the city of Paris administration. All six guilds played an important role in the French economy, but it was the merchant mercers who were key in the dissemination of French luxury goods and the latest fashions. They were at the top of the fashion hierarchy.

In addition to the large number of trades associated with the sale of textiles and trims, a substantial industry in secondhand goods also existed for those who could not afford to have their clothing custom-made. Secondhand-clothing dealers called *fripiers* were the most important members of this trade. Most had stationary stores located in Les Halles, the large marketplace in the center of Paris. The *fripiers* also had the right to sell ready-made work clothing sewn from cheap fabric, often putting them at odds with the tailors over the price limit of the fabric with which they could work. Along with the *fripiers*, itinerant street merchants, or *revendeurs*, also sold secondhand clothes. The *revendeurs* would travel from door to door buying and selling their wares. Highest ranking were the *revendeuses à la toilette*, usually women who specialized in selling used fabrics, laces, jewels, and trims they acquired from an upper-class clientele. The *revendeuses* provided ready cash to those in need of funds to pay gambling debts and other expenses. They also had a less savory reputation as a conduit between lovers, delivering messages and arranging assignations.[9]

Like the manufacturers and merchant guilds, the trades that actually made clothing also interested Colbert. In his efforts to improve the French reputation for well-made fashionable clothing, Colbert revised the structure of these trade guilds. In 1655,

During the eighteenth century, the most fashionable boutiques were located just north of the Louvre, around the gallery of the Palais Royale.

Secondhand clothiers and craftsmen involved in the clothing trades were located in Les Halles.

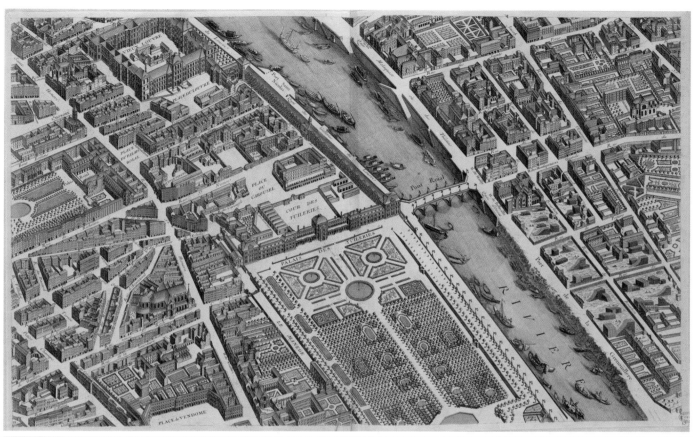

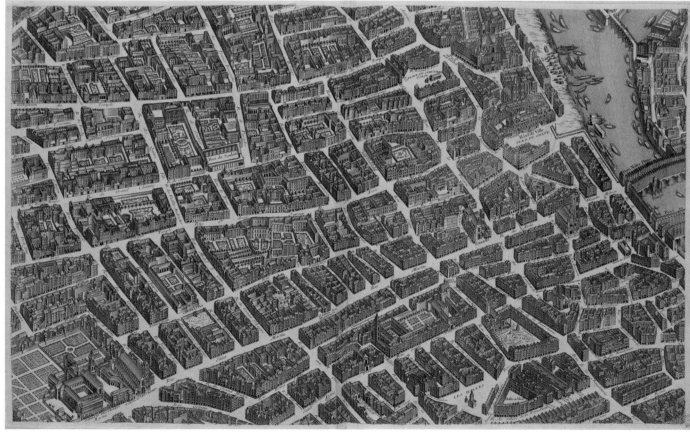

the master merchant tailor's and the doublet maker's guilds merged to create the Master Merchant Tailors and Doublet Makers, who were granted the sole right to make tailored clothes. Twenty years later, Colbert turned his attention to organizing the dressmaker's, or *couturière*'s, guild. For the first time, women were given the right to make clothing for their own sex and for children. Four types of dressmakers were established within the guild structure: those who made women's clothing, called *couturière en habit*; those who made children's clothing, known as *couturière en corps d'enfant*; those who made linen underwear, or *couturière en linge*; and those who specialized in trimming dresses, called *couturière en garniture*. To control the quality of the clothing they fashioned, the guild regulations instituted a three-year apprenticeship for the dressmakers, similar to that of tailors. Although women could finally clothe themselves, the tailor's guild retained the exclusive right to make tailored clothing such as riding habits and whalebone stays or corsets.

Since many of the trades were concentrated in specific neighborhoods in Paris, consumers could easily locate textiles, trims, and accessories and the artisans who turned them into finished garments. Certain areas of the city became associated with particular trades. By the eighteenth century, the mercers' luxurious boutiques could be found around the Palais Royale, on the rue St. Honoré, on the rue St. Denis, and in the neighborhood of St. Eustache. The secondhand-clothing shops were well established in Les Halles, while the furriers could be found on the rue des Fourreurs, the ironworkers on the rue de la Ferronnerie, and the linen sellers on the rue de la Lingerie. In the nearby *quartier de la Bourse*, the artificial flower makers and sellers' shops were located on the rue Vivienne and the rue St. Denis, easily accessible to the general public and to the mercers and fashion merchants who often used their goods to trim finished garments.

The geographic proximity of all these merchants, craftsmen, and materials made Paris the most efficient center for the development of the luxury clothing trades, while the city's proximity to Versailles and the court of Louis XIV made its merchants key players in supplying fashionable dress to the provinces of France, as well as to the courts of Europe. As the Sun King's light dimmed toward the end of his reign and he focused more attention on his inner religious life, the court at Versailles played a less significant role in the dissemination of fashion, and the younger, more fashionable members of the court spent more time in Paris. When the king finally passed away in 1715, his nephew Philippe, Duke of Orleans, acted as regent for the young King Louis XV. Philippe earned the reputation of a profligate rake who nevertheless had a sensitivity to the arts and the finer things in life. He detested the life at Versailles, preferring the more intimate, relaxed lifestyle he found away from the court, in Paris.

Fashion in Eighteenth-Century Paris

The more intimate lifestyle that characterized the court of the regent coincided with a general relaxation in dress, especially that of women. While men continued to wear the three-piece suit composed of jacket, waistcoat, and breeches, during the latter part of the seventeenth century a style of dress worn indoors, in private, by both men and women had become increasingly popular for women *outside* the boudoir. Known as a *robe de chambre* — or in England, a nightgown — it was a loosely fitted overgarment that

The woman depicted in this fashion plate wears a fashionable outer garment known as a *robe de chambre*. Its simple shape made the fabric out of which it was made the most important fashion statement.

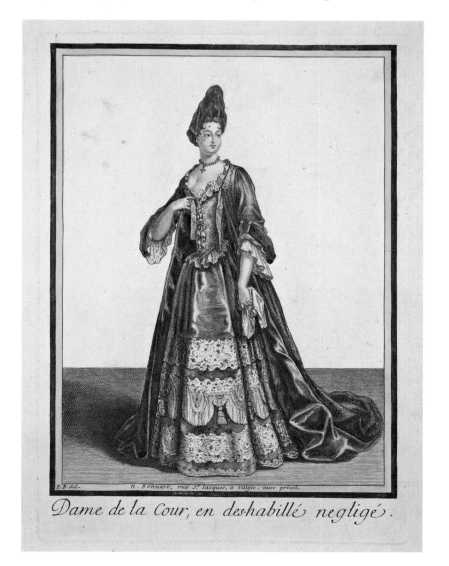

Dame de la Cour, en deshabillé negligé.

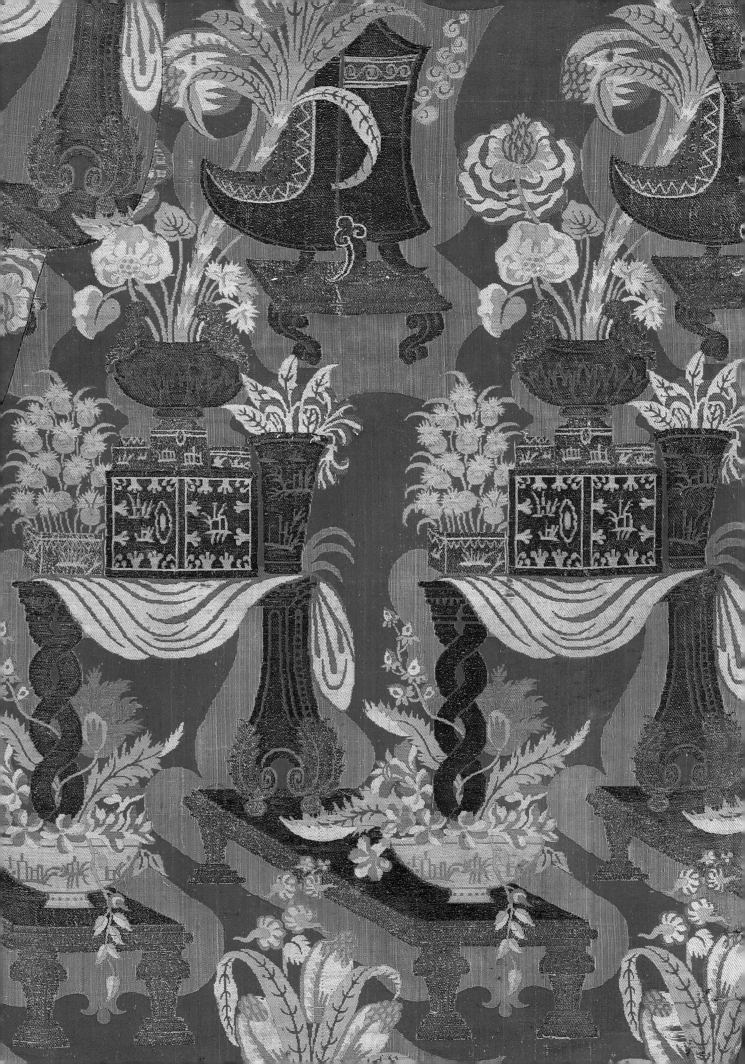

took its original inspiration from the Japanese kimono, whose shape had been introduced through the Dutch–Japanese trade during the previous century. Women wore the *robe de chambre* over a petticoat and a stiff-bodied corset, known as stays. The T-shaped garment was simply constructed, but although its lines were plain, the fabrics were anything but. Incorporating luxurious materials and exotic patterns, the silks made at the end of Louis XIV's reign mark it as one of the greatest periods in the history of textile design.

The silk industries of France and the rest of Europe responded quickly to the changes in fashion and the growing interest in elaborately patterned cloth. The city of Lyon earned particular fame for its silk designs, but Lyon was not the only weaving center in Europe. Late in the seventeenth century, the Dutch industry enjoyed great success and probably produced some of the most exotic silk designs.[10] Asian aesthetics and other sources that still defy our understanding influenced patterns now known as "bizarre" silks. These fabrics, with their indefinable motifs and very large repeats — often as long as ninety centimeters, or thirty inches — were well suited to the Asian-inspired *robes de chambre*. Over the course of the eighteenth century, because of the increasingly important role of textile designers in creating fashionable patterns, they acquired higher standing, and some of them, including Jean Revel and Pierre Rinquet, earned great fame and power. Others, such as Philippe LaSalle, actually went into partnership with manufacturers or became merchant weavers, or *marchands fabricants*, in their own right.[11]

The *robe de chambre* took on increasing formality as it moved from the boudoir to the outdoors. By the 1720s, it evolved into a new style of dress called the *robe volante*, with double box pleats at the center back that flowed loosely from the neck to the floor. This feature is often referred to as Watteau pleats, because the artist Antoine Watteau frequently painted women in the *robe volante*. In a sign for the luxury merchant Gersaint's shop (pp. 28–29), for example, Watteau depicted two women visiting the establishment in *robes volantes*. The woman in the foreground of the painting is seen from the back, a view that emphasizes the graceful lines of her dress as she peers at a painting being uncrated in front of her.

The dresses worn by the women in Gersaint's sign are made of simple striped and plain silks, not the complexly designed ones mentioned above. This simplicity reflects an important aspect of the *robe volante*'s influence on society. The fashionable nature of the new dress did not rely on the elaborate trims — such as ribbons, gold and silver fringe, and lace — that had decorated the most

European silks designed about 1700 featured exotic flowers and unexpected motifs. Their large repeats suited the simple, flowing lines of the clothing styles of the period.

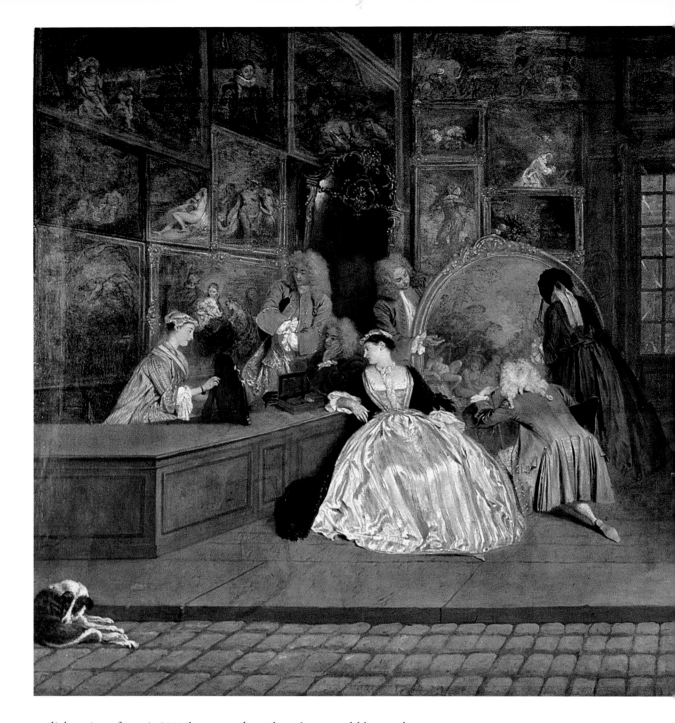

stylish attire of Louis XIV's court; the *robe volante* could be made from whatever fabric the wearer could afford. Thus, its introduction heralded a breakdown of the social order of dress. Under the Sun King, only those of the highest social and political status were permitted the ostentatious display that fashion demanded; others dressed according to their low station and humble nature. Now, women of almost any social class could be fashionable in the *robe volante*. Of course, status and wealth still had to exert themselves in some way, so the type of fabric and whether or not it was of the most current design became the primary measure of taste.

Because of the growing importance of silk design and the expanding interest in fashion among the various social classes,

Antoine Watteau painted women wearing *robes volantes* so often that the pleats at the back became identified with the artist and are commonly referred to as Watteau pleats.

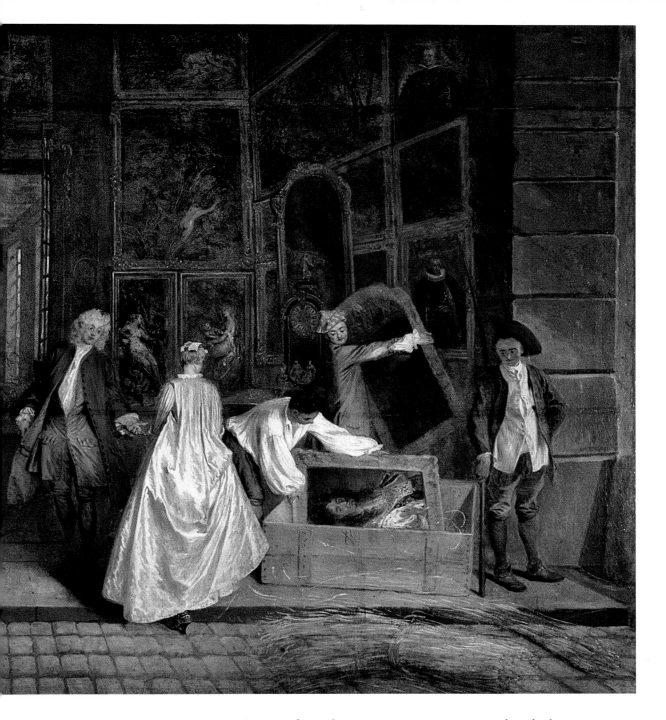

mercers achieved even greater prominence within the luxury trades during the first part of the eighteenth century. Their role as wholesalers and retailers of cloth of silk, gold, and silver, as well as of gold and silver lace, ribbons, buttons, some wool, cotton, linen cloth, and fashion accessories such as fans, gloves, and jewelry, made them key figures in the new fashion system.

The mercers who supplied the court played a particularly noteworthy role as the conduit between members of the aristocracy, who were still regarded as fashion leaders, and those in foreign courts and the provinces who were interested in the latest styles of dress. A portion of the correspondence of the silk mercer Jean-François Barbier has survived and illustrates that customers

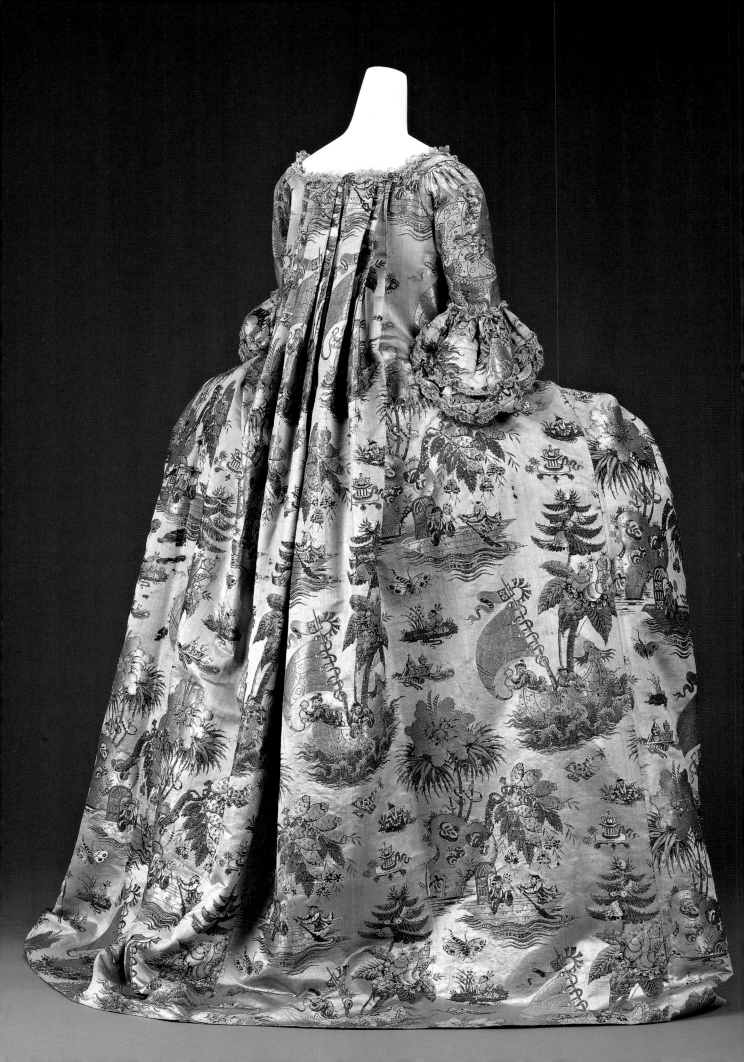

relied on Barbier for advice on the latest styles. The Countess of Demouleau, for example, wrote to him requesting fabric for a dress that would be wearable for three seasons, stating that she trusted in his honesty to recommend the colors and fabrics of the latest fashion. In another letter, Barbier was asked to send samples of fabrics for the autumn season and to indicate which pieces were most stylish.[12] At the other end of the retail spectrum, the mercers gave key advice to the textile manufacturers. Extant letters between several mercers and Lyon weavers show that the mercers' knowledge of what was popular at the court guided the weavers and designers as to what textile patterns to produce.[13]

The mercers and textile makers met the rising demands for fashionable silk patterns among different social and economic classes in a number of ways. They introduced new designs seasonally and stocked goods in a range of prices. In fact, the manufacturers would often weave a popular design in a variety of styles to suit different price points. Gold or silver thread would be included at the higher price, or left out and replaced with silk to make the cloth more affordable. Thus, without changing the set-up of the loom, which could take weeks to do for an elaborate pattern, the weaver could create one style of fabric and then weave another type simply by varying the yarns used. The silk dress and textile fragment seen here illustrate this business strategy. Both textiles were probably woven in Amsterdam (the panels' widths, structure, and designs associate them with that city) and were known as *indiennes* at the time.[14] But the fabric used to make the dress includes gold- and silver-metallic brocading yarns, adding a level of luxury and expense not found in the fragment, which is brocaded solely with silk thread.

The fabric out of which this dress was made was brocaded with silver and gold metallic yarns. The metallic threads were replaced with silk on a less expensive version of the same fabric, pictured at right.

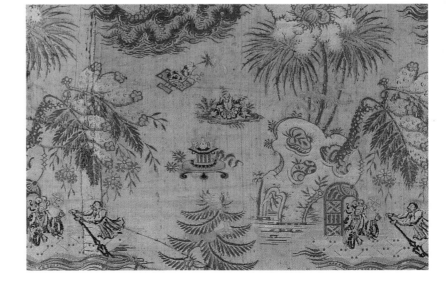

The mercer's trade continued to expand during the eighteenth century, and by 1723 twenty different subdivisions existed within the corporation. Wholesalers and merchants could specialize in silk and cloth of gold and silver; gold and silver trims such as braid, lace, buttons, and fringe; wool; jewelry made of precious metals and stones; lace, cambric, and lawn; raw silk; animal skins; tapestries, carpets, and other furnishing textiles; iron and metalwork; hardware such as tools, cutlery, and locks; luxury furnishings, including paintings, bronzes, furniture, and clocks; mirrors; ribbons, fans, and other fashionable trims; tools for writing, including paper, ink, sealing wax, and penknives; tin and copper work; waxed cloth, umbrellas, and hats; mercery; toys; snuff boxes; or devotional items.[15] The mercers had become the primary source for any kind of luxury ware, and it was to their shops that one came to find the latest in fashion.

As the mercers became more and more significant in the luxury goods trade, they also developed a range of techniques to market their wares and make them desirable. Those at the top of the industry recognized the role of their shops as a gathering place for the fashionable elite. They decorated the boutiques elaborately, signaling their preeminent status in the transmission of fashion. The names of the shops immediately suggested the luxurious and exotic nature of the wares. Barbier, for instance, called his shop A la Barbe d'Or. Other mercers who showcased imported goods took names like A la Pagode and Au Grand Turc.

One of the most famous shops in Paris, Le Petit Dunkerque, opened in 1767 and was run by Charles Raymond Granchez. Granchez specialized in English goods that had become fashionable in Paris during the second half of the century, including jewelry and metalwork from the London silversmith Thomas Gray and ceramic wares from Wedgwood and Bentley. He sold small luxury items such as decorated boxes, shaving and sewing kits, and buttons, as well as larger objects such as chandeliers, vases, garnitures for chimneypieces, candlesticks, teapots, fountains for making tea, and even mechanical toys. With its mirrored ceiling and back wall, gilt-mahogany furnishings, and lanterns in the shape of griffons, his shop was itself a destination.

The mercers were largely wholesalers and retailers who were not allowed to manufacture goods, only to sell finished products. However, they did have the right to finish items — a process known as *enjoliver*, or to "pretty up." Those who sold furniture added the lacquer and porcelain panels, as well as brasses and other ornamentation that trimmed the most stylish examples. Other mercers who retailed exotic imported Asian ceramics added ormolu mounts. Similarly, the silk

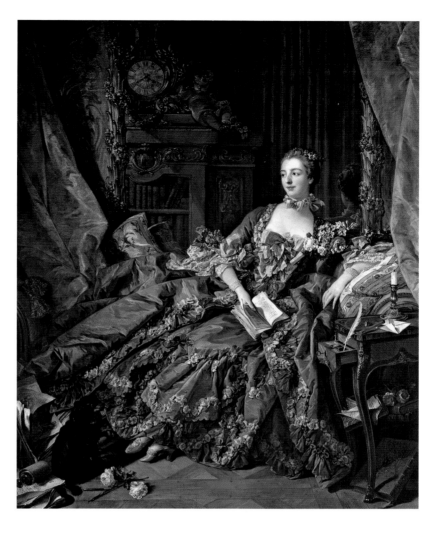

Dress trims had become an important fashion statement by the middle of the eighteenth century, as can be seen in this 1756 portrait of Mme de Pompadour, Louis XV's mistress.

merchants who retailed trims and accessories gained the right to trim garments with the chic ribbons, fringes, and galloons seen on the clothing of the court. For those who catered to the dress trades, this right to *enjoliver* their goods became particularly significant, especially as the eighteenth century progressed and the focus of fashion switched from the design of the fabric to how the dresses were trimmed.

By the middle of the century, the importance of textile design in fashionable dress began to give way to an increasing demand for trim. The *robe volante* had evolved into a new style of dress now referred to as the *robe à la française*. This dress was very similar to the earlier design, except that its waistline was more fitted in the front. It usually consisted of two parts: a petticoat and an overdress that opened down the front. Often, a matching triangular stomacher was worn over the stays at the center front and attached to the sides of the overdress's bodice. In this portrait by François Boucher, Mme de Pompadour wears a *robe à la française* with a stomacher covered in ribbons.

The height of popularity of the new dress coincided with

silk designs featuring depictions of serpentine branches of flowers, often interlacing with ribbons. A range of trim styles developed to complement these patterns, which reigned supreme from the 1750s through the 1760s. One of the most stylish kinds of trim involved three-dimensional passementerie known as *agréments*, made to resemble the flowers illustrated in the silks. These trims adorned the petticoat, the front opening of the overdress, and the stomacher.

The Fashion Merchant

The division of the mercer's trade that sold trims and accessories began to play an ever greater role. These fashion merchants, or *marchandes de modes*, as they came to be known, evolved slowly out of the mercer's corporation as interest in fashionably trimming women's dresses surpassed the focus on the textile patterns themselves. This facet of the trade also became associated with women, and often the wife or widow of a mercer undertook this side of the business.[16] By the time the guilds were again restructured in 1776, the status of the *marchandes de modes* merited incorporation into their own guild with the feather and artificial flower sellers. Along with the dressmakers and linen sellers, the new guild of Marchandes de Modes, Plumassières, et Fleuristes was one of the few female corporations.

According to Louis Sebastien Mercier, who chronicled late eighteenth-century Parisian society, the *marchandes de modes* were at the pinnacle of the fashion pyramid. Their position was due not only to their importance in supplying the fashionable dress trims that were so vital during this period, but also to their ability to actually trim finished garments and accessories such as hats. Mercier referred to them as "*poètes d'enjoliver*" and stated that they were no longer mere artisans, but artists.[17] He was fascinated by the profession's rising status, the creativity of the women involved, and their expanding role in setting new styles.

The names of several fashion merchants have survived the centuries. Two of the best known were Mlle Pagelle, who was the preferred fashion merchant of Mlle du Barry, the last mistress of Louis XV, and the de Beaulard family, who catered to many of the court aristocrats. The most famous name of all to survive is that of Rose Bertin. Marie-Jeanne Bertin was born in Abbeville in 1747 and probably apprenticed with a dressmaker in that city, Mme Barbier. By the time Bertin moved to Paris in 1770, she had changed her name to Rose. She opened a shop on the quai des Gesvres, which was known for its modest boutiques with low prices. Given her provincial background, this was probably a sensible location in which to establish her reputation. It didn't take long for her to make a name for herself supplying imaginative dress and hat trims and to acquire the means to relocate. By 1773, she moved her shop to the center of the fashionable world, near the rue St. Honoré, and she soon earned the status of the preeminent fashion merchant in Paris.

During the reign of Louis XVI, from 1774 to 1792, women's informal clothing was characterized by a decrease in the width of the skirt and an increase in the size of headwear. Formal and ceremonial dress increased in skirt width as well as in elaboration, and like informal dress, was worn with extravagant hats. The fashion merchants, with their right to *enjoliver* their wares, found themselves uniquely positioned to meet the needs of their clientele. Bertin and other merchants with imagination and a good eye became ever greater figures within the fashion trades. Clients began to rely on their sense of style, and those top merchants whose patrons numbered among the aristocracy of France — perhaps even Queen Marie Antoinette — were sure to provide the latest in fashion in their shops. Of course, talented dressmakers and tailors had long been important to members of the court in creating and setting new fashions, but it was not until the end of the eighteenth century that the influence of those who furnished fashionable goods began to overshadow that of the aristocrats themselves. Some *marchandes de modes*, like Bertin, began to take on airs, to the disapproval of their colleagues and some members of the aristocracy.

According to Mme Campan, lady in waiting to Marie Antoinette, the Duchess of Chartres introduced Rose Bertin to the queen in 1774 during a visit to the chateau at Marly. Campan's memoirs also state that by this time Bertin was famous, or infamous, for the complete change she had effected in French women's dress.[18] The queen soon became dependent on Bertin and her taste, scandalizing the court in the process. Since the time of Louis XIV, the dressing of the king and queen had been an important daily ritual. Only the most favored courtiers were admitted to the morning and evening ceremony, and an attendant's status was revealed by which garment he or she had the privilege of handing to the king or queen. Marie Antoinette never enjoyed the ceremony of the French court and evaded its strict etiquette whenever she could. She shocked her ladies in waiting by inviting Rose Bertin to participate in the morning ritual. However, she had enough respect for court

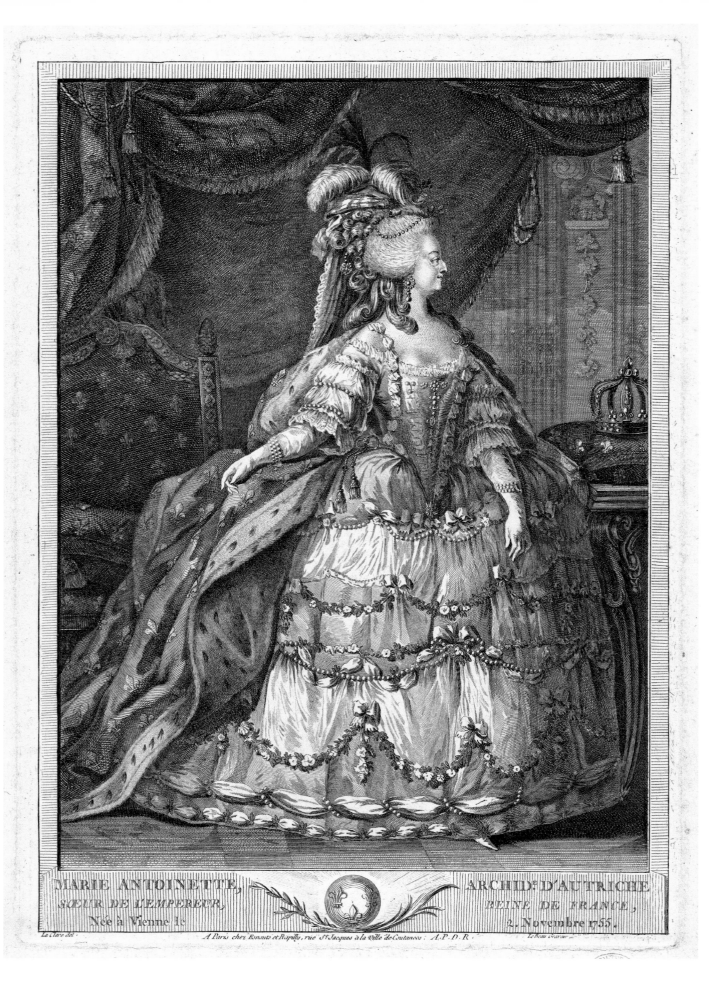

MARIE ANTOINETTE, ARCHID.ᵈᵉ D'AUTRICHE
SŒUR DE L'EMPEREUR, REINE DE FRANCE,
Née à Vienne le 2. Novembre 1755.

Le Clere del. A Paris chez Esnauts et Rapilly, rue St. Jacques à la Ville de Coutances. A.P.D.R. Le Beau Graveur

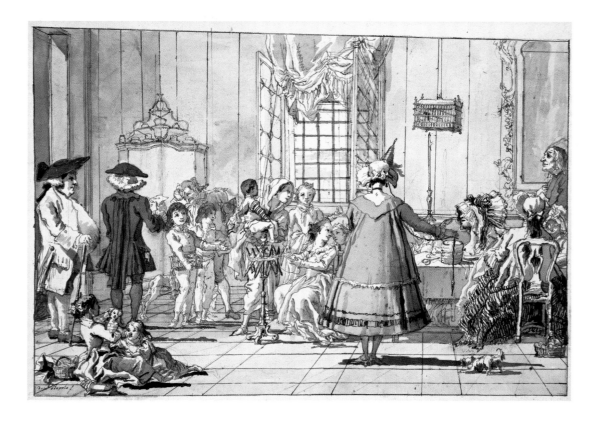

Fashion merchants'
boutiques such as this
Italian shop drawn by
Giovanni Tiepolo were the
source of the most stylish
dresses and hats during the
late eighteenth century.

etiquette to not bring the merchant into her bedroom; instead, the queen interrupted the ceremony of dressing and left her ladies in waiting to join Bertin in a small chamber or cabinet. The two would then confer about her dress, creating new styles that her retinue would rush to imitate. Although dressing according to one's rank still played a role, members of the court worked hard to keep up with the fashions set by the king and queen; imitating the royals' dress was a sign of loyalty that, as in Louis XIV's time, would be rewarded with favor and possibly those important court sinecures.

Bertin's close association with Marie Antoinette made her shop one of the most essential in Paris, and she did not hesitate to take advantage of the connection. In the tradition of mercers who supplied the royal family, she labeled herself Marchande de Modes de la Reine. While her notoriety inevitably made her sought after, she also employed traditional methods of attracting clients to her shop, Au Grand Mogul. The name itself followed the convention of appealing to the fascination with the exotic, and the setting and décor were suitably grand. In its first location at 13, rue de Riche-lieu, near the Comédie-Française, the shop was on the third floor, and Bertin rented out the first two. A porter dressed in green livery trimmed with gold greeted patrons and ushered them upstairs into a luxurious world decorated with Bohemian glass and gold and

Marie Antoinette sought
out the most successful
Parisian fashion merchant,
Rose Bertin, to trim her
court dresses.

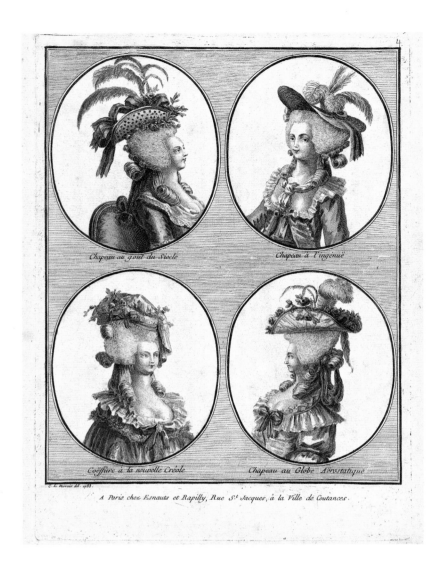

Chapeau au gout du Siecle

Chapeau à l'ingénue

Coeffure à la nouvelle Créole

Chapeau au Globe Aérostatique

A Paris chez Esnauts et Rapilly, Rue St Jacques, à la Ville de Coutances.

The fashion merchant specialized in trimming hats that, at the end of the eighteenth century, reached extraordinary proportions.

white paneling. In 1789, the boutique moved down the street to number 26, where the décor was presumably just as splendid.

Bertin not only stocked dress and hat trims, including ribbons, flowers, laces, and feathers, but also featured some ready-made accessories such as shawls, fichus, and handkerchiefs. However, it was not necessarily the merchandise that brought people through the doors but the knowledge that they could discover the most fashionable methods of trimming dresses and hats. Bertin earned particular celebrity for her creative and imaginative hats, in a period when headdresses reached extraordinary height and contained everything but the kitchen sink. She often introduced new headdress styles, and patrons had to visit her shop to see her latest creations.

Innovation and imagination were important capital in achieving success as a fashion merchant. Fame rested on the ability to trim and ornament stylish garments, a skill that set the *marchandes de modes* apart from the other fashion trades that provided the

Visitors to Paris often sent drawings home to their families in order to illustrate the latest French fashions. Count Axel Fersen sent this drawing of Marie Antoinette wearing a redingote to his sister, Sophie, in Sweden.

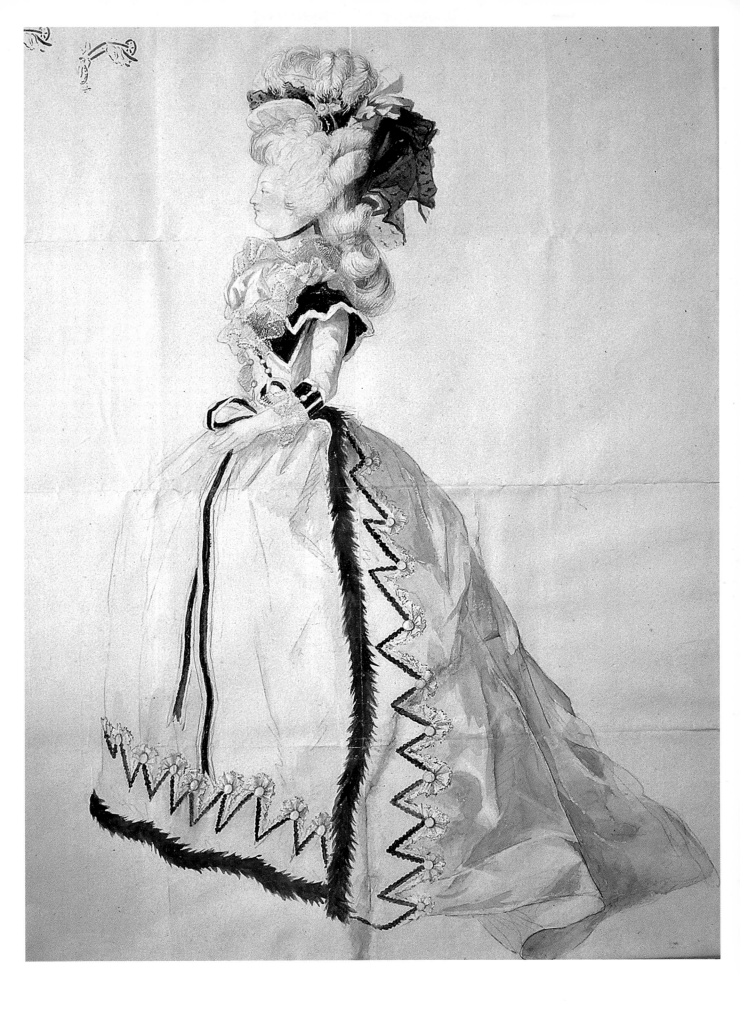

necessary components. Archival records show that Rose Bertin worked with over 120 different suppliers, including hat makers, hosiers, lace makers, silk mercers, linen sellers, cord makers, ribbon weavers, flower makers, feather sellers, jewelers, glove makers, furriers, button makers, and fan makers, as well craftspeople such as dressmakers, linen sewers, and embroiderers. The fashion merchant had literally become the center of the fashion trades, surrounded by all the suppliers and craftspeople she needed to create her goods.

Bertin and other *marchandes de modes* used conventional means to inform foreign clients of the latest looks from Paris. Seasonally, Bertin would dress a *poupée de mode* and send the doll on the road to Italy, Spain, England, Sweden, and Russia. She also traveled throughout Europe herself, meeting with important customers. Other fashion merchants did the same, and some actually established stores in foreign capitals. In addition to their store in Paris, for example, the Beaulard family ran a shop in Moscow called Maison de Moscow that was managed by the youngest son, Aimard Beaulard.

Distant clients also used intermediaries to conduct business with fashion merchants. Members of foreign courts often relied on diplomats and their wives to keep them up-to-date on the latest styles and to execute commissions for them. Letters and drawings were sent back and forth to communicate about the fashions. Count Axel Fersen, an influential Swedish diplomat to the court of Louis XVI, served as an intermediary between the Swedish court and the *marchandes de modes* of Paris. He sent a beautiful drawing of Marie Antoinette in the latest fashion to his sister, Sophie, to illustrate the current French style. The sketch may have served as inspiration for Sophie's dressmakers or as a point of order for Fersen, who could have commissioned something similar from a French fashion merchant.

Along with private intermediaries, Bertin and others worked directly with commission and shipping houses, known as *maisons de roulage et commission*. These *commissionaires* specialized in shipping and exporting goods to specific countries in Europe and abroad. A vital aspect of the French export market, they had been in business since the seventeenth century. They not only served private clients but also played a key role in the French luxury economy, by redistributing goods no longer in style with the court and fashionable elite to provincial and foreign markets such as Peru and Mexico, where they were retailed for knock-down prices. This outlet opened up additional markets to the luxury merchants and helped insulate them from sudden changes in fashion: even if goods were no longer fashionable in Paris, they could be sold in the provinces or overseas.[19]

A New Consumerism

One of the most influential developments in spreading changes
in fashion during this period occurred in the printing trades. The
growth in consumerism and expanding markets created an atmosphere in which fashion periodicals could flourish. As a result, new
fashion journals and prints appeared regularly in the last quarter of
the eighteenth century and were distributed throughout Europe. One
of the first and most successful, *The Ladies Magazine*, was launched
in London in 1770 and continued in publication until 1825. In Paris,
Le Cabinet des Modes, ou les Modes Nouvelles appeared in 1785. The
journal was published twice a month and included a selection of
plates illustrating the latest fashions in dress, hats, furniture, and the
decorative arts, along with lengthy descriptions of each. Often, the
text gave the name of the shop in which the object could be found.

In the first edition of *Le Cabinet des Modes*, the publishers
wrote that they hoped their enterprise, one of the most agree-
able they had undertaken, would be especially pleasing to those
outside of France — in Italy, Spain, Germany, England, and
Scandinavia — who would no longer have to spend large sums of
money on *commissionaires* or have fashion dolls or mannequins
made in order to keep abreast of the latest French fashions. The
editors claimed their publication would detail the current fashions for a modest price. They asserted it would provide the same
service to those in the French provinces, whose business in Paris
made up perhaps one of the most important branches of commerce
in the capital. The editors' pride in Paris and its standing as the
most fashionable city in the world was evident in their declaration
that no other city could match Parisians' genius, character, taste,
and above all, desire to please and to distinguish themselves.[20]

The plates that appeared in the first issue of the journal
included a woman dressed in a formal gown, or *habit de bal*, with
a fitted bodice and full skirt. She carried a black mask in one
hand and wore a large hat, characteristic of the period, trimmed
with a pouf of Italian gauze, rose ribbons, and a garland of
laurel leaves. Plate 2 illustrated a man wearing an overcoat with
mother of pearl buttons, a hat *à la Androsmane*, a vest of black
silk patterned with green flowers, wool breeches the color of
sulphur, and to finish off the look, blue-and-white striped stockings (p. 42). Plate 3 depicted a porcelain table clock and candela-
brum that could be found at M. Granchez's Petit Dunkerque.

La Gallerie des Modes et Costumes français dessinés d'après

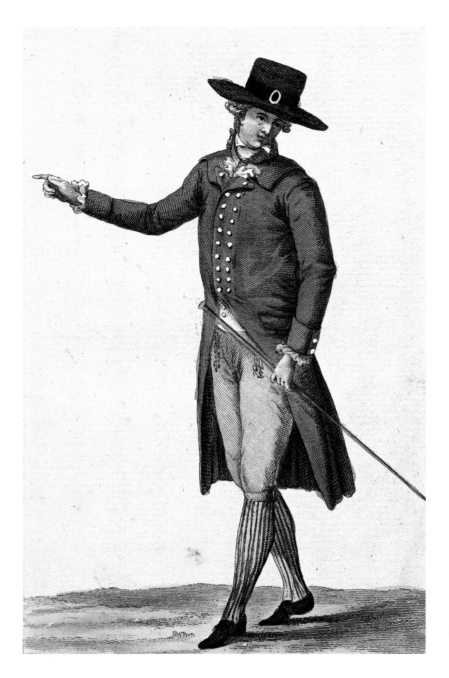

Fashion periodicals enjoyed
great popularity at the end
of the eighteenth century.
This plate from the first
issue of *Le Cabinet des
Modes* illustrates the latest
in men's daywear.

nature, first published in 1778, was one of the most luxurious
fashion periodicals. Each folio released by the publishers, Esnauts
and Rapilly, comprised a series of six plates. The earliest editions
featured four different headdresses per plate, but the seventh folio
introduced full figures. As in *Le Cabinet des Modes*, merchants'
names were often included; one plate from the periodical identifies
the work of Rose Bertin. The publication's title stressed the fact that
the fashions depicted were taken directly from original examples.

This link between the plates and real examples remained
important throughout the late eighteenth century and continued

Fashion plates often
included the names of the
fashion merchants whose
work was depicted.
The hat illustrated in this
plate from *La Gallerie des
Modes* was trimmed by
Rose Bertin.

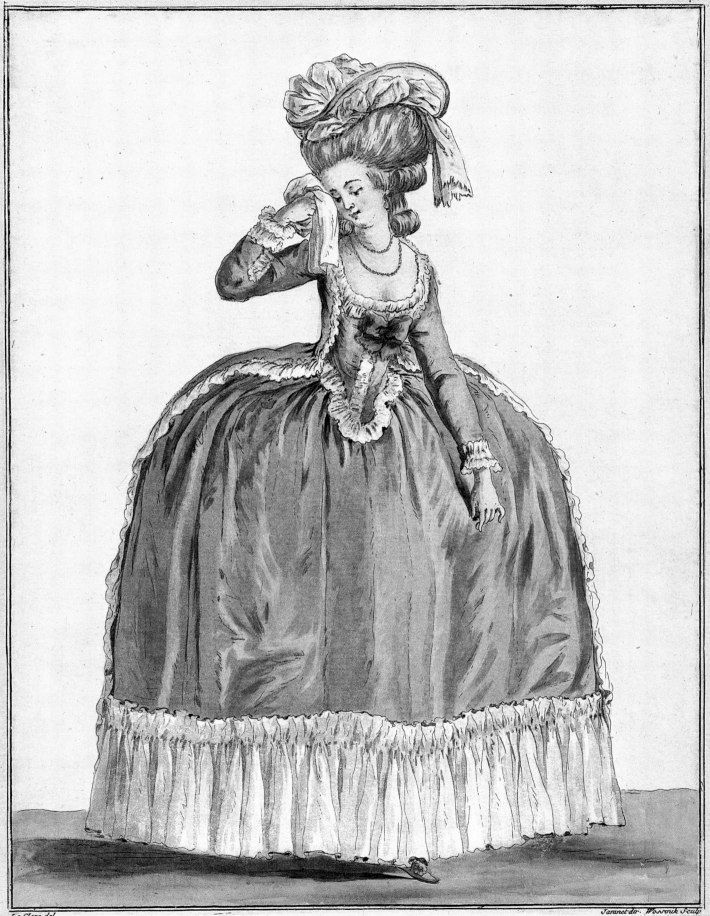

Le Clere del.   Jannet dir. Wowrnik sculp.

Robe à la sultane simple telle qu'elle se porte actuellement sans grande parure Cette robe est dégagée du
devant et laisse voir la jupe entiere par derriere elle forme la polonaise détroussée et descend jusqu'à terre
comme le Lévite Coefure Chapeau bonet de Gaze inventé par M.lle Bertin.

a Paris chez Esnauts et Rapilly, rue S.t Jacques a la Ville de Coutances. A.P.D.R.

into the nineteenth. For instance, the English book *The Fashions of London and Paris during the Years 1798, 1799, and 1800*, published in 1801 by Robert Phillips, included all the fashion plates from the journal *The Magazine of the Female Fashions of London and Paris*. According to the book's introduction, "The leading feature of the publication is to exhibit only the dresses which are actually worn in the most fashionable circles of London and Paris."[21]

The fashion plates of the late eighteenth century illustrate a new phenomenon in the clothing of the period — the evolution of novel styles of dress beyond the classic *robe à la française* that had remained fashionable throughout most of the century. In the 1770s, a fascination with anything English held sway in Paris, and the *robe à l'anglaise* was the first new type to be introduced. The back of this dress was fitted close to the body, as the English preferred. Other styles quickly followed and took on the names the *robe à la turque*, the *levite*, the *chemise*, and the *sultan*.

The chemise dress was particularly significant. Derived from the basic women's undergarment, it was gathered at the neck, arms, and waist and was primarily used for casual wear. The painter Elizabeth Vigée-Lebrun scandalized the public when she exhibited a portrait of Maire Antoinette in a chemise dress. Despite the unseemliness of its intimate origin, the chemise evolved into the most fashionable style of dress during the last decades of the eighteenth century. Its simple lines, recalling the garments worn in ancient Greece and Rome, harmonized with the Neoclassical style then popular in the decorative arts.

Just who introduced these new styles of dress is unclear. The fashion merchants had the right to make only simple outer garments such as mantles and capes. Dressmakers maintained the privilege to sew women's dresses, but whether they introduced the innovations is unknown. The two professions did work closely together, and perhaps the new styles were a result of that collaboration.

The last decades of the eighteenth century also saw fundamental changes in the fashion economy. As the French monarchy went into decline, the Christian moral philosophy of dress no longer held sway. At the same time, Enlightenment theory, the philosophical school of thought during the period, promoted the individual over the social hierarchy. The new philosophy encouraged the accumulation of riches and the right to dress as one could afford; individuals were no longer morally required to dress according to social position. This sartorial equality blurred the distinction between the classes and resulted in a tremendous increase in personal spending on clothing. Daniel Roche, in his

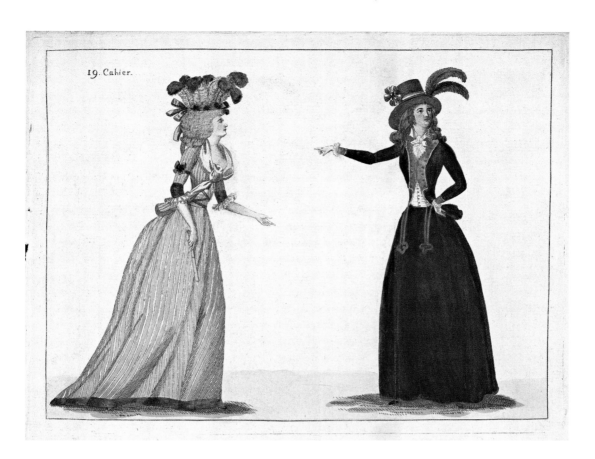

19. Cahier.

Plates included in magazines from the late eighteenth century often featured new dress styles. For the first time, the way in which a dress was cut became of fashionable interest.

research on dress of the eighteenth century, found a 233 percent increase in expenditures on dress by the nobility and gentry and a 215 percent increase by wage earners in the larger urban centers.[22] Technological advances in the textile and related trades also made clothing more affordable, allowing people from many different social classes to keep up with changes in fashion.

The role of the court in setting and promoting new styles had continued under Louis XVI and Marie Antoinette; the queen's escalating influence on fashion and her close work with Rose Bertin played a key role in moving the fashion economy. However, the French Revolution, which removed Louis XVI from power in 1792, suspended the hegemony of the court and sent some fashion professionals like Bertin wandering in exile. Despite her peripatetic lifestyle, Bertin continued her business creating fashionable garments for the courts of Europe and the French aristocrats who had fled the country. She returned to France in 1800, when the unrest had calmed, financially better off than when she had left. By then, Napoleon Bonaparte had wrested control of the French government from the Directory, which had been established in 1795 to quell the revolutionary terror of Robespierre. Napoleon and his wife Josephine replaced the Directory with an imperial court. While Napoleon focused his

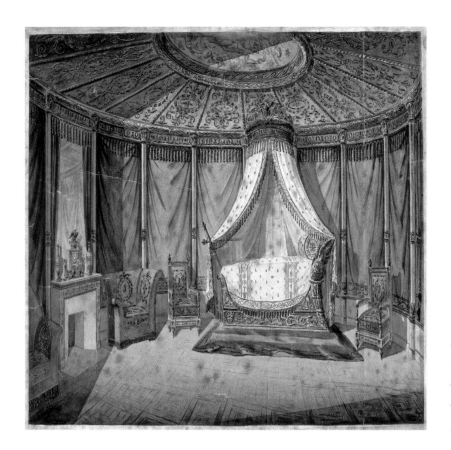

One of the ways Napoleon revived the French luxury trades was by refurnishing the French palaces, such as Malmaison.

attention on reestablishing the French army, reviving the French economy, and restructuring the French state — from its schools to the judicial system — Josephine took on the role of fashion leader.

When Napoleon crowned himself emperor of France, he recognized the importance of the luxury trades to the economy. To support them, he set about refurnishing the palaces at Versailles, Malmaison, Fontainebleau, and the Tuileries. He commissioned silks from Lyon, as well as tapestries and furniture from the Gobelins. He also encouraged Josephine's interest in fashion. With the help of professionals such as the fashion merchant Hippolyte Leroy, Josephine set about creating new styles that featured Lyon silk, Alençon lace, and other French luxury goods. Under her influence, the plain muslin Neoclassical chemise popular about 1800 gave way to more elaborate gowns.

The reestablishment of a French court and its accompanying ceremony necessitated a return to ornate dress and luxurious trappings. For ceremonial purposes, Napoleon encouraged courtiers to wear the richly embroidered three-piece man's suit traditional in the seventeenth and eighteenth centuries. By doing so, he brought work to the Parisian embroiderers who had nearly gone out of business during the revolution. The women of the court wore gowns with detachable trains of silk velvet or satin,

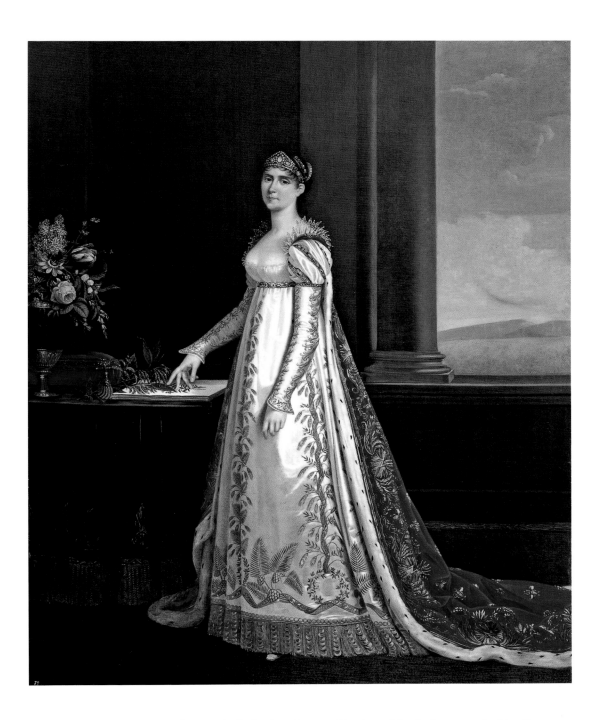

A connoisseur of luxurious dress, Josephine helped to revitalize the fashion trades in France.

often embellished with metallic thread in designs symbolic of Napoleon's empire, such as lilies, acanthus, and palmettes.

Although Napoleon revived elements of prerevolutionary French ceremony, one change he did not reverse was the suppression of the guild structure that had occurred by 1799. Despite the fact that the corporations had dissolved, countless dressmakers, tailors, fashion merchants, and textile mercers flourished during the first half of the century by meeting the demands of the new imperial court and of the aristocrats and foreigners now returning to

Paris. Many continued to work in the traditional manner, running small shops open to clients who desired custom-made garments finely crafted in the most innovative and fashionable styles. Others expanded their trade, taking advantage of the fact that there were no longer guild restrictions on what they could make or sell.

Ready-to-Wear and the Emergence of One-Stop Shopping

By the 1820s, some mercers and even tailors began to sell men's ready-made clothing, such as work clothes, vests, dressing gowns, and redingotes, and women's ready-made mantles and capes. These garments did not require a close fit, so they could easily be made in stock sizes. Several tailors began producing ready-made suits for the lower classes and even the bourgeoisie, but it was still a hand-craft industry, and not mechanized. Over the course of the century, men's clothing became more uniform and easier to mass-produce. Dark wool jackets, often worn with buff leather breeches or even trousers — which were a new addition to fashionable men's wear — became male wardrobe staples, and the manufacture of ready-made suits increased.

Ready-to-wear dresses for women took longer to become available. Some were made for the lower classes by the 1870s, but high-end ready-to-wear for women was not successful until the early twentieth century. Women's interest in maintaining their own individual style through the selection of fabrics and trims, plus the need for their dresses to have a close fit, meant that the custom dressmaker was still essential. Nevertheless, the expansion of ready-to-wear was a significant change in business practice.

Another key development was the growth of the boutiques run by mercers and fashion merchants into large establishments that provided everything necessary to clothe a family. Several businessmen — primarily mercers, but some tailors as well — began to aggressively enlarge their operations along English models, which featured more advanced retail methods, including the production of ready-to-wear and increased marketing, in order to meet the consumer needs of an expanding, wealthier middle class. One of the first Parisians to emulate the English approach was an astute businessman named Pierre Parissot. Parissot traveled to England in 1826 to familiarize himself with the traditional English store known as an "outfitter."[23] Specializing in a range of products, an outfitter sold ready-made men's clothing along with trunks, needles, canes, umbrellas, and even medicine — everything a traveler might need.

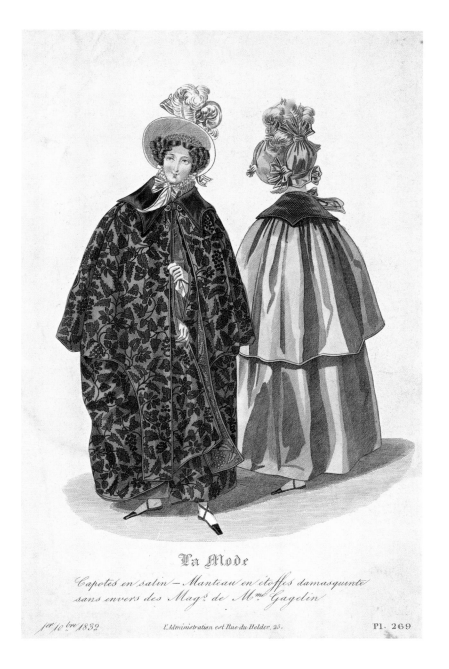

La Mode

Capotes en satin — Manteau en étoffes damasquinté
sans envers des Mag.s de M.me Gagelin

1.er 10.bre 1832   L'Administration est Rue du Helder, 25.   Pl. 269

Capes and mantles, which did not require a close fit, were the earliest examples of women's ready-to-wear.

The concept of one-stop shopping had never before been practical in France, because the corporations had strictly controlled what could be sold and manufactured by their members, and they vigilantly monitored other tradesmen to make sure they didn't sell or produce anything they shouldn't. Now that such restrictions were no longer in place, Parissot capitalized on the mercantile freedom to launch a new type of store in Paris. La Belle Jardinière opened in 1827 near the flower market on the quai aux Fleurs — close to the Temple, where an important secondhand-clothing trade existed. Parissot began by offering fixed prices and ready-made work clothes that did not depend on fit, including overalls, smocks, and aprons.

He adopted more efficient and profitable sewing methods, subdividing labor and cutting more than one layer of cloth at a time.

Parissot's shop quickly expanded to meet the rising demands of the poor and middle classes, who had developed a taste for new garments rather than secondhand clothing. In 1855, La Belle Jardinière advertised "all kinds of clothing within the reach of people of modest means under these three headings: work clothes, daily wear, Sunday clothes, from pea jackets at 4.75 francs, cuir-laine trousers at 5 francs, trousers at 20 francs, all the way to frock coats at 60 francs."[24] The store experienced great success, and after twenty years it occupied more than twenty-five neighboring buildings. In 1866, when it moved across the river to the quai de la Messagerie, the company did a business of more than twelve million francs and employed more than four thousand workers.[25]

La Belle Jardinière's fixed prices and expansion into ready-to-wear reflected a growing trend in the development of Parisian retail. Other merchants, particularly mercers, had begun to carry a range of fashionable goods at fixed prices, including men's ready-to-wear vests, paletots and redingotes (types of men's overcoats), and women's ready-made lingerie, shawls, and outerwear, along with the traditional mercer's wares. Soon known as *magasins de nouveautés*, these expanded stores prospered in the economic boom of the first empire, benefiting from the increasing interest in fashionable dress by the growing middle class. By 1803–4, the *Almanach du Commerce de Paris* listed that *nouveautés* (the latest fashionable goods) could be found at one mercer's shop and five silk merchants. Ten years later, the *Almanach*'s section for silk merchants was titled *Merciers des soireries et nouveautés*, and by 1822 the *magasins de nouveautés* had established their independence.[26] They were the new fashion mecca.

The *magasins de nouveautés* operated differently than the boutiques of the mercers, secondhand-clothing dealers, and drapers of the past. Following the English model, they sold a large volume of goods at low prices; clearly labeled the merchandise with fixed rates, eliminating the need to bargain; provided *entrée libre*, or the right to enter the shop without buying anything; and allowed customers to exchange merchandise or return it for a refund. These new policies, combined with lavish interiors and enticing window displays in which merchandise was artfully draped and lit by oil lamps at night, held great appeal for shoppers. The large stores eliminated the need to visit several merchants, and with the addition of tailors and dressmakers to the staff by mid-century, made a separate trip to a clothing craftsman unnecessary.

Parisian stores known as *magasins de nouveautés*, such as La Maison Popelin-Ducarre, sold fashionable accessories as well as textiles and trims.

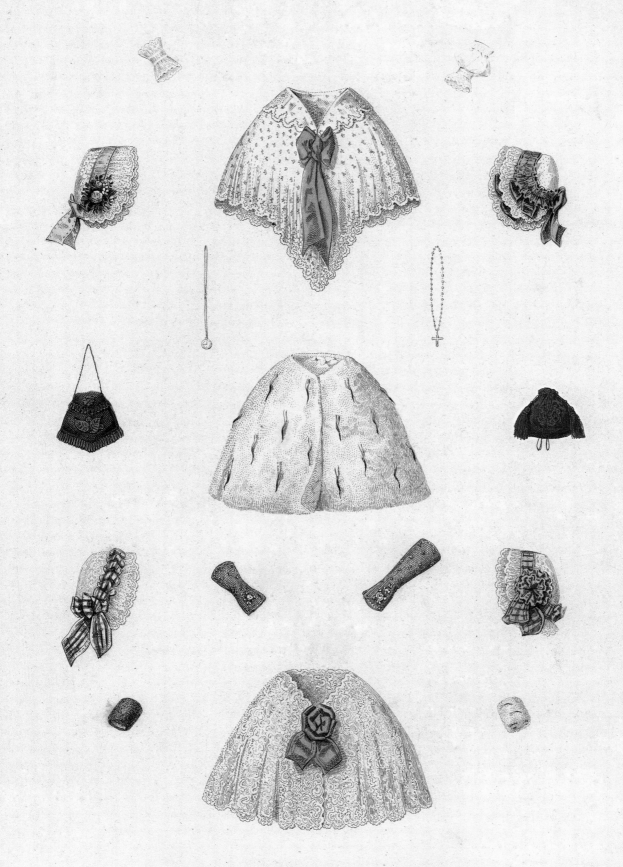

LE MONITEUR DE LA MODE.

Journal du Grand Monde

Décembre, 1846.

PARIS, Rue neuve Vivienne, 43.

Eventually providing one-stop shopping for men's, women's, and children's clothing, the stores were the precursors to the *grands magasins*, or department stores — such as Au bon Marché, La Samaritaine, and Galeries Lafayette — that dominated the Paris retail scene during the second half of the nineteenth century.

Although descended from the mercer's and fashion merchant's shops, the *magasins de nouveautés* evolved to more closely resemble the shopping galleries of the previous centuries, such as those near the Palais de Justice and the Palais Royale. In those galleries, various merchants specializing in a particular ware sold their goods behind counters. Abraham Bosse's illustration of the shops near the Palais de Justice (see p. 15) shows the counter of a silk mercer alongside a linen seller and a book seller. Following this example, the *magasins de nouveautés* were furnished with a series of counters, each selling a different type of good (the use of the plural term "*magasins*" reflects this arrangement).

One of the earliest stores was the Petit Saint Thomas, which opened in 1810 at number 34 on the rue du Bac and later moved to number 23. The shop's proprietors were innovators, and in 1844 the Petit Saint Thomas became one of the first stores to issue a catalogue. Though not illustrated, the catalogue listed all the merchandise in the shop and where it could be found. Each type of fabric was sold at a separate counter. The managers set aside several areas for silk fabrics, such as plain silks, patterned silks (*façonnées*), and silks for mourning dress and half mourning. Two counters offered shawls — one cashmere shawls and another winter wraps made of silk damask or plain silk. Another counter was devoted to *les confectionnés*, or ready-made capes and mantles for women. In all, the shop contained twenty-one "*magasins*." Shoppers could find ready-made lingerie crafted by a tailor employed by the store, stockings, gloves, cravats, fichus, and more.[27]

The *magasins de nouveautés* became extremely popular with tourists, as well as with the increasingly wealthy French people from the provinces and the city. Several catered specifically to visitors. One of the largest and most successful was A la Ville de Saint-Denis. The shop opened in 1845 at the corner of the rue du Faubourg St-Denis and rue du Paradis-Poissonière, near the new train stations, the Gare de l'Est and the Gare du Nord. Its proximity to the stations attracted the many visitors brought to Paris by the new rail system, and the store quickly grew. By 1870, it occupied space in five buildings. About 1865, the building at number 1-*bis*, rue de Paradis was transformed into a large central court featuring a

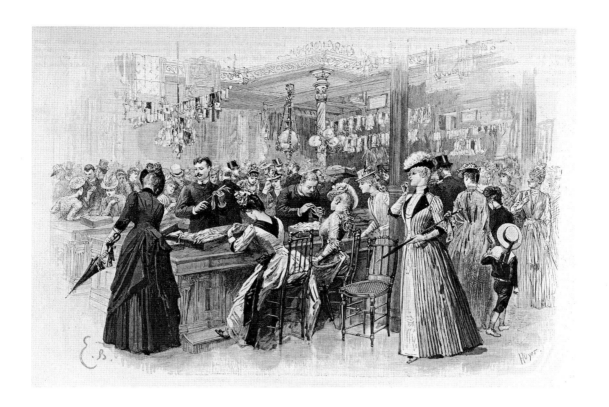

Magasins de nouveautés were organized with counters that specialized in various goods. This plate illustrates the glove counter at Au bon Marché, which originated as a *magasin de nouveautés* and later developed into Paris's first great department store.

grand staircase that opened onto four floors. In 1869, the proprietor installed the first elevator in a Paris store, alleviating the need for clients to climb three flights of stairs to find the counters where fine bedding and men's and children's ready-to-wear clothes were sold.

While A la Ville de Saint-Denis and other stores catered to visitors to the city, some specialized in the export trade. These shops operated in the tradition of the *commissionaires*, facilitating the shipping and export of their goods to foreign clients. Many, such as Popelin-Ducarre, Maison Lassalle, and la Compaigne Lyonnaise, were located on the rue Vivienne. Maison Lassalle was one of the most important shops dedicated to foreign clients. It originally sold religious articles to the provinces, but by the early nineteenth century its focus changed and it became the chief retailer of *robes*, or pre-patterned dress lengths. These *robes*, an early stage in the development of women's ready-to-wear, were pre-embroidered, printed, or patterned textiles with designs engineered so that when the length was cut and sewn together properly, the finished dress showcased often-elaborate patterns on the skirt and the bodice. Another house, Mathias Frères, with offices in Leipzig and Warsaw, specialized in the export of bridal trousseaus, which during the nineteenth century included custom-made day and evening dresses, lengths of fabric and lace, jewelry, fans, gloves, and shawls — everything a new bride needed to take her place in the fashionable world.

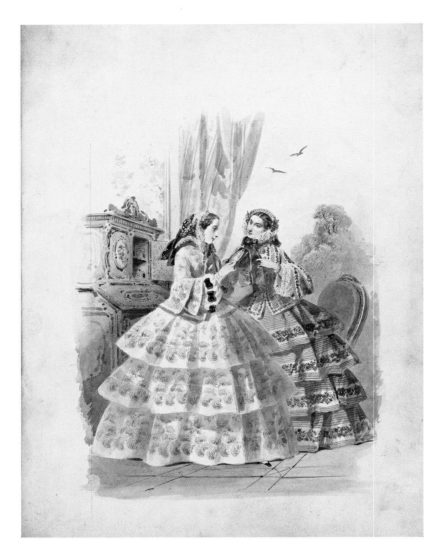

Some *magasins des nouveautés* specialized in *robes*, fabrics pre-patterned to create dresses trimmed with floral ruffles and borders such as those illustrated in this design for a fashion plate.

Certain of the shops on the rue Vivienne also specialized in the sale of model dresses, or *patrons modèles*, to foreign dressmakers and stores in London, New York, and Berlin who could then copy the French styles for their clients. It is unclear just what the *patrons modèles* were at this time, but they seem to have been paper or muslin patterns for French-designed dresses and outerwear. They were shipped in boxes to the foreign dressmaker or merchant, who would stitch them together to illustrate the latest Parisian fashions to their clientele. The individual pattern pieces would also provide a guide for the dressmaker to follow.[28] According to the fashion periodical *L'Album* of January 5, 1822, buyers from America and England would arrive at the shops in the spring and the fall to purchase models for reproduction. Some Paris dressmakers advertised dates on which they would show *poupées de mode* and *patrons modèles* in rented showrooms in cities such as London and St. Petersburg. [29]

As the century progressed, catalogues took on growing

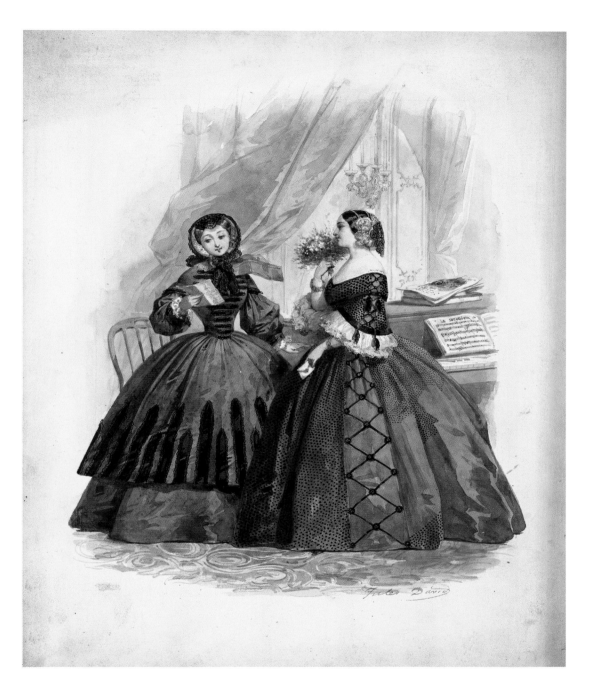

Jules David painted this illustration for the fashion magazine *le Moniteur de la Mode*, which was established by La Maison Popelin-Ducarre as a marketing tool.

importance for the stores that catered to a foreign clientele. Beginning in 1839, La Maison Popelin-Ducarre — which specialized in embroideries and eventually offered *nouveautés confectionnées* such as ready-made mantles and lingerie, as well as embroidered robes and wedding trousseaus made up by in-house dressmakers — published a free monthly catalogue called *Le Journal spécial des nouveautés de la Maison Popelin-Ducarre*. Sent to "all the courts and all the first families of Europe,"[30] it included fashion plates of the latest styles offered by the house (see p. 51). In 1843, Popelin-Ducarre transformed the catalogue into a fashion journal

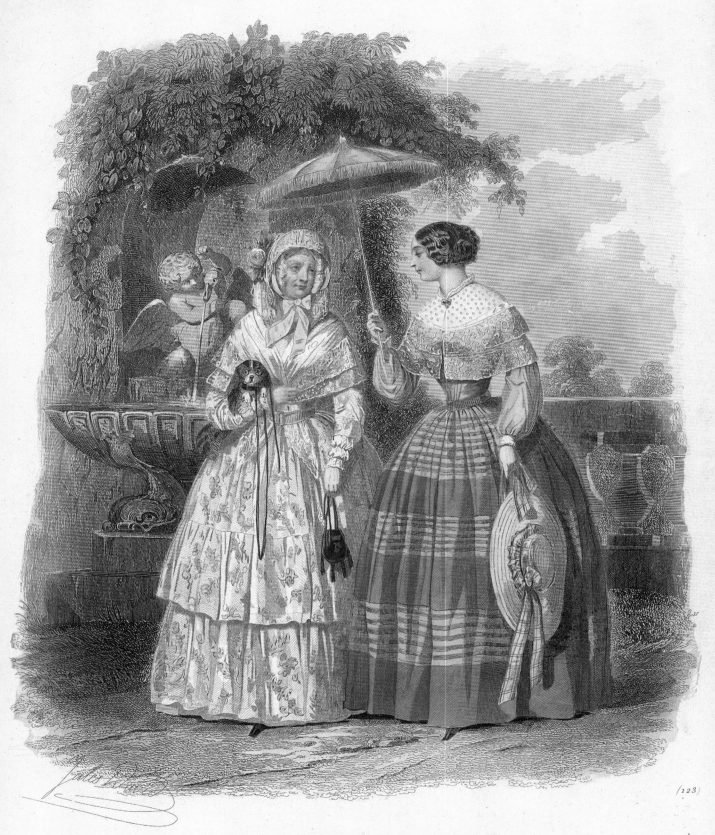

LE MONITEUR DE LA MODE.
Journal du Grand Monde

Toilettes de la Maison Popelin Ducarre rue neuve Vivienne, 41.

Chapeaux de Mme Bidault rue de Choiseul, fleurs de Mertens rue Richelieu, 96.

Ombrelle de Mottet Jne Boult Poissonnière, 7.

Bureaux du Journal, 43, Rue neuve Vivienne

PARIS.

New York E.B. Strange et Brother.   London at the Moniteur Office F. Durnus 15 Greek Street Soho.

and renamed it *le Moniteur de la Mode*; it would remain in publication until 1913. A famous fashion illustrator of the time, Jules David, became associated with the catalogue and continued to provide illustrations for *le Moniteur* until his death in 1892.

One of the most important and fashionable *magasins de nouveautés* was La Maison Gagelin. In 1828, Charles-Louis Gagelin, a merchant of *nouveautés* from Versailles, purchased a shop located at 93, rue de Richelieu in Paris. Gagelin continued in the tradition of the shop's previous owner, selling shawls and luxurious fabrics, laces, embroideries, and trims. He retired in 1839, and the business passed into the hands of his nephew Octave Opigez and Louis-Léonard Chazelle. As Chazelle and Opigez took on a number of investors, the shop grew considerably in size and significance. It enjoyed particular popularity with wealthy foreigners coming to Paris to look for the latest fashions. Like Popelin-Ducarre, La Maison Gagelin expanded to include women's ready-made capes and mantles.

Nineteenth-Century Fashion Trends

While retailers began offering some ready-made garments to clients, most women continued to frequent dressmakers to have their clothing custom-made. Talented and creative dressmakers took on increasing prominence as a trend toward more sophisticated cuts and more elaborate trim developed. The emphasis on the cut of clothing had begun with men's tailors, who prided themselves on providing a good fit. Since the fall of Napoleon in 1815 and the restoration of the monarchy under Louis XVI's brother, Louis XVIII, and then Charles X, men no longer wore ornately embroidered waistcoats, breeches, and jackets for ceremonial wear. The dark wool suit had become the norm for most occasions, including formal ones. The quality of the cloth and fit of the garment became the marks of a well-dressed man.

By the 1820s, women's clothing reflected the same interest in cut and fit. During the first two decades of the century, dressmakers fit garments by inserting drawstrings at the waist, neck, and sleeves that the wearer could easily adjust. As the century progressed and the cut of clothing grew in sophistication, new patterns allowed garments to fit more closely to the body — or to the corset, which was now an essential item of dress. Innovative technologies, including cutting tools, fitting systems, and paper patterns, were developed to aid the tailors and dressmakers in their work.

The dresses illustrated in this *le Moniteur de la Mode* fashion plate could be custom-made at La Maison Popelin-Ducarre. The shop also furnished many of the accessories, or *nouveautés*, pictured.

The July Revolution of 1830 overthrew the repressive regime of Charles X, and Louis Philippe succeeded to the throne. Louis Philippe repudiated the divine right of monarchs and became known as the bourgeois king. He and his wife, Louise Marie Adélaïde de Bourbon-Penthiève, ruled quietly and did not hold the lavish entertainments and ceremonies typical of previous reigns. Louise Marie was not interested in fashion or the extravagant lifestyle enjoyed by most royals, and women's clothing during the 1840s reflected a new simplicity. When an economic crisis led to Louis Philippe's abdication in 1848, rather than place his grandson on the throne, the National Assembly proclaimed the Second Republic. Louis Napoleon Bonaparte was elected president of the republic, and in a coup d'état on December 2, 1851, he declared himself president for life. Within a year, he had promoted himself to emperor and instituted the Second Empire. He married Eugénie de Montejo de Guzman, a stylish woman of Spanish-Scottish descent, and together they established a new and sparkling court in Paris.

The return to a lavish court lifestyle initiated a renewed interest in ceremony and dress. Eugénie, like Marie Antoinette before her, became the focus of fashion. She spent liberally on her bridal clothing, which was made by two of the most important dressmakers of the era, Mmes Palmire and Vignon — who as mortal enemies divided their responsibilities between her trousseau and her wedding dress. Napoleon III supported Eugénie's attention to fashion. Like his namesake, he understood the economic importance of the luxury industries, and he encouraged elaborate ceremony, sumptuous balls, and extravagant entertainments.

Franz Xavier Winterhalter's portrait of Eugénie surrounded by eight of her thirteen ladies in waiting is a study in mid-nineteenth-century dress. Probably made by the most fashionable dressmakers of the 1850s, the dresses are pure confections of fabric, lace, and ribbons that represent the height of fashion in 1855 Paris. Their full skirts worn over petticoats appear even wider because of the layers of ruffles or silk net trim. Seated to Eugénie's right, the Princesse d'Essling wears a pink taffeta *robe à disposition*, like those for which La Maison Lassalle earned its fame. The fabric is patterned with a white floral design engineered to border each ruffle edge. The other dresses worn in the portrait reveal the growing fashion for trimming dresses with lace, net, and ribbons.

Chic dressmakers enjoyed great popularity with visitors to the city, as well. Women from around the world traveled to Paris in ever-greater numbers to finish their wardrobes with the most fash-

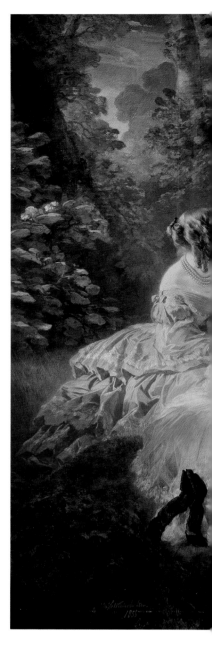

Franz Xavier Winterhalter's depiction of the empress Eugénie and her ladies in waiting shows them wearing the height of midcentury fashion, featuring tightly fitted bodices and full skirts.

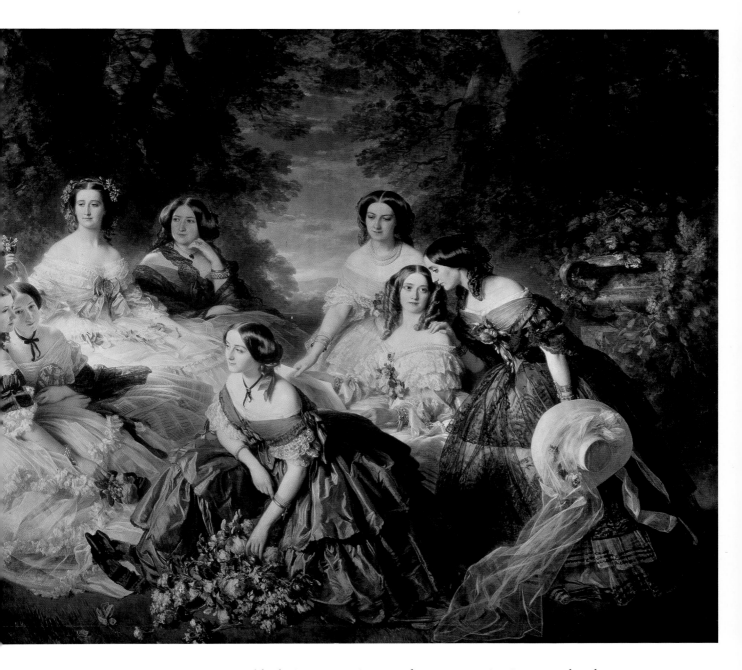

ionable designs. Americans such as Mrs. Benjamin S. Rotch, who
lived in Paris while her husband was studying painting there, were
able to keep their friends and relatives apprised of the latest fashions,
as well as offer shopping services. The Rotches socialized with the
cream of Parisian society, attending many of the glittering court
balls held by Napoleon III and his new wife Eugénie. When they
returned to the United States, Mrs. Rotch brought with her a collection of important headwear and dresses she had purchased in Paris.[31]

American families took pride in dressing their daughters in the
best Paris had to offer. Mrs. William Amory of Boston, in an 1865
letter to her son Ned, who was then traveling in Europe, reflected on

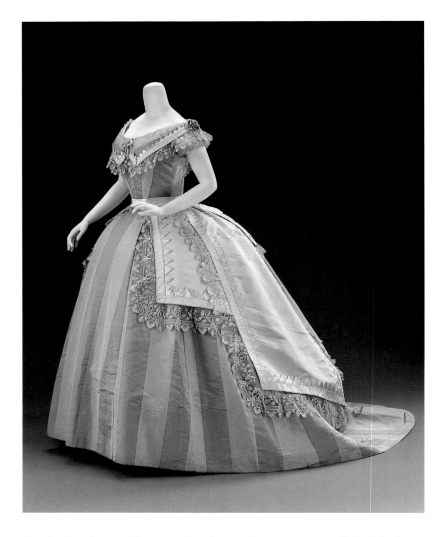

Mme Roger, one of Paris's most fashionable dressmakers, made this gown for Fanny Crowninshield, of Boston. Many Americans traveled to Paris to acquire the latest in stylish dress.

the death of one of her two daughters: "I go over my whole life, how ambitious I was for my two little girls — how I taught them their first lessons, helped them as they grew-up — worried over their *dress* thinking no expense too great & nothing too good."[32] At about the same time, Fanny Crowninshield's (later Mrs. John Quincy Adams II) parents bought her several Parisian gowns during travels to Europe. They purchased at least two gowns by Mme Roger, a rival of Palmire and Vignon, and one of Paris's leading dressmakers.[33]

The two Roger dresses illustrate the elaborate ornamentation that became stylish during the 1850s and 1860s and the elegance in design achieved by the best Parisian *couturières*. According to family history, Fanny wore one of the dresses to a ball given in Boston in honor of the Prince of Wales, later Edward VII; she danced the fourth set, a quadrille, with the prince. Mrs. Adams's granddaughter later described her as "an obsessed clotheshorse" who would often order dresses for specific occasions, as well as buy a season's worth of ensembles during a trip — a testimony to the allure of Paris fashion.[34]

François Claudius Compte-Calix created original watercolors from which fashion plates were engraved. He depicted actual garments, such as this burnoose from Maison Gagelin and dress by Mme Ghys.

No 15

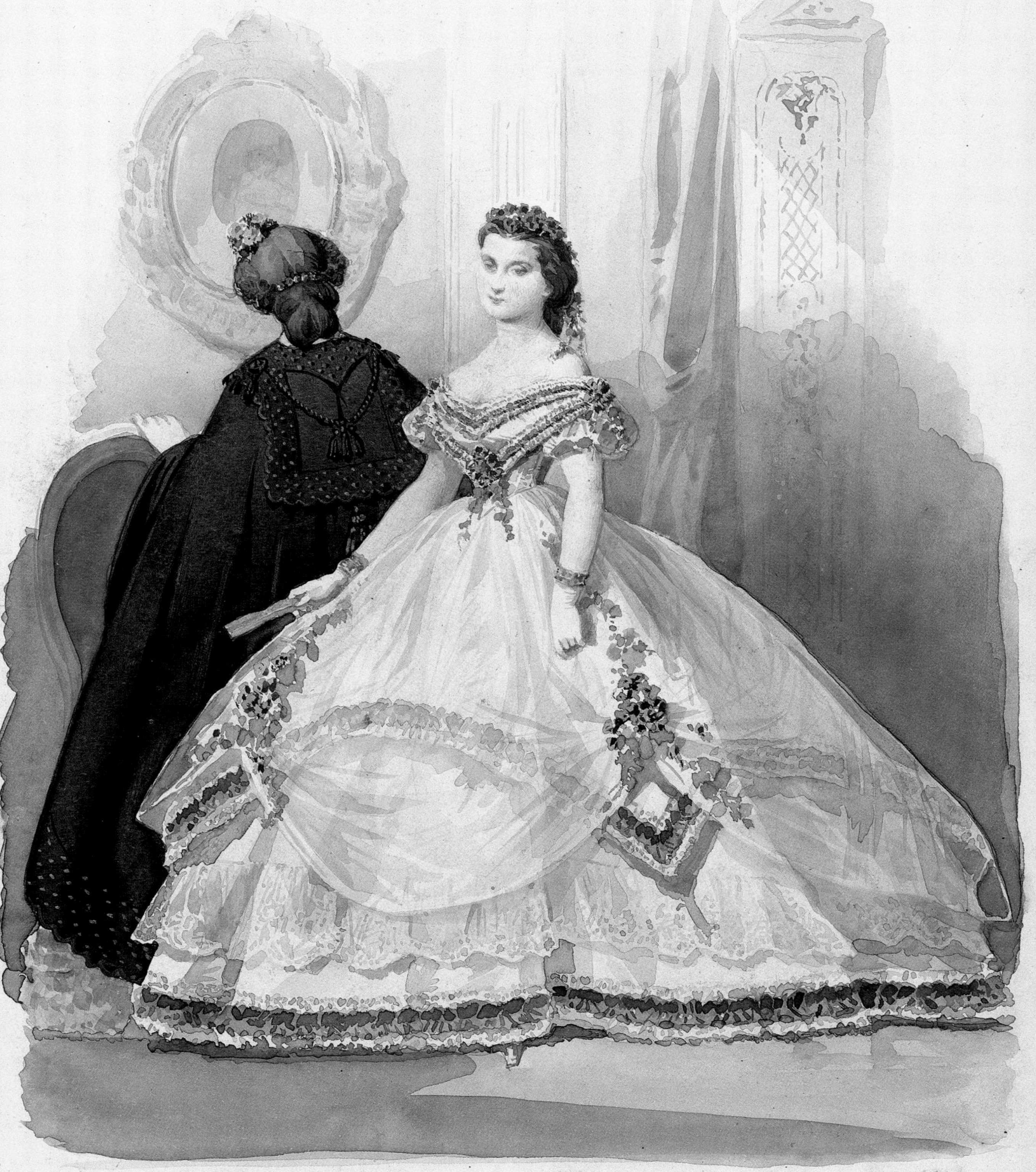

Modes —

Robe, Alexandre Ghys — Burnous Gagelin

The attention that both the court and the increasingly wealthy bourgeoisie gave to fashion created an environment in which change and innovation flourished. Women sought novelty, and those dressmakers with imagination flourished. The most fashionable dressmakers were also some of the most innovative business women. Both Mmes Roger and Palmire stocked fabric in their stores, in competition with the *magasins de nouveautés*. Others shipped clothing to the provinces and abroad or sold *patrons modèles* to foreign buyers for copying. Mme Roger was one of the first dressmakers to advertise ready-made clothing for women and children. In the Paris trade directory *Almanach-Bottin du Commerce* of 1850, her advertisement reads, "Mme Rodger & Cie., Ladies Dressmaker. Only house in Paris where ready-made wear for ladies and children can be found, 26 rue Nationale Saint Martin."[35]

The increasing interest in novelty encouraged the emergence of a new profession, that of *dessinateurs en costumes et robes*, or fashion and costume designers.[36] These artists, such as Charles Pilatte, Léon Sault, and Emile Mille, provided dressmakers with designs that could be copied for clients or used as inspiration. The dressmaker Mme Alexandre Ghys donated her archive of such designs to the Galliera Museum in 1879.[37] Several are annotated on the back with changes made in consultation with the client — an indication of one way they were used, as a starting point in discussing the design of the garment to be made.

These designers didn't work exclusively; depictions of the same dress drawn by Charles Pilatte exist in both Mme Ghys's records and the couturier Charles Frederick Worth's archives, now housed in the Victoria and Albert Museum.[38] In addition, the artists supplied fashion periodicals with drawings that, unlike the designs made for dressmakers, showed figures wearing actual dresses in elaborate and elegant settings. The journals emphasized that their fashion plates depicted real dresses, often attributing the clothing to fashionable dressmakers or *magasins de nouveautés* from Paris. Ironically, some of the dresses may have been inspired by the artists' own designs.

The Couturier

The involvement of men within the sphere of ready-to-wear and as *dessinateurs en costumes et robes* was paralleled by the developing role of male dressmakers, or couturiers, within the world of women's fashion. The *magasins de nouveautés* often employed men to oversee the women's clothing counters, and one of the most influential couturiers in the development of nineteenth-century women's fashion, Charles Frederick Worth, began his career in this way. The Englishman arrived in Paris before 1846 in search of a position at one of Paris's more influential *magasins de nouveautés*. After a year or two of struggle, he finally found a job as a salesclerk with La Maison Gagelin, where his charm, knowledge, and native tongue must have served him well with English-speaking clients from the United States and Great Britain.

Worth began to work closely with the *demoiselles de magasin*, the shopgirls who modeled the women's ready-to-wear capes, mantles, and shawls. These girls served an apprenticeship with the store and then began working as house models. Initially compensated with room and board, they were given a salary once they became more experienced. Worth ultimately married one of Gagelin's shopgirls, Marie Vernet, and it might have been his close working relationship with Marie that led to his career as a dressmaker.[39] As he draped shawls and mantles onto a live model, he pondered the best style of dress to wear underneath. According to his son Jean-Philippe, he began to design simple but well-cut dresses and had them made up for Marie to wear when modeling.

Gagelin's customers greatly admired the dresses, and with their encouragement, the ownership eventually allowed Worth to make up muslin *patrons modèles* for cloaks and simple dresses. Customers could then choose a model and have it custom-made to their size, using fabrics purchased from the shop. According to Jean-Philippe Worth, the muslin models were immensely successful, and the house permitted Worth to open a full-fledged custom dressmaking department. One of the most interesting features of the department was the salesroom where Worth could show prospective clients, including foreign buyers, his models made up in a variety of materials and trims carried by the store.

In addition to the new dressmaking salon, Gagelin also profited and earned fame for its ready-to-wear efforts around this time. It was the only firm to show women's ready-to-wear at the London Exposition of 1851, possibly under the influence of Worth. The company exhibited several mantles titled *Chambord* and *Mathilde* — by the mid-nineteenth century it was already common for houses to name their models — along with embroidered silks from Lyon and shawls.[40] La Maison Gagelin acknowledged Worth's contribution to its achievements in 1853, when he was made an associate. In the Paris Exposition of 1855, Gagelin exhibited "Fashionable accessories. Court trains. Models and forms: models for reproduction for the manufacturers in France and abroad." The catalogue also stated that the house exercised a certain influence on the development of elegant women's ready-to-wear, through its "multiple models, often pleasing and in good taste, that it creates and puts into circulation."[41]

Despite the store's accomplishments, by the end of 1857 conflict had arisen between Gagelin's associates, and Worth left to start his own business. The dress department continued and became very successful in spite of Worth's departure. By 1867, it employed between eighty and one hundred seamstresses on site and maintained at least ten offsite workshops, each retaining between one hundred fifty and two hundred seamstresses who worked to supply the shop and keep up with orders. Gagelin also expanded its sales of *patrons modèles* to dressmakers, custom shops, and the growing ready-to-wear trade, exporting as many as seven hundred thousand throughout the world.[42]

The store's growth was part of a larger trend: by 1867, the women's fashion industry had developed into a significant branch of French commerce, worth about fifty-five million francs and employing over seventeen thousand people.[43] Foreign manufacturers, dressmakers, and retailers with custom shops all looked to Paris as the source of fashion and to its *patrons modèles* as the model on which to base their work. The report from the 1855 Exposition indicates that the only women's ready-to-wear shown originated in France. According to the authors, women's ready-made clothing was manufactured everywhere, but because foreign manufacturers copied their clothing from Paris designs or models, they understood that they would not benefit by exhibiting their wares, which were simply imitations of the French.[44]

Within the atmosphere of luxury and high society encouraged by Napoleon III and his wife Eugénie, this expanding women's clothing industry created the perfect environment for a man of Worth's talents to succeed. His creativity ensured he was a favorite with the women of the French court, and his experience working with foreign clients made him a magnet for foreign buyers and for women traveling to Paris to find a wardrobe. With the financial backing of an expatriate Swede, Otto-Gustave Bobergh, Worth et Bobergh opened for business in the fall of 1857. The store followed the model that Worth had established for Gagelin's dress salon, and it was listed in Paris trade directories as a "Maison Spéciale, Robes et Manteaux Confectionnés, Soieries, Haute Nouveautés." In addition, the shop could be found under the headings "Couturiers" and "Nouveautés Confectionnées,"[45] amid other names includ-

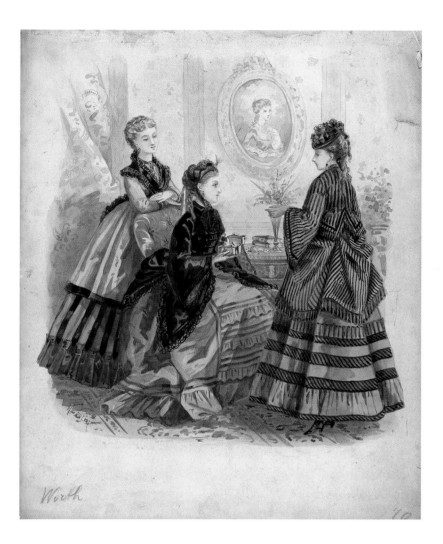

This watercolor by Héloïse Colin depicts dresses and mantles designed by Charles Frederick Worth, Paris's first couturier.

ing Pingat, Felix, and Duchoud, who also set up shop at this time and enjoyed great success, especially with foreign clients.

Like Gagelin, Worth et Bobergh custom-made dresses, sold fabrics and trims, and offered models for reproduction. However, Worth's shop differed from the traditional dressmaking establishment in that women had to select their designs from his collection of models; they did not consult with Worth on developing the design of their clothing. Women no longer dictated or even collaborated. Rather, Worth became the dictator of fashion. The age of the couture had begun, and it was centered in Paris.

Worth et Bobergh started out small, occupying a second-floor apartment at 7, rue de la Paix. However, Worth soon came to the notice of the empress Eugénie, who ordered several dresses after seeing his creations on Pauline, princess von Metternich, who was a fashion leader at the court. In a now-familiar pattern, Worth capitalized on his connections with the imperial family and the fashionable members of its court to launch his creations. Once Eugénie began wearing Worth's gowns and using him exclusively for her formal wear, his success was assured; anyone with pretensions to being well dressed visited M. Worth on the rue de la Paix. His clients included the czarina of Russia, the empress of Austria, the queens of Spain, Italy, and Sweden, and the queen of Madagascar, Ranavalova. Indeed, women from every court in Europe patronized Worth. Some of his best clients, though, were Americans, including Mrs. J. P. Morgan, Isabella Stewart Gardner, and Mrs. Potter Palmer, who didn't balk at his prices and usually paid in cash.

While the Americans favored several Parisian houses — Mme Roger, Emile Pingat, and Laferrière, among others — Worth remained the top choice, and women flocked to his shop. Joseph Primoli, the nephew of Mathilde Bonaparte, Napoleon III's cousin, wrote, "I have been with mother to Worth's. He is the great couturier in fashion. He charges sixteen hundred francs for a simple little costume! Ladies arrange to meet at Worth's and they talk politics as they sip tea. At Worth's, the faubourg Saint Germain sits between two kept women, and the world of officialdom meets the faubourg Saint Germain. Perhaps M. Worth does not even realize what he is doing, but he is reconciling all political parties and mingling all social classes."[46]

The wealthy Bostonian Isabella Stewart Gardner described the shop itself after a visit in 1867. She and her husband entered by climbing a red-carpeted stair lined with flowers. The first salesroom — furnished with overstuffed chairs and couches and cabinets exhibiting snuff boxes, fans, and other curios from Worth's personal collection — stocked black and white silks. The next room presented a rainbow of silks in all colors and was followed by rooms for velvets and woolen goods. Another showroom was devoted to Worth's model dresses, displayed on wooden forms.[47] At the back was the *salon des lumières*, a windowless room lit by gas where women could try on their evening dresses in the proper light.

Behind the showrooms and dressing rooms, a series of workrooms was each presided over by a *première* who supervised a specific aspect of the business, such as cutting the cloth, draping it, and stitching and fitting the garments. Other establishments were organized similarly. In some, the workrooms were divided according to specific types of sewing: there might be a workroom for fitting sleeves, another for making the skirts, and another for stitching the bodices.[48] This division of labor separated the larger houses from the small dressmaking establishments, making them more efficient and better able to handle the quick turnaround often demanded by foreign clients and the last-minute orders placed by the Paris elite.

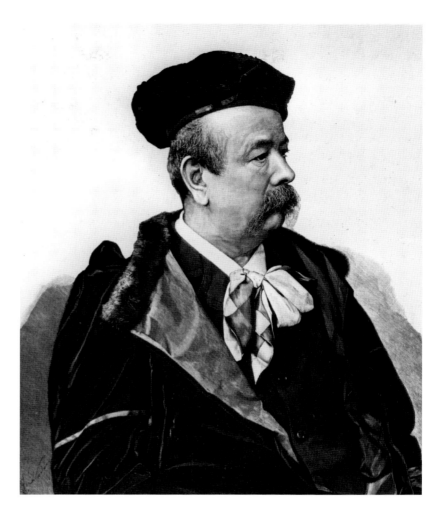

Charles Frederick Worth considered himself an artist and became the first dressmaker to dictate to women in matters of dress.

Worth presided over his shop as both creative director and fashion dictator. Jean-Philippe noted that his father had an interest in overseeing all aspects of the business, from the purchase of the silks and trims to the final fitting of the garments, making sure that everything was made to his exacting standards.[49] The designer considered himself an artist and often dressed the part, wearing a loose smock and beret. Some clients found him "respectful and sympathetic"; others thought him less polite. One customer wrote that he was "a most pronounced poseur and his affectations were extravagant almost to grotesqueness. At times he was arbitrary, brusque and even brutally rude."[50] Supremely confident in his taste and his ability to dress a woman to her best effect, Worth often bullied clients to see things his way. He once advised a short client who had her heart set on wearing dark green that she would look like an ivy bush.[51]

Male dressmakers such as Worth, Pingat, and Duchoud — as well as tailors such as Creeds of London, who dressed women and often tailored garments for Empress Eugénie — took on increasing importance in the world of women's fashion. The *maisons spéciales* that the couturiers set up provided the model for the twentieth-century *maison de couture*, where a selection of models designed by the house were shown to clients, as well as sold to foreign buyers, in an elegant, relaxed surrounding. The clothing could be displayed on wooden forms, on *demoiselles de magasin* (Marie Worth's previous role at Gagelin), or by 1870, in fashion parades.[52] The selected model dresses or mantles were then either custom-made for the client or shipped overseas to dressmakers and retailers who would custom-make them for their own clientele, or to manufacturers who would reproduce them as ready-to-wear.

One of the early problems faced by the new couture industry was the practice of copying a couturier's designs without paying to buy the model. In 1868, feeling a need to regulate this and other aspects of the industry, Worth established the Chambre Syndicale de la Confection et de la Couture pour Dames et Fillettes (Association of Women's and Girls' Ready-to-Wear and Couture). This organization oversaw the production of both couture and ready-to-wear, paying particular attention to battling piracy.

Around the same time, dressmakers and couturiers began to mark and label their garments. While the capes and mantles provided by the *magasins de nouveautés* typically had labels sewn to the back of the neck, the first labeled dresses appeared around the 1860s. Since dresses were made in two pieces, bodice and skirt, they were labeled on an interior ribbon known as a petersham band that wrapped around the waist of the bodice. Labeled Mme Roger garments exist in the collection of the Museum of Fine Arts, and labeled bodices from Worth et Bobergh and Pingat survive in many museum collections. Some American dressmakers followed the same practice: an 1860s dress labeled by the New Orleans dressmaker Mme Olympe recently appeared on the market and was sold at auction.[53] As dressmakers and couturiers gained greater name recognition and economic power as fashion leaders, the labeling of garments — often including client order numbers — became more common. Eventually, some couturiers even included their fingerprints on the labels, to more definitively establish the authenticity of their garments.

Creativity and Collaboration in the Early Twentieth Century

By the turn of the century, the couture had established itself as one of the most prestigious and important industries in France, and it was celebrated as such in Paris's Exposition Universelle of 1900.

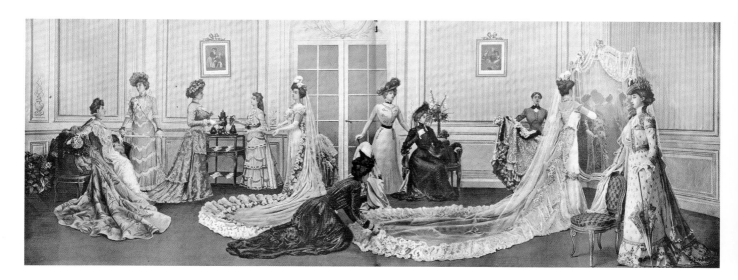

The costume pavilion at the 1900 Paris exposition displayed contemporary couture in real-life settings, including this replica of the house of Worth's fitting rooms.

Fashionable garments and/or *patrons modèles* had been shown at all of the French international exhibitions — in 1855, 1867, 1878, and 1889. But the French fashion display enjoyed particular success and prominence in 1900.

A bove the monumental gateway to the fairgrounds stood a bronze statue named *la Parisienne*, depicting a figure wearing a dress by one of the city's most influential couturiers, Mme Jeanne Paquin. Paquin and her husband, a former banker and business-man, had run a fashion house since 1891 with a combination of creative talent and business acumen that provided a model for many future houses, and Mme Paquin had become the first great female couturier. Her peers acknowledged her status by electing her to oversee the installation of the contemporary Paris couture gowns in the exposition's costume pavilion. The pavilion contained thirty dioramas, featuring clothing from the past and French provin-cial dress as well as contemporary couture garments. The couture displays were most popular, though. They included scenes such as "Departure for the Opera" and "Fitting the Wedding Gown" (which reproduced a salon from the house of Worth), as well as a diorama showing Mme Paquin herself in front of a dressing table.

The exhibition was held during a period of great artistic energy and freedom in Europe. In the early decades of the twentieth century, artists, designers, writers, composers, and choreographers were all working together in a spirit of collaboration and experi-mentation to create styles that moved Europe into the modern era. Some of the most creative minds gathered in Paris. Pablo Picasso arrived in 1904 and Henri Matisse in 1905, and other artists such as Georges Braque, Constantin Brancusi, Francis Picabia, and Fernand Léger also emigrated to the city and began experimenting with

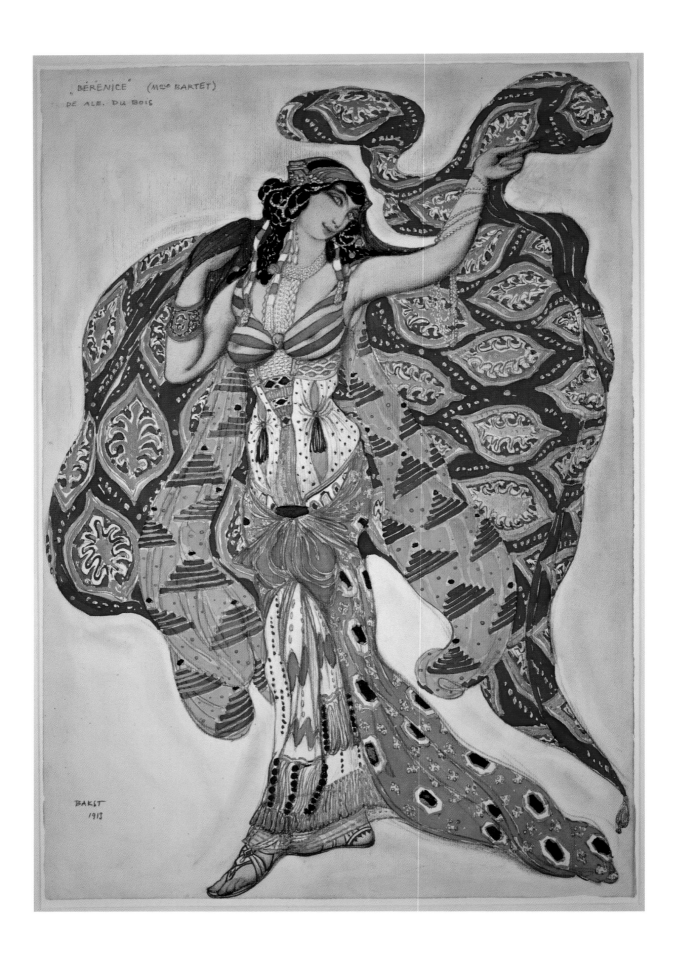

„BÉRÉNICE" (Mme BARTET)
DE ALE. DU BOIS

BAKST
1913

modernist approaches to painting and sculpture. Writers living in Paris included Marcel Proust, James Joyce, Guillaume Apollinaire, and T. S. Eliot, all of whose writings redefined modern literature.

One of the most influential artistic collaborations to hit the city was the Ballets Russes, founded by Russian impresario Serge Diaghilev. The ballets *Cleopatra* and *The Orientals* were first performed in Paris in 1909 and introduced an oriental exoticism and a profusion of brilliant color that shocked the Paris audience. The success of the Ballets Russes resulted from the teamwork of composer, choreographer, dancers, and artists. As the company settled in Paris, Diaghilev brought in local artists, designers, and even couturiers to partner with the choreographers and dancers. For the 1917 ballet *Parade*, for example, Picasso designed the scenery, and the shop of Jeanne Paquin made the costumes.[54]

Fashion designers who began their careers in these artistically fertile decades brought an unprecedented sense of creativity and collaboration to their work. One of the most innovative, talented, and influential clothing designers of the time was Paul Poiret, who epitomized the couturier as impresario and artistic leader. He counted among his friends many artists, designers, and writers, actively collecting and supporting their work. Poiret began his career by working in the design studios of Gaston and Jean-Philippe Worth (who had taken over operation of their father's house) and Jacques Doucet between 1899 and 1900. Both houses immediately recognized Poiret's creativity, but his modern tastes were at odds with their more classic styles. When he finally opened his own company in 1903, his progressive attitudes toward dress, his extravagant personality, and his openness to collaboration with his artistic friends made his house one of the most experimental in Paris.

Poiret has been credited with several important innovations, including the Art Deco fashion plate. In 1908, he invited the illustrator Paul Iribe to publish a series of ten plates illustrating his designs. Poiret felt that Iribe's simple lines and broad, flat use of color would suit his clothing. The plates were published in the 1908 book *Les Robes de Paul Poiret racontées par Paul Iribe*. Iribe printed the plates using the *pochoir* technique, in which colors were brushed onto paper through metal stencils. The technique became standard for many deluxe fashion magazines of the early twentieth century, such as *La Gazette du Bon Ton*, *Le Journal des Dames et des Modes*, and *Modes et Manières d'Aujourd'hui*.

Poiret was also one of the first modern designers to expand his business into several related areas, including accessories,

The brilliant colors and exotic oriental costumes of the Ballets Russes, as seen in this costume design by Léon Bakst, had a significant impact on artists and designers in Paris during the early twentieth century.

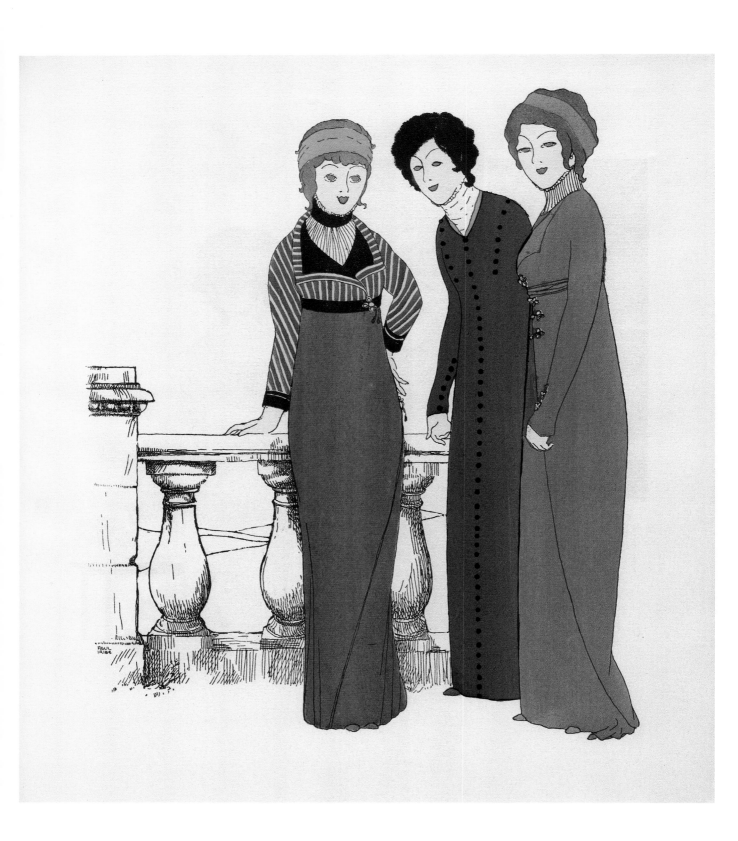

perfume, and the decorative arts. He opened a design atelier in 1911 (named "Martine," after his daughter), and he employed young women without any classic training to design textiles, furniture, and other decorative arts in a fresh, uninhibited way. Unhappy with the selection of textiles available from French manufacturers, Poiret also approached some of his artist friends to design for him. Raoul Dufy began working for him in another studio set up in the same year as Martine. Dufy designed and printed fabrics such as a beautiful rose-printed velvet that Poiret made into a coat for his wife, Denise. Dufy's work soon came to the attention of Lyon silk manufacturer Bianchini Ferrier, and the artist left Poiret's studio to design for the larger firm.

In this atmosphere of experimentation and artistic freedom, Poiret and his contemporaries began to design clothing with cuts and silhouettes that had not been seen before in the dressmaking and couture industry. During most of the second half of the nineteenth century, women's dresses were generally composed of a

Paul Poiret commissioned the artist Raoul Dufy to design fabric for him in 1911. Dufy designed and printed the velvet used to make this coat named *La Perse*.

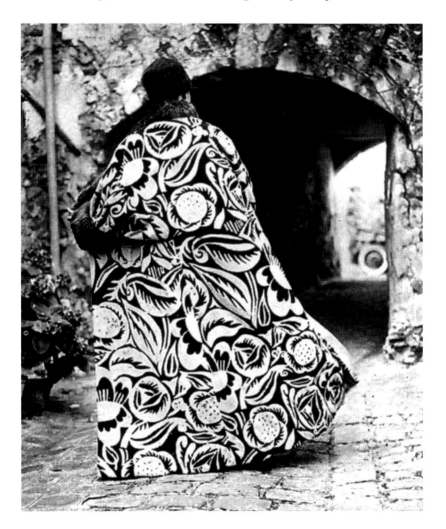

LA MODE

73

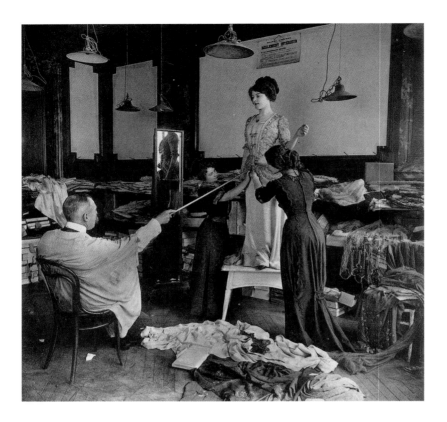

Until the early twentieth century, couturiers draped fabrics and trims on an undergarment known as a lining. The basic shape, or cut, of the garment did not change.

bodice and skirt. While the skirts and sleeves slowly expanded and contracted to change the silhouette, the basic structure remained the same; a dressmaker or couturier's creativity rested with the choice of fabrics and trims used and the draping of the fabric on the basic understructure, or lining.[55] Couturiers such as Worth had pushed the silhouettes along, but it wasn't until the turn of the century that the designers did away with the understructure and developed new ways in which to cut and fit clothing.

One of the new century's first major changes in the way women dressed was the evolution away from the hourglass silhouette that had characterized women's dress throughout most of the nineteenth century. Although Poiret took credit for bringing back the slim empire silhouette and banishing the corset, in fact several designers were involved in effecting this gradual change. Mme Paquin presented her experiments with a slimmer silhouette in her display for the Paris 1900 exhibition. And Poiret's contemporary Madeleine Vionnet, who also got her start in the workrooms of Jacques Doucet, introduced a slimmer silhouette the year before Poiret did. Vionnet looked to the fabric and the geometry of the human body for inspiration.[56] Her revolutionary cuts exploiting the bias cut of fabric resulted in clothing that draped and clung to the body. Poiret, by contrast, was inspired by the oriental and exotic clothing of the East.

Madeleine Vionnet, along with Paul Poiret, redefined the cut of women's clothing. Vionnet looked to the fabric and geometry for inspiration.

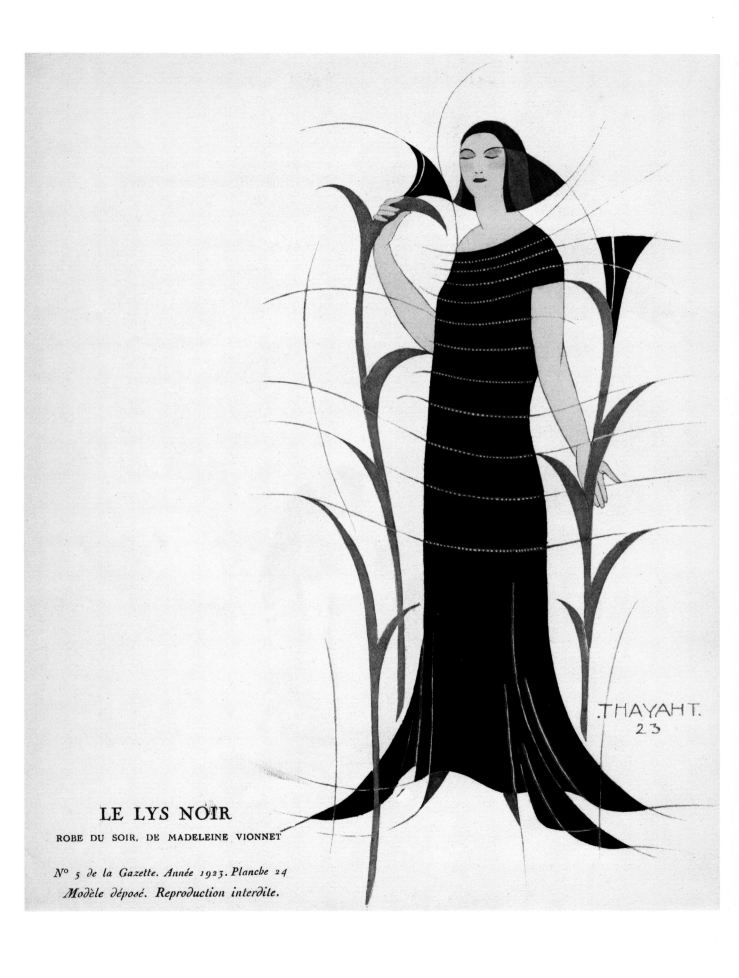

LE LYS NOIR

ROBE DU SOIR, DE MADELEINE VIONNET

N° 5 de la Gazette. Année 1923. Planche 24

Modèle déposé. Reproduction interdite.

The fame of designers such as Poiret and Vionnet spread
quickly during the early twentieth century, as fashion magazines such
as *Vogue* and *Harper's Bazaar*, as well as newspapers from around the
world, increased coverage of the new styles introduced in Paris. The
couture houses themselves adapted to their growing international
markets. The Paquins were the first to open a foreign branch, in 1896
in London. Other branches followed, in Buenos Aires and New York
in 1912 and Madrid in 1913. By 1900, Worth also had a branch in
London. Some designers traveled to promote themselves — particularly Poiret, who visited Russia in 1911 and the United States in 1913.
Denise Poiret accompanied her husband to the States, traveling with
a wardrobe of one hundred Poiret gowns to show off his work.[57]

The role of the Paris couture in setting new fashions only

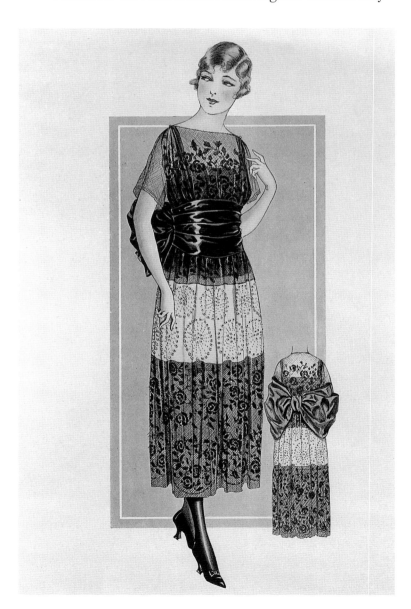

A design by Maison Paquin
inspired this 1918 model
dress offered to dress-
makers by the New York
wholesaler Harry Angelo
Company.

expanded as the couturiers' renown grew. Supplying model dresses to dressmakers and industry buyers developed into an extremely lucrative aspect of the business. Foreign department stores, dressmakers, wholesale importers, and manufacturers used the model designs and the couturiers' names attached to them to successfully market their wares in their own country. Department stores and importers who sold dry goods to dressmakers and smaller custom shops began to publish catalogues that included a photo of the Paris design along with a list of the materials needed to have it made — which they could, of course, supply. These catalogues became valuable tools for local dressmakers, who used them as both a source of inspiration and an assurance to their customers that they offered the latest word in Paris fashion.

Defining the Couture and Ready-to-Wear

As the Paris couture developed into the dominant force within the fashion world, a split occurred within the industry, dividing the couture from the ready-to-wear. Until the early twentieth century, the two had been overseen by the same organization, the Chambre Syndicale de la Confection et de la Couture pour Dames et Fillettes founded by Charles Frederick Worth in 1868. Now, the leaders of the couture felt a need to separate from the ready-to-wear industry, in order to establish a hierarchy and more effectively manage their diverging interests. In 1910, encouraged by Worth's grandson Jacques, the original Chambre Syndicale was dissolved and the Chambre Syndicale de la Couture Parisienne (Association of Parisian Couture) was created. The separation of the industries emphasized the difference between couture and ready-to-wear and formally placed couture on top.

Some of the concerns of the new Chambre Syndicale included fixing the dates of the fashion parades for the press and buyers, regulating the number of models shown, managing relations with the press, developing promotional opportunities, ensuring the labor conditions of the seamstresses and other craftspeople, and combating style piracy. To formalize procedures for the sale of model dresses, the Chambre Syndicale established that twice a year each house's salon would be turned over to buyers and press from abroad. The shopgirls would parade one after another through the store, wearing the house's new models. Similar fashion parades may have been used by Charles Worth as early as the 1870s, but it is unclear just what those parades were. The English couturier Lucille is most often credited with the first scheduled theatrical-style runway shows held for buyers and the press, and she may have held them as early as 1897. By 1903, the practice appears to have been common on both sides of the Atlantic; Lucille produced shows in her shops in London and Paris, and American department stores also staged theatrical fashion parades incorporating music and lighting.[58]

Although the evolution of the couture in Paris was interrupted by World War I, when most of the young male designers — including Poiret, Worth's grandsons Jacques and Jean-Charles, and Jean Patou — were drafted into the army, the government did what it could to keep the couture houses in business. It worked with the houses to make sure they had the fabric they needed during a time of restrictions, and it even sent couture models by Paquin, Doucet, Jeanne Lanvin, Callot Soeurs, and other designers to the 1915 Panama Pacific International Exhibition in San Francisco, to show the world that, despite the war, the couture industry was still creating fashions. Buyers continued their biannual visits to Paris, seeking the inspiration only that city could provide.

After the war, new designers such as Gabrielle Chanel, Elsa Schiaparelli, and Lucien Lelong emerged and added fresh energy to the industry. The emphasis on youth culture, the fact that more women were entering the workforce, and the increased pace of life brought about by improved transportation and communication accelerated the move toward a simpler, more youthful silhouette already taking place within the fashion industry. The short, unfitted dresses and sport suits that characterized the 1920s had an important impact on the industry, especially on fine women's ready-to-wear. Previously, the focus on fit and on complexly draped fabrics and trims in women's fine apparel made it difficult to manufacture high-end dresses that women would actually buy. Women who could afford high fashion had their clothing made by dressmakers or couturiers. The loosening up and simplification of the silhouette made the manufacture of dresses a much easier proposition, and the women's ready-to-wear industry began to flourish, especially in the United States.

Manufacturers, like the dressmakers and dry-goods suppliers, relied on the couture models to provide the *caché* needed to sell their products. Their representatives traveled to Paris twice a year and acquired designs, which they brought back to the studio to be modified for their clientele's taste and mass-produced. Often, cheaper fabrics and trims would be used, or, as was frequently the case in the United States, anonymous in-house designers would simplify

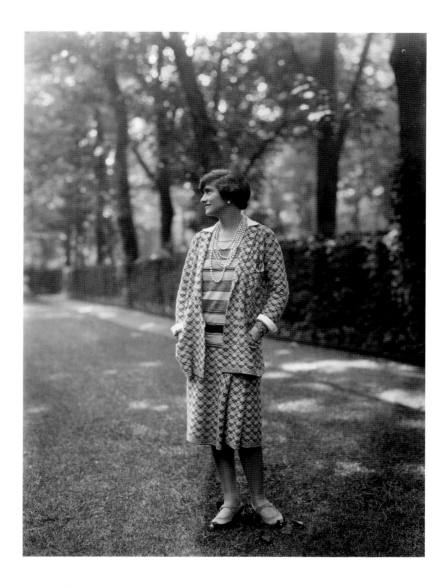

Gabrielle "Coco" Chanel designed youthful sport suits often made of wool jersey, a utilitarian fabric used during World War I.

the models to suit their countrywomen's tastes. However, the name of the couturier who designed the original model remained attached to it and was promoted to sell the new ready-to-wear fashions.

The Second World War again disrupted the business of the couture. Lucien Lelong, now president of the Chambre Syndicale, worked hard to keep the industry in business and in Paris. During the occupation, the Germans proposed merging the Paris couture with the ready-to-wear industries already established in Berlin and Vienna. Lelong went to Berlin to convince them that their plan to move the couture houses, their workers, and their machinery, and to split them between Vienna and Berlin, would never work. He argued that if the couture businesses alone were moved, they could not survive, because the houses relied on numerous small Parisian merchants and craftsmen to provide the accessories, trimmings, and embroideries they needed to do their work. The supportive role of these small craft businesses within the high fashion world had not changed since the time of Rose Bertin. Lelong persuaded the Germans of the unfeasibility of their plan and returned to Paris, reestablishing his house despite the continued German occupation. He hired two young designers to help him in this task, Pierre Balmain and Christian Dior.

Under Lelong's guidance, the couture industry maintained itself during occupation. However, it was impossible for foreign buyers to continue their biannual trips to Paris. Because of German regulations, the twenty houses that remained open for business each showed only about a hundred models per year; in the past, the numbers could reach as high as three thousand. Cut off from their supply of French designs, the foreign buyers had to rely on home-grown talent to create new fashions.

In the United States, serious efforts were made to encourage native design talent. American designers had long been a part of the industry, but in general they worked anonymously.[59] When the U.S. manufacturers could no longer access the French designs, they became dependent on their in-house designers, and with the help of department stores such as Lord & Taylor, as well as the fashion press, these designers gained increasing renown. Names such as Norman Norell and Charles James, as well as those of sportswear designers Claire McCardell, Claire Potter, Tom Brigance, and Tina Leser, became familiar to many women, threatening the French industry and the dominance of Paris and its couture houses.

When Paris was liberated in 1944, those who supported the growing American fashion design industry remained optimistic that the Parisian dominance of the profession had finally been broken. However, Paris's enduring reputation as the place where new fashions were set was hard to extinguish. Many of the couturiers who had fled during the occupation, including the Italian Elsa Schiaparelli and the Englishman Edward Molyneux, returned to the city. Both Schiaparelli and Molyneux showed collections in the autumn of 1945. In that same year, Pierre Balmain also presented his first independent collection.

Lelong's other assistant, Christian Dior, with the backing of financier Pierre Boussac, introduced his first line in 1947 in Paris. Dior's collection, now known as the New Look, was a huge success. The ultra-feminine dresses set the fashion of the time, with their nipped-in waists and full skirts, and struck a cord with women looking for a new femininity after the deprivations of the war. Dior's success, and that of the rest of Paris's couture houses, brought back to Paris all the attention that had slowly seeped away during the war years. High-end ready-to-wear manufacturers in the United States and other

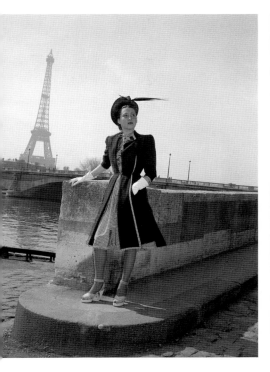

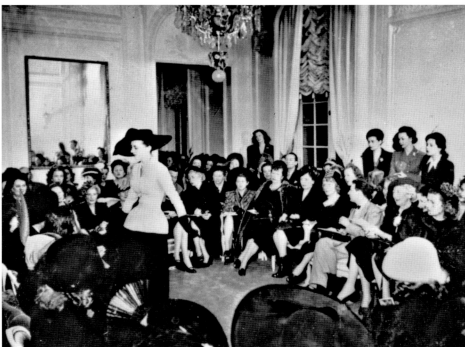

Pierre Balmain opened his couture house in 1945. This design from his 1947 collection, with its slim profile and restricted use of fabric, reflects the wartime silhouette.

Christian Dior opened his own house in 1947 and showed ultra-feminine styles that featured yards and yards of fabric. The success of the collection, dubbed the New Look, ensured that Paris remained the center of fashion.

countries again looked to the Paris couturiers as the creative force in the fashion industry and again relegated their in-house designers to the back room. However, the American sportswear industry that had become successful during the war remained strong, paving the way for the development of New York into a major fashion center with the growth of the American designer ready-to-wear industry in the 1960s.

Despite the increasing importance of the fashion industries in New York, Rome, and London, Paris continued as the undisputed leader throughout the 1950s. Couturiers such as Christian Dior, Cristóbal Balenciaga, Jacques Fath, Jean Dèsses, and Madame Grès created some of the most beautiful clothing ever made by the couture industry. In spite of their success, by the end of the decade the young daughters of couture clients saw their mothers' clothing styles and habits as less relevant to their lifestyles, and they sought their own style of dress. They turned to smaller boutiques that were opening in London and New York and sold more youthful clothing.

During the 1960s, couturiers kept making beautiful clothes, but the growth of the ready-to-wear industry, competition from small boutique lines such as the young Englishwoman Mary Quant's, and buyers' diminishing patience for the time and effort necessary to fit custom clothing all brought about a decline in the industry. Some couturiers such as Balenciaga closed shop, while others such as Yves Saint Laurent and Pierre Cardin expanded into designer ready-to-wear, or *prêt-à-porter des couturiers*.

The Fédération Française de la Couture, du Prêt-à-Porter des Couturiers et des Créateurs de Mode

In 1973, faced with a changed industry, the couture and the ready-to-wear again came together under the same organization, the Fédération Française de la Couture, du Prêt-à-Porter des Couturiers et des Créateurs de Mode (French Federation of Couture, Couturier Ready-to-Wear, and Fashion Designers). This Fédération, still in existence, is composed of three individual *chambres* — couture (originally founded in 1868 and revised in 1910), couturier and designer ready-to-wear, and men's wear (both founded in 1973). The Fédération's several goals include establishing synergies between the various factions of the fashion industry, specifically textile weavers, designers, and buyers; defending intellectual property rights, as copies continue to be a problem; fostering training and professional development, in part by managing the Ecole de la Chambre Syndicale de la Couture Parisienne (School of the Association of Parisian Couture) founded in 1928; solving collective problems and advising its members of legislative changes and new regulations concerning business, taxes, and trade; and, finally, maintaining Paris's role as the "world capital of creation."[60] In this last function, the Fédération oversees the biannual fashion shows of the couture, ready-to-wear, and men's wear, updates the press list from which its members prepare their show invitations, and informs journalists and buyers of the activities of the Fédération and its members.

Roughly one hundred French companies belong to the Fédération. In acknowledgment of the internationalization of fashion, there are also associate members from outside of France, specifically from Japan, Italy, and Belgium. Membership in the Fédération brings with it a legitimacy that designers can find nowhere else. Its long history, significant role in organizing the fashion industry, and location in Paris — with its enduring reputation for taste and luxury — all combine to make it the most important fashion trade organization in the world.

The Fédération's most prestigious members are the haute couture designers of the Chambre Syndicale de la Couture Parisienne. The title "haute couture" is legally protected by the French government and is granted yearly in a decree issued by a special commission of the ministry of industry. Members show their collections twice a year: the Fall–Winter couture collections in July and the Spring–Summer ones in January. Since 1997, the organization has revitalized itself by inviting some designers to become corresponding members (their candidacy must first be approved by the members of the organization), as well as by inviting other designers to present their collections during the couture shows (again, with approval by the member houses). Currently, there are two corresponding members, Valentino and Armani, and seven guest members.

Membership in the Chambre Syndicale du Prêt-à-Porter des Couturiers et des Créateurs de Mode (Association of Couturier Ready-to-Wear and Fashion Designers) and the Chambre Syndicale de la Mode Masculine (Association of Men's Wear) is less strictly regulated. Those applying for membership must submit a portfolio and be sponsored by two current members. The women's ready-to-wear Fall–Winter collections are shown in February or March and the Spring–Summer collections usually in September or October. The men's ready-to-wear collections can be seen in January and June or July.

One of the most important benefits of belonging to the Fédération is the right to show on its calendar. Each season, the Fédération sets the official schedule and coordinates activities around the showing of the collections. This coordination is key in today's fashion world, where the designer's runway show occurs only once. As recently as the early 1980s, the couture houses showed their collections repeatedly over a two-month period in the comfort of their own salons.[61] However, as the runway shows developed into theatrical spectacles by the end of the decade, this practice changed.

The management of the calendar has become even more important to ensure that everyone who needs access to the collections has it. The Fédération has worked with the French government to make sure that adequate space is available to show the collections, many of which are now held in the auditorium spaces built into the Louvre Museum renovations of 1993. The four rooms in the Carrousel du Louvre host many of the shows, while others are staged nearby in a large tent set up in the Tuileries. Other well-attended shows such as those of Dior and Chanel occur at the Grand Palais, or in out-of-the way spots chosen by a specific house.

The Fédération has evolved over the years to stay current with changes in the industry, to keep Paris central to the fashion world, and to meet the needs of its members. Its willingness to open its doors to those outside the traditional couture and fashion worlds, among them the Japanese designers Issey Miyake, Rei Kawakubo, and Yohji Yamamoto during the late 1970s and the young Belgians Martin Margiela, Ann Demeulemeester, and Dries Van Noten during the 1980s, gave these talented designers a standing they could not have acquired elsewhere. At the same time, their

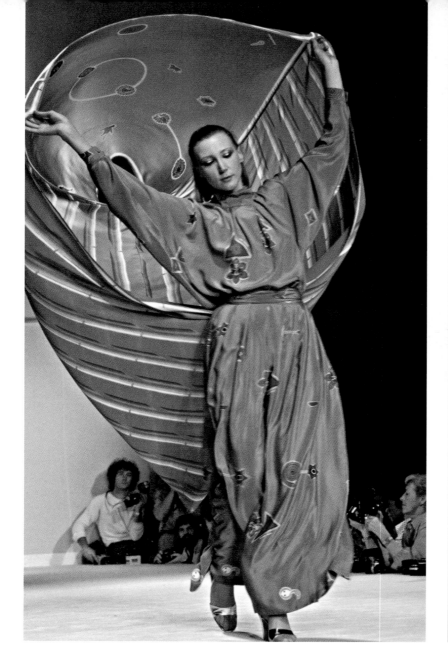

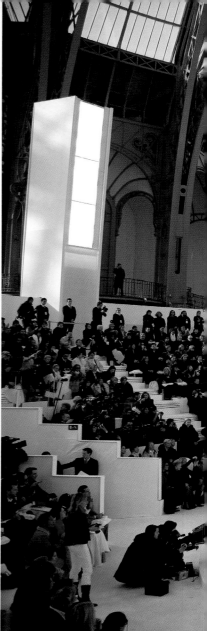

presence in Paris brought new and exciting work to the runways.[62]

Today's Fédération follows in a long tradition of fostering creativity and smart business practices to reinforce Paris's status as the capital of fashion. Colbert and Louis XIV laid the foundation in the seventeenth century by establishing and controlling the industries related to the production and sale of luxury goods — and concentrating them in Paris, to make that city the place to acquire the most luxurious and fashionable goods available. By cultivating a desire for French fashion, Louis's court supported the industry and increased its exports. Subsequent governments have employed similar political and economic practices to sustain Paris's dominance of fashion.

Alongside the government support, the French people's respect and admiration for creativity, tempered with a Gallic practicality,

During the 1970s, the French fashion establishment opened its doors to foreign companies and invited designers such as Issey Miyake, of Tokyo, to show their collections alongside those of the French houses.

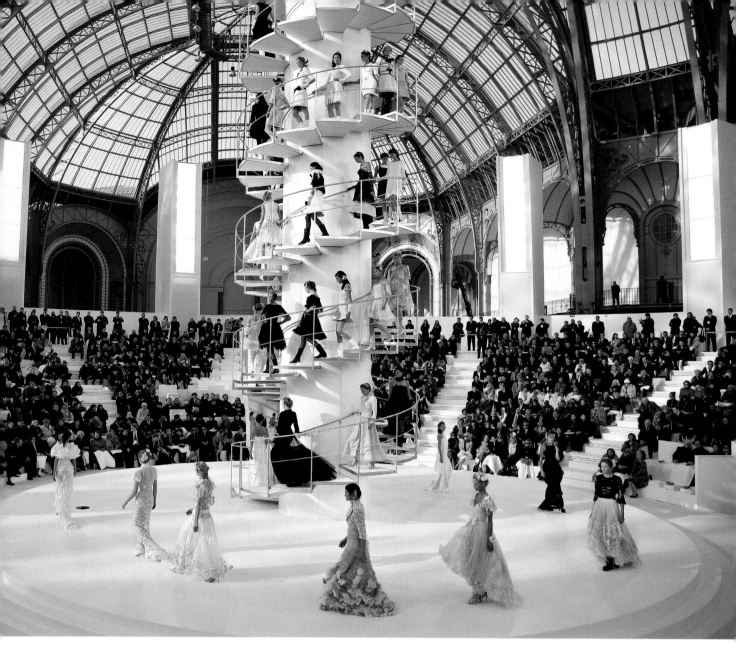

Extravagant fashion shows have replaced the weekly parades that the French houses held until the early 1980s. Chanel showed its Spring–Summer 2006 collection in the Grand Palais and featured a circular runway and stair.

has supported the industry's survival, even in more recent times when the couture has frequently run at a loss. In 1988, the Syndicat Confédération Géneral du Travail (General Confederation of Labor of France), a French trade union, commented in a press release that, "Haute Couture is not clothes for sale but a research laboratory of creation and also functions as publicity that is vital for other related activities of a couturier. It should not be the houses' goal to make profits from the couture business."[63] It is this creative edge that has nurtured Paris's preeminent role within the fashion world. The great names in the history of French fashion — Rose Bertin, Hippolyte Leroy, Charles Frederick Worth, Paul Poiret, Madeleine Vionnet, Christian Dior, Cristóbal Balenciaga, Yves Saint Laurent, and now all of the designers represented in this book — stand out for their creativity and their ability to lead the way into the future.

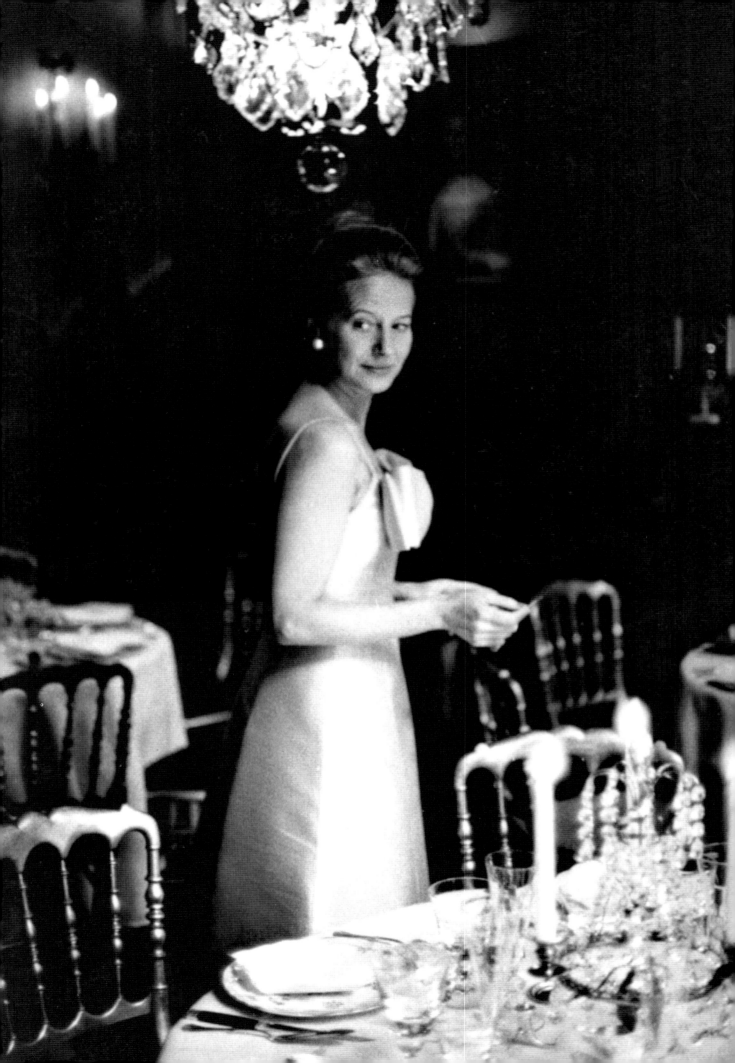

Haute Couture and Ready-to-Wear: A Recent History

DIDIER GRUMBACH

On December 14, 1910, at the instigation of Jacques Worth, the couturiers and ready-to-wear manufacturers (*confectionneurs*) of Paris split into separate camps, after half a century of coexistence.[1] This split resulted in the French fashion system as we now know it, with those who sold ready-made clothes on one side and those who custom-made garments to their clients' measurements on the other. Until 1940, however, there were other, more subtle distinctions at work within the fashion industry. Those with a place on the official calendar of fashion showings published by the Chambre Syndicale de la Couture Parisienne, the industry's professional association, were called *grands couturiers*, while those who sold their models to foreign buyers, usually without holding runway shows, were considered *moyenne* (midlevel) *couture*. The term *petite couture*, finally, was used for the neighborhood seamstress.[2] These practices had been forged by longstanding convention and finally changed only under rather unusual circumstances.

By 1941, the war had brought about a severe shortage of raw materials in France, particularly of fabric. A rationing system was instituted. As a way of getting dressmakers more fabric than their ration books allowed, it became necessary to define the haute couture industry more precisely. Lucien Lelong, president of the Chambre Syndicale at the time, sent a questionnaire to its membership; the responses he received helped determine the adopted criteria, which were ratified by the minister of industrial production in 1943. Otherwise put, the definition of "haute couture" was shaped by the national manufacturing predicament. We should note that designer ready-to-wear did not yet exist in France; until the late 1950s, 60 percent of Frenchwomen wore clothes made to

Princess Ghislaine de Polignac became the first French stylist. Working for Galeries Lafayette, she helped to make department store clothing acceptable to the fashionable elite for the first time.

measure. Haute couture remained competitive and privileged, while the concept of couturier ready-to-wear was still in its infancy.

Couture and Ready-to-Wear

Runway shows were devoted solely to haute couture, since in most people's minds the creation of new designs belonged exclusively to couture. In 1956, Raymond Barbas, president of the house of Patou and then-president of the Chambre Syndicale, drafted a request for aid in obtaining fabric. Appended to his application was a document containing three brief sentences, highlighted and underlined, that very clearly express the relations between couture and ready-to-wear at that time: "The life's blood of couture, the source of the public's profound interest in it, is creative design. And design happens at such a pace, seasonally and continually, that it precludes any recourse to industrialization. If creativity could exist in an industrial atmosphere, couture would have changed its way of operating a long time ago." This postulate met no objections from the ready-to-wear manufacturers, nor, needless to say, from the couturiers.

And yet the signs of a new age were already starting to appear. That same decade, on their return from the United States, Max Heilbronn and Raoul Meyer, future presidents of the Galeries Lafayette and sons-in-law of the department store's founder, Théophile Bader, challenged the assumption that no Parisian woman of taste would ever buy her wardrobe in a department store.[3] The two men had visited Bloomingdale's and been amazed at the elegant clientele that flocked to the Green Room, where Madge Carroll presided. Why not try to do the same thing in France, and hire a fashion director?

Heilbronn went looking for a woman from the Paris jet set, ideally someone who had never held a job before. He eventually chose Princess Ghislaine de Polignac, a familiar figure in the society pages, witty and spirited, precisely the kind of woman all the couturiers dreamed of having as their "jockey."[4] Historically, she was the first French stylist (though the term itself did not come into use until 1960, and the function it designated was still rather vague).[5] Ghislaine de Polignac's job was to preview all the ready-made and couture collections, and from them select the elements of what would become the Galeries Lafayette "style." Innovation was not yet a part of her job, as that would mean challenging sacrosanct haute couture. However, she stripped the dress designs of superfluous frills and decreed that true chic could be had with a basic black sheath dress. Gradually, the simple, pretty outfits that the princess wore with ballet slippers "to go to work" began catching on like wildfire in so-called high society.[6] One day, running into the princess, the duchess of Windsor accosted her: "What a beautiful coat, Ghislaine. Don't tell me it comes from Galeries Lafayette!" "But of course, your highness." At that, the duchess immediately ordered two coats in size 38, one in pink and one in blue. In 1954, such an event was seen by the ready-made dressmakers as a gift from the heavens. Ready-to-wear decidedly had a future.

Fashion specialists began sprouting up in the major department stores, just as stylists were flourishing in the industrial sector. It is in this category that we should place Christiane Bailly and Emmanuelle Khanh, two former models for Balenciaga. In 1962, at Pharamond, a restaurant on rue de la Grande-Truanderie, they presented a joint collection under the label Emma-Christie. Actually, the two stylists were alternately presenting their own designs. Although each was only half the label, the introduction, under its designers' names, of a kind of fashion for the street and in the street was something new and important in France. The international press titans *Life* and *Look* reported on the historic moment with wonder.[7]

"Style Versus Couture" could have been the title of the runway show that the Fashion Group of Paris organized in Neuilly in 1965. In the first part, stylists Emmanuelle Khanh, Michèle Rosier, and Christiane Bailly were represented by models with a "neurasthenic" look. After that, ready-to-wear collections from Castillo, Jean Patou, Madeleine de Rauch, and Philippe Venet were worn by professional models, offering a stereotype of Parisian chic. Two irreconcilable concepts of elegance were on display, each leaving half the audience enthusiastic and the other half outraged.

In 1966, Hebe Dorsey, fashion columnist for the *International Herald Tribune*,[8] invited our three heroic stylists to New York for the April in Paris Ball; they were escorted by Paco Rabanne, who had become famous for his metallic dresses. This time, their presentation was a complete flop, and people quietly began leaving the room.[9] Fortunately, the humiliation was mitigated by congratulations from Diana Vreeland, then editor-in-chief of American *Vogue*, who came to their hotel the following day with her entire staff to inspect their collections more closely.

This was a pivotal moment: haute couture was still a profitable enterprise, and it was therefore still essential to safeguard it against counterfeit. Photographers were banned from runway shows, sketches were confiscated, and the police commissioner

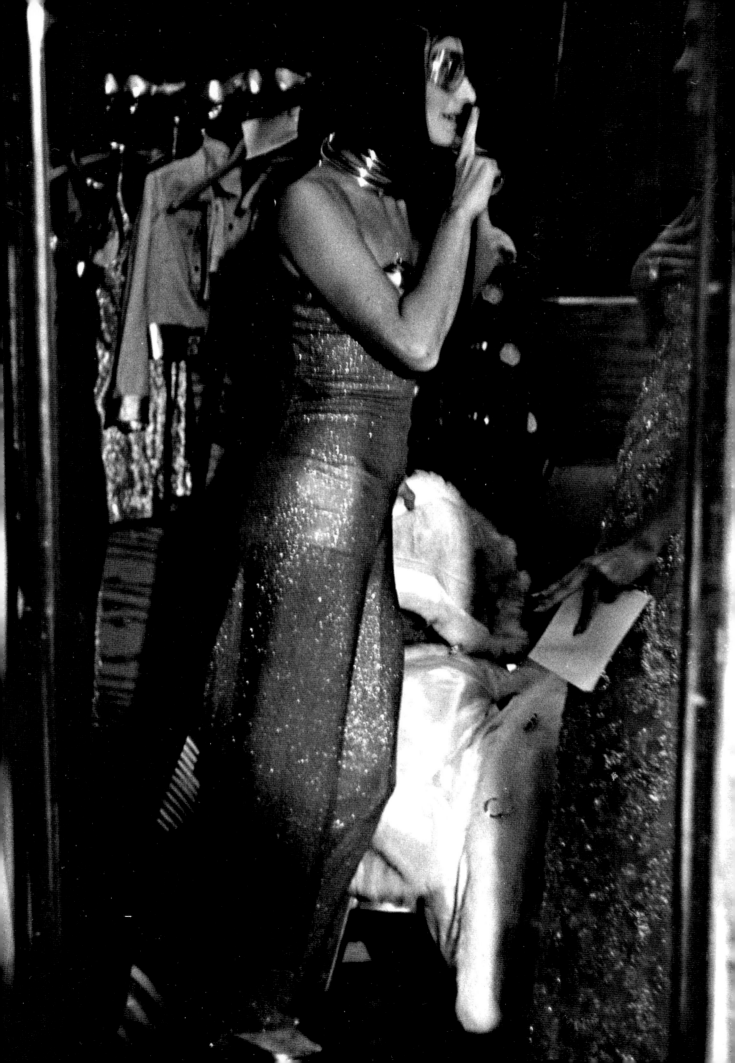

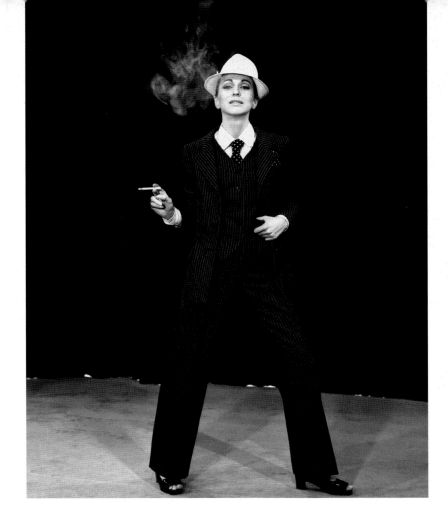

Yves Saint Laurent's ready-to-wear line *Rive Gauche* offered suits for women modeled after men's wear and in step with the concurrent women's equal rights movement.

Emmanuelle Khanh wore a dress of her own design at a fashion show for the 1966 April in Paris Ball, in New York. While the fashion show was not well received by the guests, Khanh returned to Paris and found success designing for the French ready-to-wear industry.

was frequently called in. The Chambre Syndicale made sure that press release dates were strictly observed, much to the pleasure of the couturiers.[10] When a magazine borrowed a prototype to photograph it, for example, it had to commit in writing not to publish the photo until the date specified by the Chambre board — which corresponded to when the design would be put on the market. This helped ensure that any knock-offs would not become available until long after the original was delivered. Failure to observe this rule entailed prosecution of the journalist in breach and possibly the couture house's exclusion from the Chambre.

Ready-to-wear, on the other hand, was not considered an important part of the couturiers' operations, but rather constituted a marginal slice of their overall sales. Moreover, until the mid 1960s, ready-to-wear was only a pale echo of haute couture. Until that time, the couture houses' "boutique" collections were listed on the calendar of women's ready-to-wear, kept by the Fédération Française du Prêt-à-Porter Féminin (French Women's Wear Trade Association), with no thought of doing things differently. Only in 1973, at Pierre Bergé's instigation, did the calendar of ready-to-wear by couturiers and fashion designers become part of the same system as that of the Chambre Syndicale. Meanwhile, in 1966–67, André Courrèges, Yves Saint Laurent, Hubert de Givenchy, and Emanuel Ungaro had launched a more creative line of ready-to-wear that immediately met with international success. At the same time, the number of haute couture houses fell that year from thirty-nine to seventeen. Couture's traditional clientele had suddenly discovered ready-to-wear: Saks Fifth Avenue, Bergdorf Goodman, Marshall Field, I. Magnin, and other stores closed their made-to-measure departments and used their purchasing budgets on ready-to-wear lines by their former couture suppliers, who were more exclusive and better suited to their way of doing business.

Nonetheless, for decades, on the model invented by Christian Dior,[11] designers such as Hubert de Givenchy, Pierre Cardin, Yves Saint Laurent, and Emanuel Ungaro considered haute couture an art unto itself and ready-to-wear something best left to specialists. As such, Saint Laurent in 1966, Ungaro in 1967, and Givenchy in 1968 signed worldwide contracts licensing their ready-to-wear lines to C. Mendès, a manufacturing consortium specializing in couturier ready-to-wear. Madame Grès (in 1957) and Raymond Barbas for Jean Patou (in 1964) had already taken such a step with the same company. Valentino followed suit in 1974, as did Chanel in 1976.

Following the terms of the agreement, it was C. Mendès that produced and distributed the garments and invoiced the retailers for each of these labels; in exchange, the label received a royalty payment. For their part, the couture houses produced, distributed, and sold their haute couture designs only to their individual clients. Their exclusive custom trade, as regulated in 1945, allowed them to pursue fruitful licensing agreements for every type of industrial product. In 1984, the Christian Dior company's earnings, not counting perfume, was 4,400 million francs (about 800 million dollars), 93 percent of which was generated by its 184 licensees. Haute couture and fashion furs, taken together, accounted for a mere 1.5 percent of the total, and the rest came from distribution deals.

It was a similar situation for Yves Saint Laurent. In a Paris stock exchange application filed on July 6, 1989, we find: "A good use of the brand consists in licensing to a select number of manufacturers the exclusive rights to manufacture and sell, under the Yves Saint Laurent label, products designed and perfected by Yves Saint Laurent . . . Contracts are granted for a given product, territory, and set amount of time . . . In 1988, the total income from these licenses rose to 280 million francs," or about 50 million dollars. It's clear that in such a model, only the licensing department was turning a profit. This systematic shift of the use of prestigious labels to their licensees risked having negative effects on French industry. Chanel president Alain Wertheimer, after having hired Christian Legrez (formerly of Dior) to develop his licensing business, was the first to realize that the revenues the licenses generated were not worth the brand dilution and loss of control this practice entailed. In 1981, he took back total control of all Chanel activities and terminated its licenses. Several years after the fact, he had shown that André Courrèges, who (like his mentor, Cristóbal Balenciaga) condemned the practice of licensing, had been right. In 1965, for the Spring–Summer 1966 season, Courrèges presented three collections in one: *Prototype* (haute couture), *Couture Future* (ready-to-wear), and *Hyperbole* (diffusion, or less expensive ready-to-wear, and knitwear). No one before him had dared show together designs made by hand and in the factory, which for fifty years had been separated into distinct industries.

Chanel would not take its reforms quite so far and still today maintains two separate divisions and runway shows for its couture and ready-to-wear lines. It goes without saying that Chanel's strategy was timed to match the opening of the global markets. The protectionist attitude privileged the process of territorial licenses. The free-exchange attitude, on the other hand, favored authenticity and differentiation. These days, innovation comes before marketing.

In recent years, the financial consortiums LVMH and PPR have favored an industrial policy for their branches that generates high margins and protects their brand. Therefore, the most prestigious high-fashion houses, such as Chanel, Dior, and Yves Saint Laurent, are today the largest French exporters of ready-to-wear. Haute couture has become a valuable asset and, for the houses that have preserved it, a competitive advantage, a standard for all the products — ready-to-wear, accessories, and perfume — that carry the label. Hebe Dorsey had already predicted this in 1972: "There is no doubt that couture and ready-to-wear are gradually sliding together. As the techniques of mass production improve, good ready-to-wear clothes will offer the elegance and finish that only haute couture could offer in the past. But this does not mean the end of haute couture: it will simply become the most luxurious end of the ready-to-wear market."[12]

Stylists, Manufacturers, and Fashion Designers

While couture was integrating its ready-to-wear lines, new trend-setters began appearing on the scene. During the 1960s, ready-to-wear designers and stylists began enjoying a certain credit

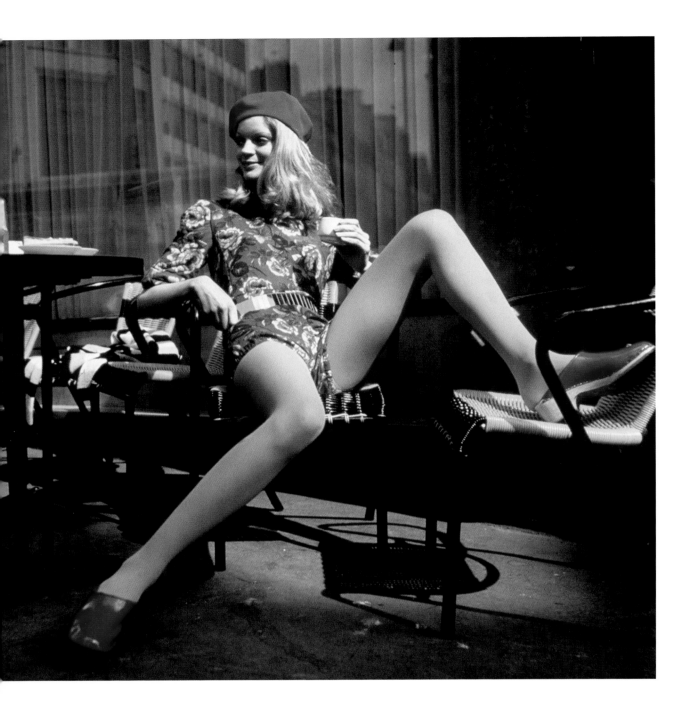

in the press — though not with the mainstream public — that
largely matched the success enjoyed by couturier ready-to-wear.

Still, while stylists such as Emmanuelle Khanh and Christiane Bailly contributed to the success of the houses that employed
them, they remained in the shadows because their names weren't
on the labels whose images they helped shape.[13] As an example,
for the Fall–Winter 1965–66 collection, Emmanuelle Khanh gathered in the Palais des Glaces the designs she had created for her
various clients. The models, gliding along the ice on skates, showed

Emmanuelle Khanh
designed active women's
wear for French ready-to-
wear manufacturers. This
1971 romper was manufac-
tured by C. Mendès.

off a variety of labels in joyful disorder: everything from Cacharel sportswear, Rottenberg furs, and Skidress skiwear to Bistrot du Tricot knitwear, Neyrat umbrellas, and Brezin handbags.

In 1971, a company was created as a branch of C. Mendès that put manufacturers (who naturally tend toward specialization) in touch with "artistic" stylists (who are by nature multitalented). Emmanuelle Khanh, who along with the celebrated English designer Ossie Clark was the first to join, protested the term "stylist," which implied that the manufacturer retained control over the product. According to her, if the designer signed her work, she should have complete control over its creation and be able to impose her decisions on the manufacturer. The company was therefore named Créateurs et Industriels (C&I).[14]

The Spectacle of Runway Shows

In April, the first C&I runway show was held in the salons of C. Mendès, in an overheated room. Emmanuelle Khanh's models opened the ceremony, stalking the showrooms to the beat of music that poured out of transistor radios hanging from the arms of a cohort of nonchalant young women . . . The spectators burst out laughing. Then it was Ossie Clark's turn. Drunk since morning, the girls, who had been brought over specially from London, planted themselves before the audience members and began insulting them in a cockney slang so crude that, before long, Baroness Ordioni of *Le Monde* and her colleagues could no longer pretend they didn't understand English.[15]

The Fall–Winter 1971–72 season marked the acknowledgment of ready-to-wear designers. Salle Wagram, Jungle Jap, Dorothée Bis, and Ter et Bantine banded together to organize a friendly "fashion contest" that set in motion a crowd of wild enthusiasts, models, journalists, and friends. Kenzo, Jacqueline Jacobson, and Chantal Thomass were on the verge of international renown. At the same time, at the instigation of Tan Giudicelli, Mic-Mac organized a runway show in which transvestites took the place of models, to the public's amused stupefaction. As for Karl Lagerfeld, he invited journalists to lunch in a club on rue Sainte-Anne to have them admire Mario Valentino's pumps, on the feet of models perched on mile-high heels wobbling over the tabletops.

The sudden break with the established and highly regulated order of the haute couture world inevitably caused waves of indignation. Needless to say, the trend these presentations were taking did not meet with unanimous approval.[16] But nothing could match the C&I runway show of April 1, 1973, held at the Paris stock exchange. Art director Andrée Putman and press officer Sylvie Grumbach organized, on a Sunday (which was unheard of), a continuous runway parade from ten in the morning until five in the evening, in a frenetic "happening" that alternated jugglers and designers amid "well-lubricated" buffets, before a crowd of enthusiastic supporters. It was at this show that Issey Miyake made his first Paris presentation.[17]

The Market Goes International

This was the beginning of the markets' internationalization. In November 1973, a so-called society event in Paris had enormous repercussions in New York. At a gala soirée given by the Baroness Marie-Hélène de Rothschild, ostensibly to benefit the Château de Versailles, five American designers — Bill Blass, Oscar de la Renta, Anne Klein, Halston, and Stephen Burrows — were invited to measure their talents against five of their French counterparts: Cardin, Givenchy, Marc Bohan for Dior, Saint Laurent, and Ungaro.

The fact had to be faced: Paris haute couture was no longer the uncontested favorite. Even if the rivalry wasn't made explicit, it was clear that a new adventure in fashion was beginning. Benjamin Shaw, who had been Pierre Balmain's American licensee in 1951, was financing new American designers such as Oscar de la Renta, Geoffrey Beene, Donald Brooks, and later Stephen Burrows. Gunther Oppenheim, Pierre Cardin's licensee, struck a deal with Anne Klein, who passed away shortly after the Versailles show. Maurice Rentner, a major buyer of French couture models, helped launch Bill Blass, while the house of Jane Derby became Oscar de la Renta.

In 1974, Fédération president Pierre Bergé invited the group of C&I designers, including Jean Muir from London and Issey Miyake from Tokyo, to be on the official calendar of showings. On October 18, 1975, for the Spring–Summer 1976 season, a single invitation announced runway shows by Christiane Bailly, Roland Chakkal, Jean-Charles de Castelbajac, and Issey Miyake, under an inflatable tent installed on the roof of the Marché Saint-Honoré parking structure. That same day, the calendar of "designers" also included Claude Montana and Thierry Mugler, who set up shop at the Hôtel Meurice and the Grand Hotel, respectively. Meanwhile, at Angelina, Michel Klein presented his first collection, and at 4, rue du Marché Saint-Honoré, the "Créateurs Grandes Ondes" presented knitwear collections by then-unknown designers such as Jean Paul Gaultier and the Argentine duo Pablo & Delia.[18]

Mixing the Genres

Beginning in the 1970s, then, creative fashion design, which until then had been considered strictly a part of couture, gradually made its way into ready-to-wear. Technology evolved with lifestyles, something that couturiers understood quite well; the kind of work that was best done on a sewing machine was considered the province of ready-to-wear; the kind that could only be done by hand was classified under couture. This was the reasoning of houses that were competitive in both disciplines — and reflects what Courrèges had been calling for since 1965.

The Crédit National's report of December 1971 ("The Influence of Haute Couture on the Textile Industry") noted that four major fashion houses — Yves Saint Laurent, Courrèges, Pierre Cardin, and Nina Ricci — planned to present a single Fall–Winter collection in April 1972 that would include both couture and ready-to-wear.

On January 21, Robert Ricci sent a letter to his clients that read, "Given that it is irrational and artificial for a designer and his team to create, every three months, for each season, two different collections that must neither repeat previous work nor fall out of style, we shall present on the dates indicated below a single, highly important collection. This collection will express the totality of our house's message, and consequently will include both the designs intended for the future 'Boutique Edition' and those that, by their nature and the conditions under which they were made, shall remain specifically haute couture."[19]

When Yves Saint Laurent was interviewed by Felicity Green, he had this to say: "What a relief . . . I always give birth in pain. Now the agony will be only twice a year instead of four times."[20]

As for Pierre Cardin, he told Claude Berthod in an interview for *Elle* on the same subject, "Down with the tyranny of idiotic dates. Individual clients? In January, summer is the last thing on their minds. The ready-to-wear manufacturers? For them, summer 1972 already began in October 1971 — which is when you have to be thinking about next winter's fashions if you want to see them on the street. That's what I'm working on now. Haute couture or ready-to-wear? For me, these terms have no meaning. Ideally it's all about creation. Ideas, dreams. To realize them, I need an elite staff. I will

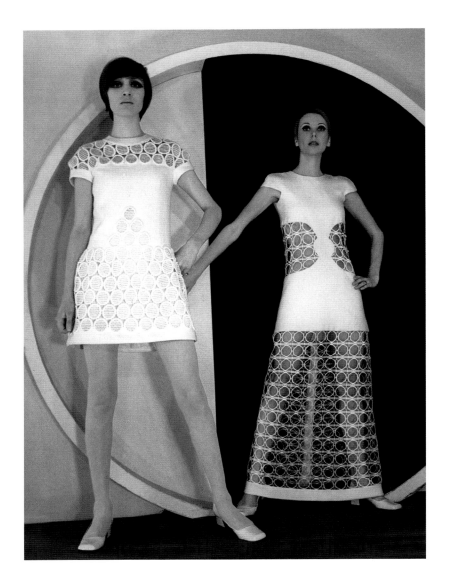

Pierre Cardin's experimental designs blurred the boundaries between ready-to-wear and couture.

never split off from my workshops. Seamstresses and forewomen who know how to dress the world's most demanding women . . . and who know how to adjust, like no one else, the fabrics that we send to the factories." When Berthod asked if he worried whether this mix of genres and dates would spell the end of haute couture, Cardin said, "If couture dies out, it will die of pride — the pride of the designers, each one draped in his 'exclusive' fabrics, who can't quite bring themselves to come down off their perches in order to standardize the presentation dates and fight counterfeits effectively."[21]

Yves Saint Laurent withdrew from the debate, leaving Robert Ricci and Pierre Cardin to set their plan in motion. Pierre Bergé, for his part, thought their stance was too radical and premature. To his mind, modifying the practices of haute couture so drastically was not the most urgent thing. Far more crucial was to associate haute couture with the young designers who excited the press. On Novem-

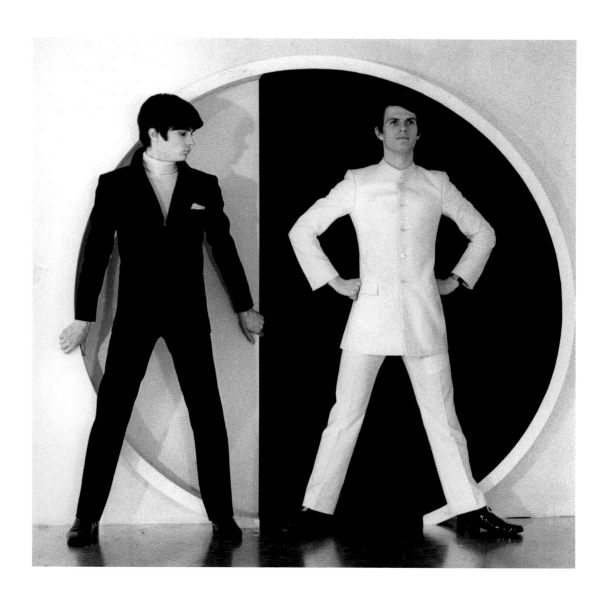

ber 15, 1973, the Chambre Syndicale du Prêt-à-Porter des Couturiers et des Créateurs de Mode was created, with Pierre Bergé as president; he would later participate in the new Fédération Française de la Couture, du Prêt-à-Porter des Couturiers et des Créateurs de Mode. The haute couture houses that had their own ready-to-wear lines were joined by Chloe, Dorothée Bis, Sonia Rykiel, Kenzo, and Emmanuelle Khanh — all of them finally gathered in the same professional organization, the first since 1910.

In 1978, Angelo Tarlazzi, Chantal Thomass, Jean-Charles de Castelbajac, Anne-Marie Beretta, Claude Montana, Jean Paul Gaultier, and Thierry Mugler joined the new Chambre Syndicale in a single bloc.[22] Thus, rather than mixing haute couture and ready-to-wear, they integrated the ready-to-wear designers into the couture system. The ultimate results would be the same, but the means of reaching them were different.

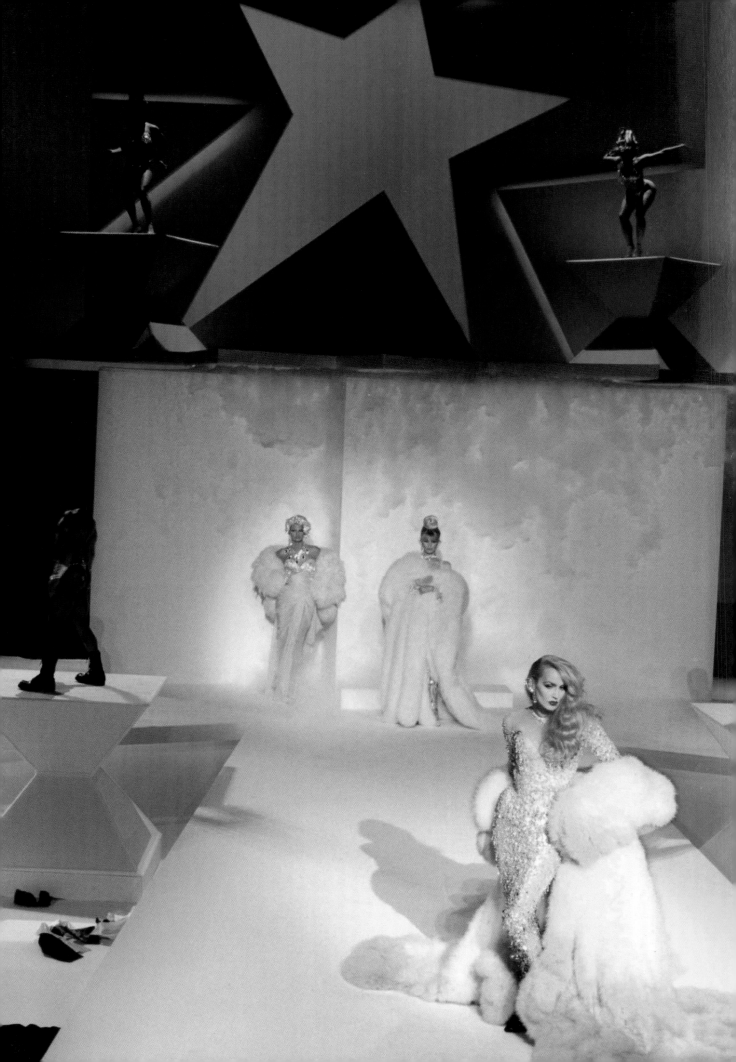

For the Fall–Winter 1978–79 collections, Stephen Burrows and Scott Barrie were inscribed on the Paris ready-to-wear calendar.[23] They ended up withdrawing, but that same year, on November 20 in Tokyo, a major event took place: at the invitation of Hanae Mori, a show titled "The Best Six" grouped together Issey Miyake from Tokyo, Stephen Burrows from New York, Thierry Mugler from Paris, Gianni Versace from Milan, Jean Muir from London, and, of course, Hanae Mori.[24]

In 1979, the ABC television network broadcast its choice of the top ten designers at the end of the century.[25] The program — rediscovered in 2004 by the dynamic fashion writer Florence de Monza — shows just how much joy, freedom, and hope inhabited the fashions of those years.

At the end of the broadcast, Thierry Mugler gave a remarkable demonstration of just how crucial a role the runway show, the product, the image, and the profile of the founding designer play in creating a new label. Mugler is so exacting, and his vision so synthetic, that he himself must oversee every component down to the last detail. For him, fashion is the excuse. He is first and foremost an actor and a showman, his own photographer, director, stage manager, and producer. He personally works on the sound, lighting, and casting, as well as on the collection — whereas each of these activities is normally handled by different individuals, many of them specialists at their task.

On March 22, 1984, to celebrate his house's tenth anniversary, he presented his collection at the Zénith, before a paying audience of six thousand: only he could have coordinated such an outsized spectacle. And for his twentieth anniversary, in 1995 at the Cirque d'Hiver, as a kind of early farewell, he staged a memorable epic that was not merely a fashion parade but also a work of art in its own right. To help offset the dizzying cost overruns, the event was broadcast live and in its entirety on Paris Première and on many stations throughout the world — a first. The amount of media coverage it received was considerable. It was a major success, and live broadcasts became the rule, a habit — we might even say a "bad habit."

Indeed, though such an approach might prove interesting for one or two labels, it naturally can't maintain the same level of interest when extended throughout the entire profession. Who are these costly spectacles intended for? Certainly not the clients — for as Pierre Cardin said, "In March, they're not particularly concerned with the winter collections, and in October, they couldn't care less about summer clothes." As for the buyers, they preferred placing their orders in the calm of the showroom; those huge media extravaganzas were no concern of theirs.

Thierry Mugler, the first to create theater on the French runway, dubbed his Fall–Winter 1995–96 collection *Le Cirque d'Hiver.*

In 1995, the Fédération's board of directors decided to create a subcommittee aimed at redefining the future of the profession.[26] To reinvigorate the ranks of the couture houses, it was decided that the Fédération would review applications by designers who wanted to present their collections on the couture calendar, and these applications would then have to be ratified by the members of the Chambre Syndicale de la Couture Parisienne. Ultimately, therefore, it was the couturiers themselves who would select the new invitees. The accepted designers would have to know couture, but they would be free to mix into their runway shows some of their new ready-to-wear designs as well.

Thierry Mugler and Jean Paul Gaultier were the first invitees, for the Spring–Summer 1997 collections [27] (Yohji Yamamoto was also invited, but did not accept). The invited members could acquire the status of full members after two years of attendance, a new vote, and an official request to the ministry of industry.[28]

The appearance of Mugler and Gaultier on the calendar, and the arrival of John Galliano at Dior and Alexander McQueen at Givenchy, caused a sensation among the world's fashion reporters and sparked renewed media interest in haute couture — for the excitement elicited by true demonstrations of "living art," as these presentations are, will always supplant the interest aroused by even the most seductive advertising campaign.

In their wake, with each succeeding season, Josephus Thimister, Adeline André, Viktor & Rolf, Maurizio Galante, Anne-Valérie Hash, Felipe Oliveira Baptista, and others displayed their talents — "off calendar" at first, before being invited by their fellow couturiers. And thus the trade-guild connection, which had been broken for too long, was reestablished: Martin Margiela, who started as Gaultier's assistant; Gaultier, as Cardin's assistant; Cardin, as Dior's assistant; Dior, as Robert Piguet's assistant; Piguet, as Poiret's assistant; and so on. Prestige, talent, skill, sponsorship, and calendar. Couldn't Lanvin, Nina Ricci, and Balenciaga resume their places in the haute couture calendar? The selection of houses included in this book, while necessarily partial, is ultimately in line with tradition and in synch with the future.

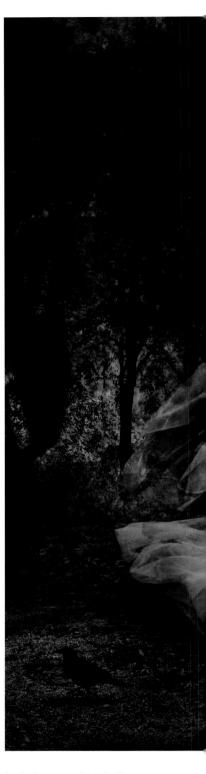

By the late 1990s, Paris fashion shows resembled theatrical extravaganzas. In 2005, John Galliano's Fall–Winter haute couture collection paid homage to Christian Dior.

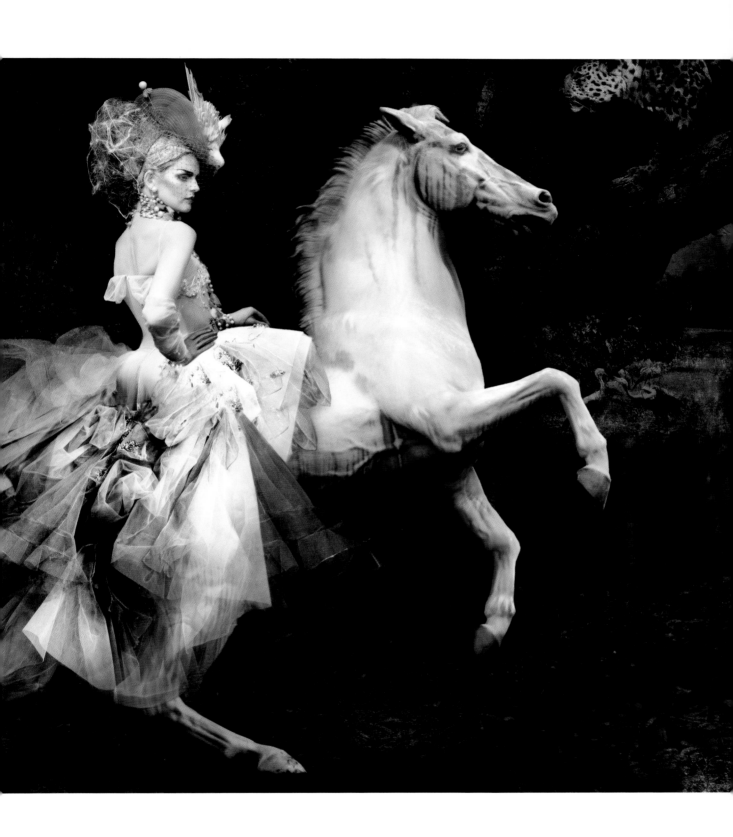

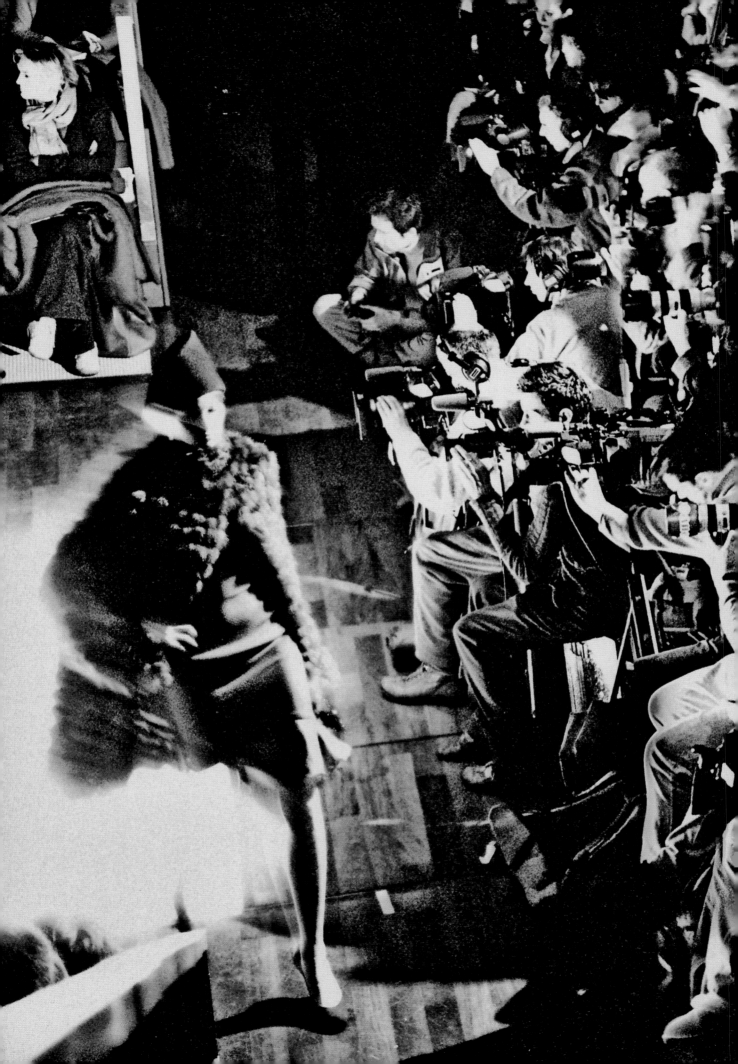

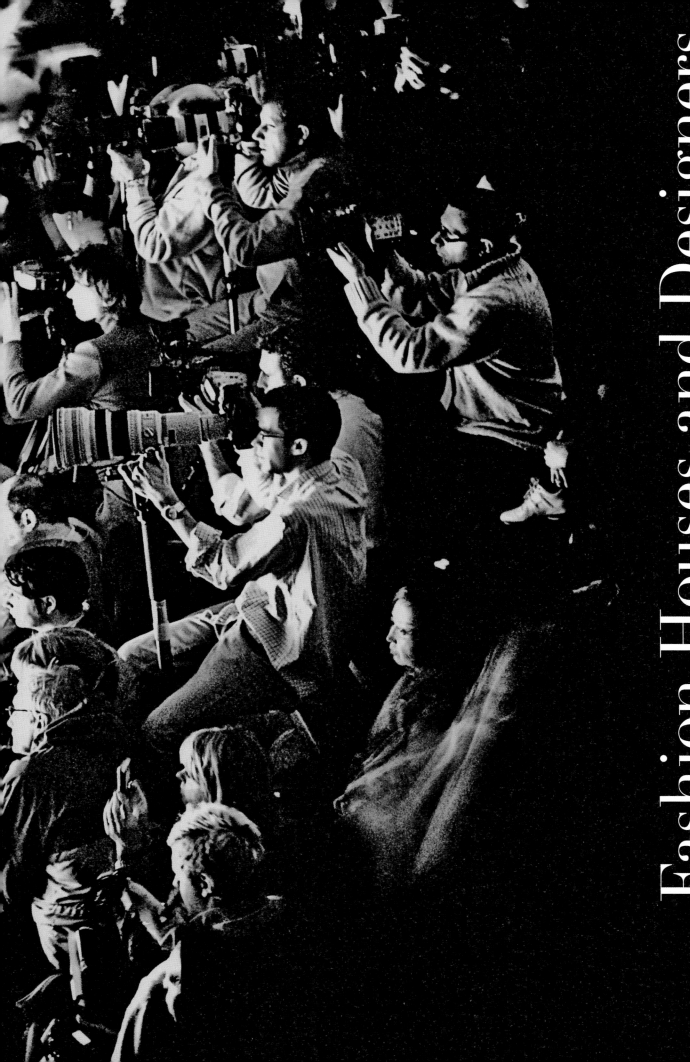

Fashion Houses and Designers

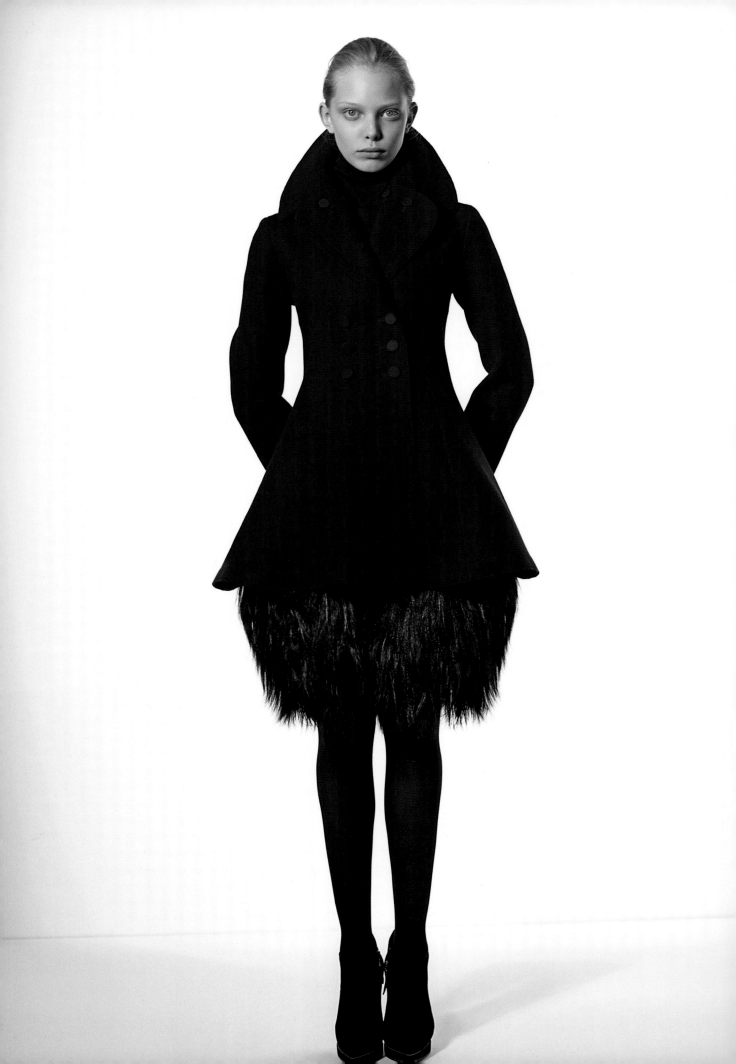

Azzedine Alaïa

The French architect Jean Nouvel once said, "If there is one artist who is extremely interested in the architecture of the female form and who knows how to display it, it is Azzedine Alaïa."[1] Alaïa's brilliance at sculpting dresses that hug the female body like a second skin earned him such monikers as King of Cling and Titan of Tight during the 1980s. Since then, Alaïa has quietly honed his craft, exploring designs that respond to the female figure through sophisticated tailoring. His deceptively simple, yet complex garments combining exquisite draping and painstaking construction have secured him a place as one of the most innovative and influential designers of the past thirty years. Alaïa continues to create on his own terms. In the early 1990s, he stopped presenting seasonal collections, preferring to design at his own pace; he shows his new fashions at his atelier according to his own schedule.

Azzedine Alaïa was born in Tunisia in 1940 and was introduced to fashion by his mother's midwife, Mme Pinot. A devotee of fashion and the fine arts, Mme Pinot subscribed to several fashion magazines, including *Vogue*, which she shared with her young aide. It was with her help that Alaïa entered the Ecole des Beaux Arts in Tunis at the age of fifteen, intending to study sculpture. Dissatisfied with that subject, he left school and took a job as a dressmaker's assistant, copying couture dresses for fashionable ladies in Tunis. Through this work, Alaïa became acquainted with the designs of Madeleine Vionnet and Cristóbal Balenciaga. He eventually acquired examples of these important couturiers' works and would continue to find inspiration in their innovative contributions in the years to come.

In 1957, Alaïa moved to Paris, where he had secured a job

Alaïa's Fall–Winter 2006–7 collection features exquisitely tailored sculptural jackets, here paired with a richly textured goat-hair skirt.

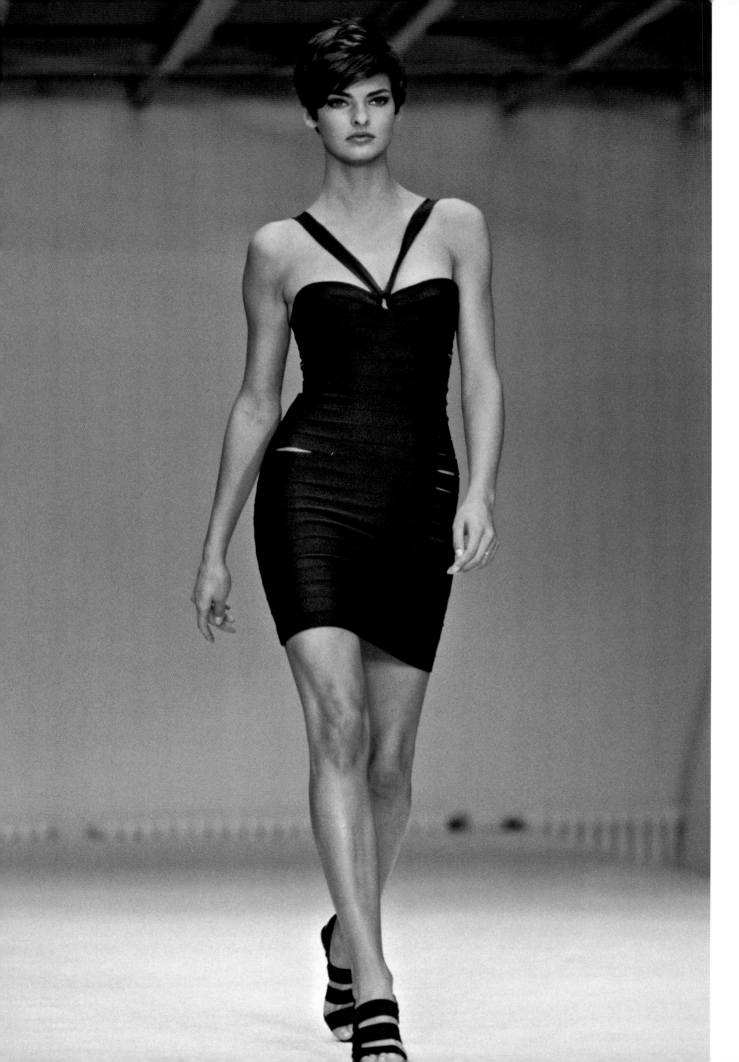

with the house of Dior. This position lasted only five days. However, two seasons in the tailoring workroom at Guy Laroche strengthened the designer's dressmaking skills. From 1960 to 1965, he lived in the house of the Comtesse de Blégiers, where he served as dressmaker. Word of Alaïa's sartorial skills spread, and he began to build a private dressmaking business. In 1965, he opened his own shop at 60, rue de Bellechasse in Paris, where he entertained discerning private clients such as Simone Zerfuss, Greta Garbo, the French actress Arletty, Cécile de Rothschild, and Louise de Vilmorin. Alaïa continued to work with this private clientele until 1979, when several of his creations appeared in *Elle* magazine. He launched his first ready-to-wear collection in Paris in 1981.

Both darling and enfant terrible of the fashion press during the 1980s, Alaïa held sway by creating some of the most iconic garments of the decade. This was the era of power suits and aerobic workouts. Alaïa was among the earliest proponents of viscose, and he created stretchy viscose dresses and body suits, as well as sculpted leather jackets and nipped-in bustiers that were unapologetically tight and sexy, glorifying the newly toned bodies of the decade. Complicated dressmaking skills underpinned these alluring designs. Unlike traditional dresses that hung from the shoulders, Alaïa's garments used the body itself as an integral support — a forward-thinking concept of dress construction.

Alaïa was also a true innovator with knitwear, who "did for stretch, what many years before Coco Chanel had done for jersey."[2] He manipulated heavy viscose jersey into concentric bands that both revealed the body and hugged it like soft armor, culminating in his Bondage Dress of 1990. Women with the right figure adored his designs, and increasing numbers of supermodels and celebrities, including Tina Turner, Paloma Picasso, and Jacqueline Schnabel, joined the ranks of admirers. Grace Jones defined a new type of powerful, exotic beauty when she wore an Alaïa hooded knit dress with asymmetrical ties to the French Fashion Oscars in 1985. Among Alaïa's most innovative designs from the mid-1980s were dresses that spiraled seductively around the woman's figure.

In the 1990s, Alaïa stepped back from the public limelight, while quietly refining his unique artistic vision. His production habits tend to put him at odds with the industry. He disparages advertising and refuses to produce collections every six months, yet he maintains a steady and devoted client base. A true iconoclast, he refurbished an old factory in the trendy, yet somewhat inaccessible Marais district in Paris in the mid-1980s, establishing

At the forefront of experimentation with new materials, Alaïa manipulated heavy viscose jersey into concentric bands to craft the body-hugging Bondage Dress of 1990.

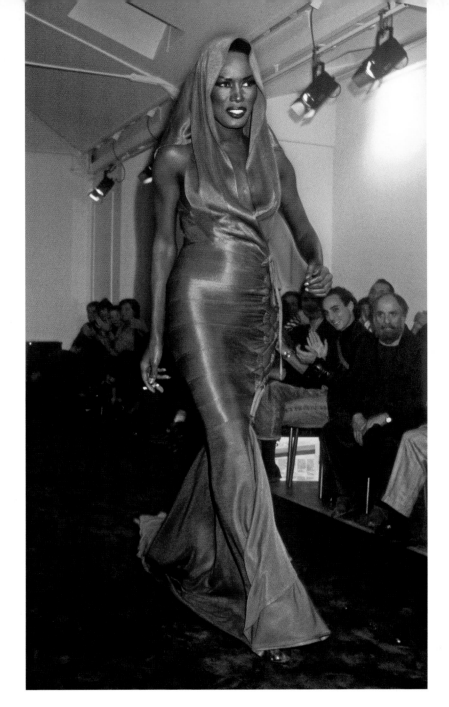

Grace Jones, one of the many celebrity admirers of Alaïa's designs, wore his hooded viscose jersey dress to the French Fashion Oscars in 1985.

a combined showroom, studio, and living space where he could explore his fashion ideas at all times of the day and night.

Construction has remained at the core of Alaïa's designs. He actually considers himself a *batisseur*, or builder, of dresses, a reminder of his early interest in sculpture and his enduring commitment to perfection in cut and fit.[3] Yet his dresses are not merely innovative; they embody the legacy of traditional couture craftsmanship, developed over years of work. Tailoring is one of his great strengths, and he painstakingly works out his ideas on a live model. Alaïa cuts the pattern, selects the fabrics, and assembles the prototype for every single garment himself — an impressive feat, considering some of his dresses contain over forty

Alaïa's first haute couture collection, presented in 2003, included a modern version of his iconic spiral zipper dress from the 1980s.

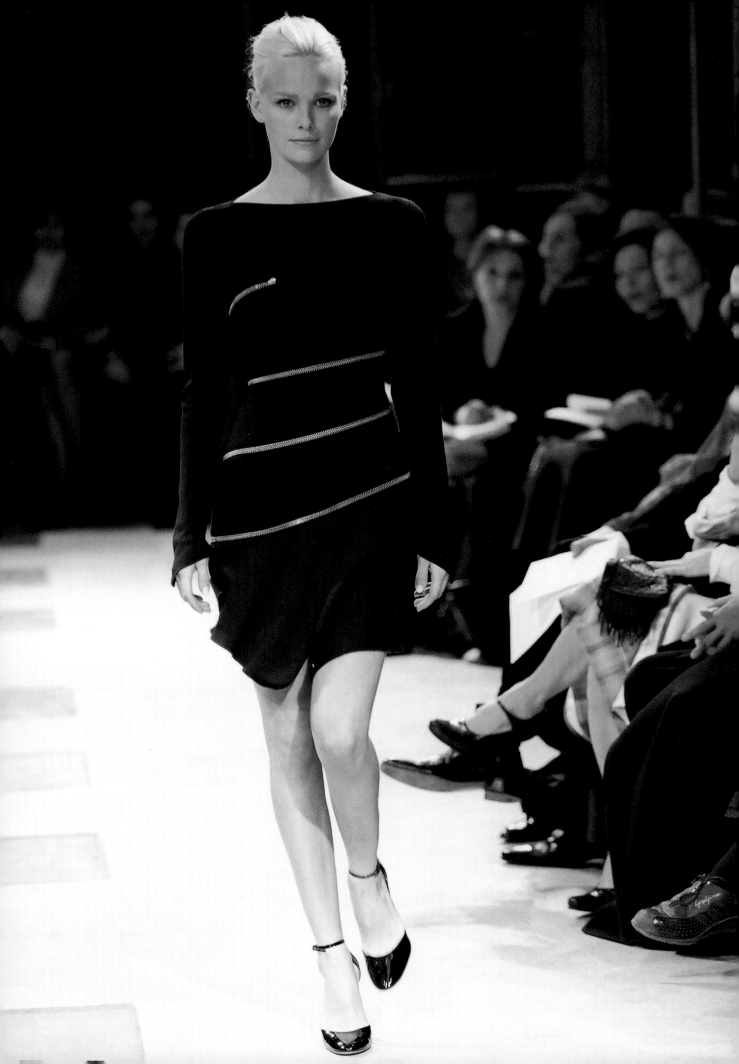

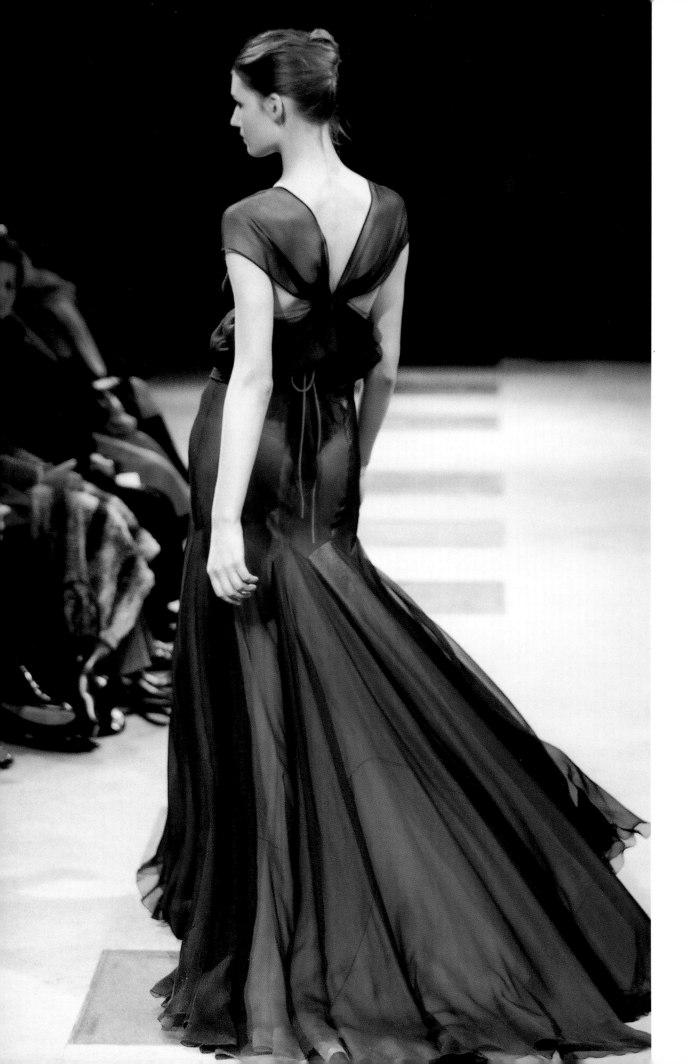

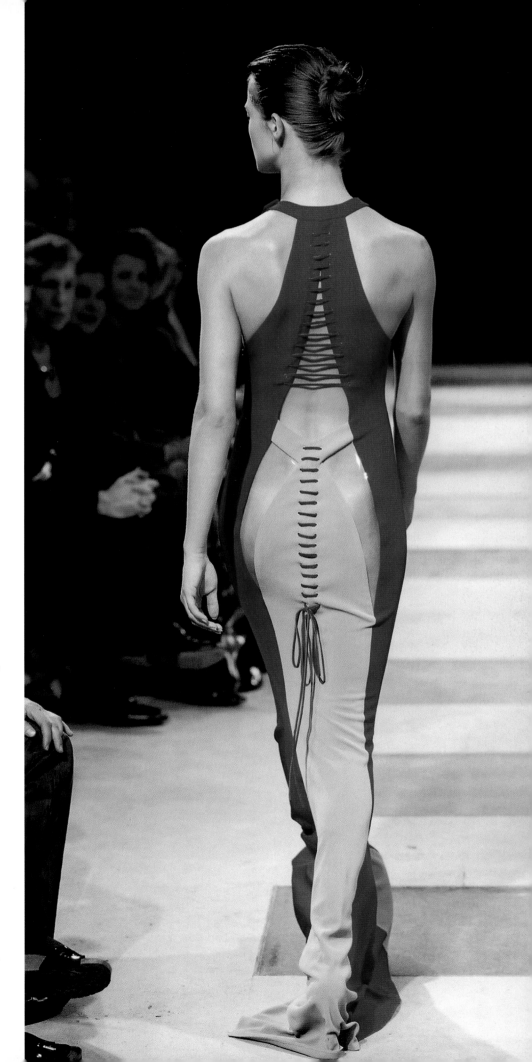

The evening dress at left, from the 2003 haute couture collection, showcases Alaïa's skills as both a forward-thinking innovator and an extraordinary dressmaker in the couture tradition.

Alaïa's commitment to perfection in cut and fit is evident in evening dresses that comprise multiple pieces carefully orchestrated to create a second skin that envelops the body.

pieces, all carefully joined to create a unified mesh that envelops the body. This rigorous process of draping directly on the live model can sometimes take weeks of work for one design.

In 2000, Alaïa entered into a new partnership with Prada. In keeping with his offbeat style, this arrangement preserves the designer's independence and artistic control, while opening doors to the financial security of the Prada group. Alaïa also recently welcomed to his atelier former staff of Yves Saint Laurent's couture workroom, which closed following Saint Laurent's retirement. Alaïa still closely oversees the production of all of his garments, though. His recent collections prove he has not forgotten how to make a woman look sexy. In 2003, he showed his first haute couture line, which included updated spiral zipper dresses, leather bustiers, and sensual gowns that went beyond the newest revivalist trend and looked sharply to the future.

Alaïa continues to refine his extraordinary skills as a dressmaker. Most recently, he has concentrated on perfecting the expressive effects of ruching, creating long dresses in silk knit that have been ruched by hand into rippled pleats. He explores traditional techniques like this with an utterly modern sensibility. A fashion critic for the *New York Times* recently wrote: "For the lesson of Mr. Alaïa is that though he possesses one of the largest archives in Paris, he never looks back; though he is not called a couturier, he is the best kind of one. To go into his studio after the haute couture shows is to feel that you have not seen anything genuinely modern until that moment."[4] So great are the accolades for Alaïa that he has been the subject of two museum retrospectives — at the Groninger Museum in 1998 and the Guggenheim Soho in New York in 2000. Plans are also afoot to establish a museum of Alaïa's renowned archives. Yet despite all the fanfare, Alaïa focuses, as always, on his enduring obsession with clothing the female body. — LDW

In his recent collections, Alaïa has experimented with the effects of ruching, creating elegant silk dresses with hand-pleated details.

While Alaïa draws inspiration from traditional couture techniques, such as bias-cut construction, he creates sophisticated garments that are utterly modern in sensibility.

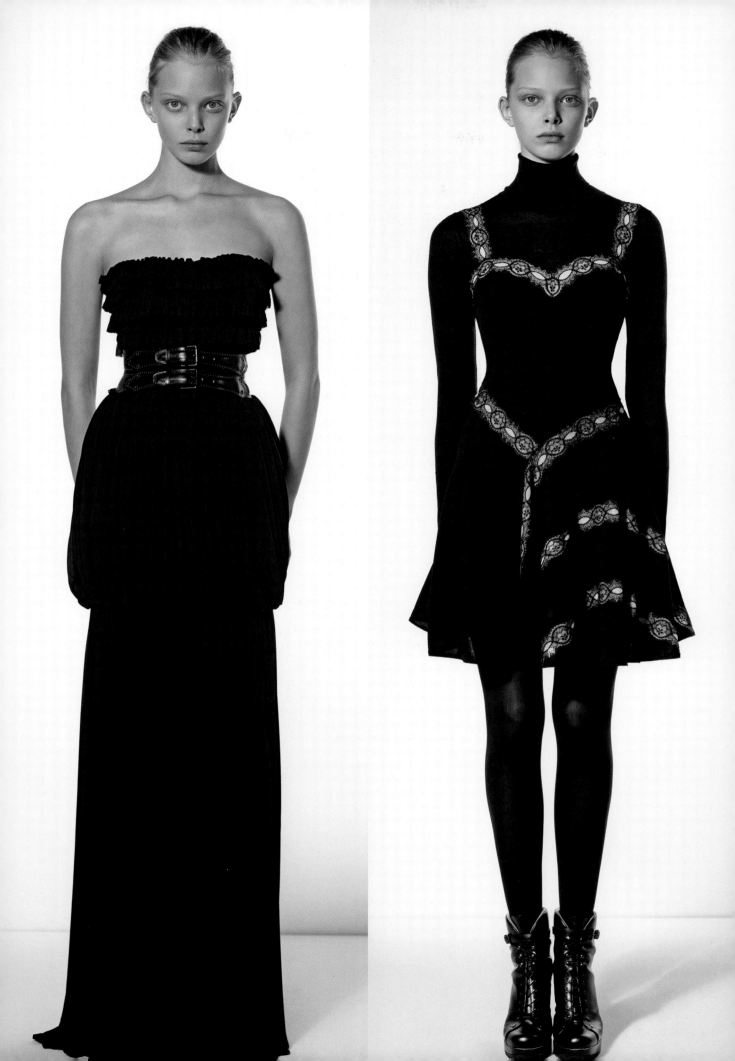

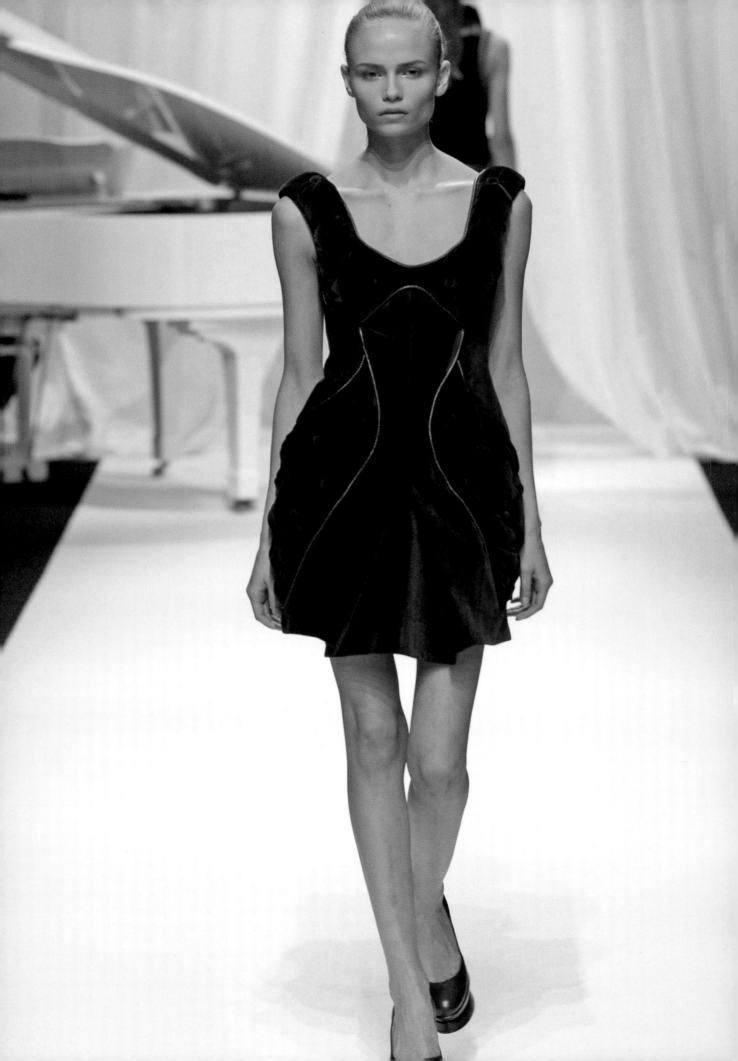

Hussein Chalayan

Hussein Chalayan approaches fashion from a conceptual and intellectual point of view. His garments challenge traditional notions of what clothing is and can be, and they express abstract ideas about identity, technology, memory, and emotion. Throughout his career, he has explored the body's relationship to the built environment, modern society, and geographic and cultural boundaries, yielding clothes that are "minimal in look but maximal in thought."[1] He collaborates across disciplines with architectural engineers, industrial designers, artists, and musicians to create poetic, meaningful, and intellectually rigorous installations and runway shows that often suggest fine or performance art rather than fashion. One of Chalayan's greatest strengths as a designer, however, is that the clothes themselves are beautiful and wearable. "It's so disappointing when people assume my clothes are difficult," he says. "They're not. I love seeing people in my clothes, and I often do . . . My clothes should be something women wear because they like them, because they enjoy the intimate space between my clothes and their bodies. That, to me, is very important."[2]

Chalayan was born in the Turkish community of Nicosia, Cyprus, in 1970 and moved to the United Kingdom at age twelve with his father, who enrolled him in an English boarding school. He later studied fashion design at Central Saint Martin's College of Art and Design, in London. Chalayan first came to public attention in 1993 with his degree collection, *The Tangent Flows*, which exemplified his idea-driven and process-oriented approach to design. He covered a series of garments with iron filings, buried them for several weeks in a garden, and exhumed them just before the show. An accompanying text explained the ritual of burial

Hussein Chalayan's Fall–Winter 2006–7 collection, *Repose*, incorporates elements and materials recalling the comfort of plush upholstered furniture.

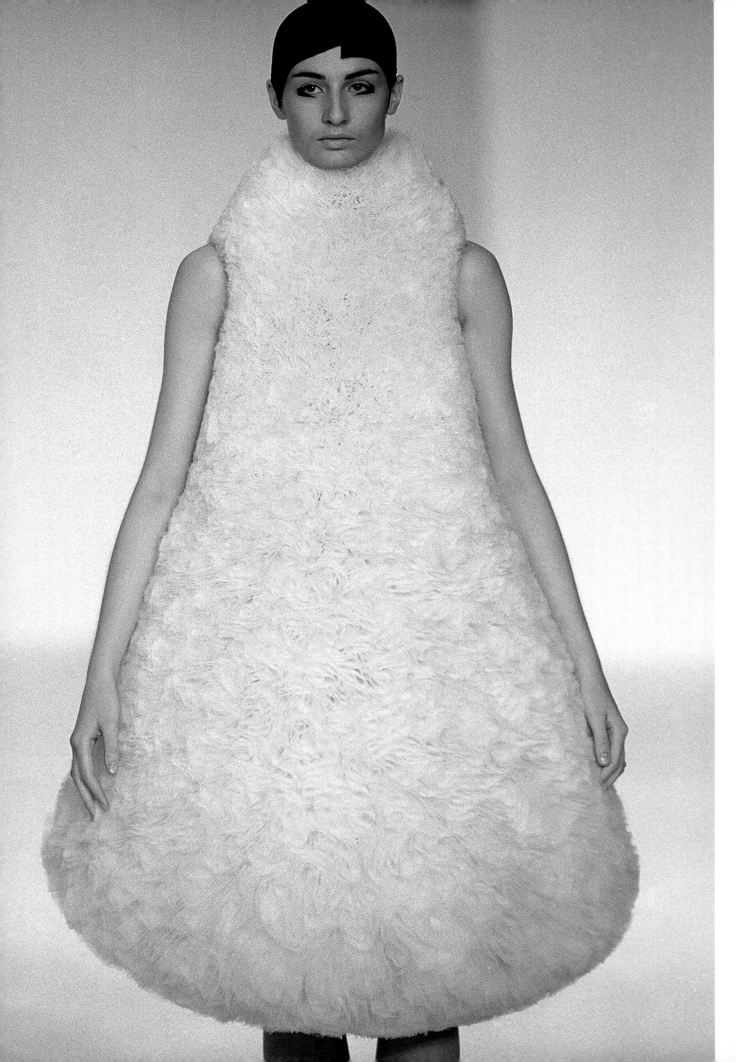

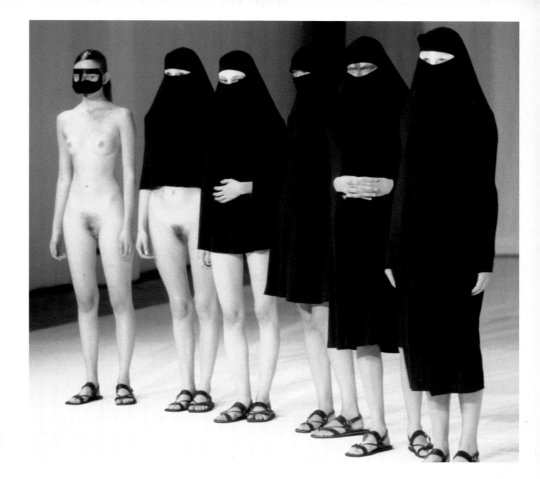

With this 1998 series of dresses based on the traditional Islamic chador, Chalayan challenged his audience to rethink cultural definitions of modesty.

The Spring–Summer 2000 collection was inspired by the forces and processes that create forms in nature. This dress was gradually cut down from a large bale of tulle, as mountains are shaped by erosion.

and resurrection, which referenced life and death while subjecting the garments to the natural processes of rust and decay.

Chalayan's collection was selected for display in the windows of Browns, an influential London designer boutique. The following year, he began to present his own independent collections in London. He gradually built a reputation in the fashion world, winning the Absolut Creation Award (sponsored by Absolut Vodka) in 1995, designing collections for the New York knitwear company TSE beginning in 1998, and being named Designer of the Year at the British Fashion Awards in two consecutive years, 1999 and 2000.

Taking no interest in fashion trends, Chalayan prefers to use each collection to explore particular ideas or questions that fascinate him, letting the exploration dictate the results. His approach to his powerful runway shows is similar: "I am really not up to date with what is going on in the art world or performance world. I just do what is good for my work."[3] Some of his most dramatic shows have addressed the theme of cultural displacement and the interaction between conflicting ideas and cultures. His Spring–Summer 1998 collection, *Between*, presented a series of dresses based on the traditional Islamic chador, with veils of varying lengths. The first model was naked except for a small yashmak covering her face, and each of the following models wore a slightly longer chador, ending in a full-length version. By showing various degrees of body exposure,

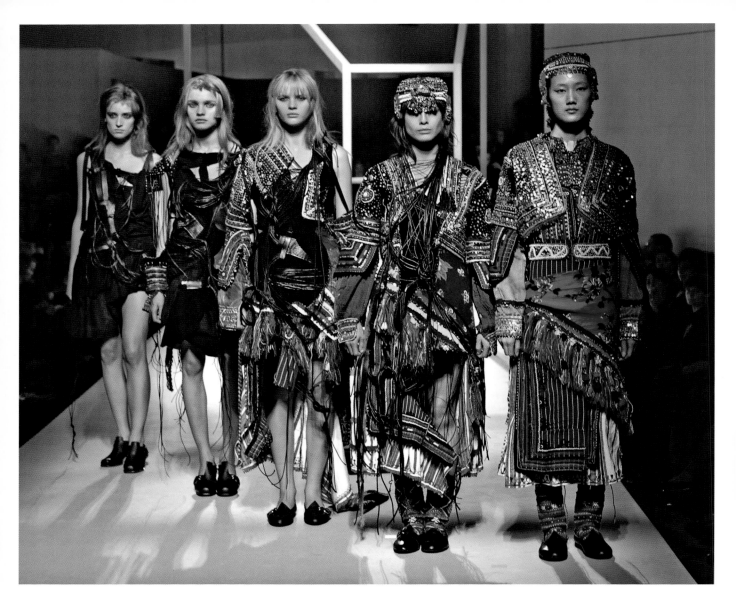

while keeping the models' faces covered, Chalayan challenged his audience to rethink both Middle Eastern and Western definitions of modesty. Similarly, in his Fall–Winter 2002–3 collection, *Ambimorphous*, he introduced a series of ensembles in which a traditional, heavily embroidered Turkish costume gradually transformed into a stylish black "Western" coat, dramatizing how the standardization of modern dress can erode personal and cultural identity.

The refugee crisis in Kosovo inspired Chalayan to explore the reality of evacuation during war in his Fall–Winter 2000–2001 collection, *Afterwords*. To Chalayan, events in Kosovo recalled his own experience growing up in Cyprus, which was forcibly divided into Greek and Turkish zones in 1974. Shown on a bare white stage set with a living room of 1950s-style tables and chairs, the collection addressed the idea of hiding and camouflaging personal possessions from an impending raid and the possibility of carrying them away as clothing. At the end of the show, models removed the covers from the chairs and wore them as dresses; they folded up the chairs and carried them

This series of ensembles showing the transformation of a traditional Turkish costume into a stylish modern garment dramatized how cultural identity can be lost and reconstructed.

The *Afterwords* collection included furniture that could be transformed and carried away as clothing, referencing the nomadic existence of war refugees.

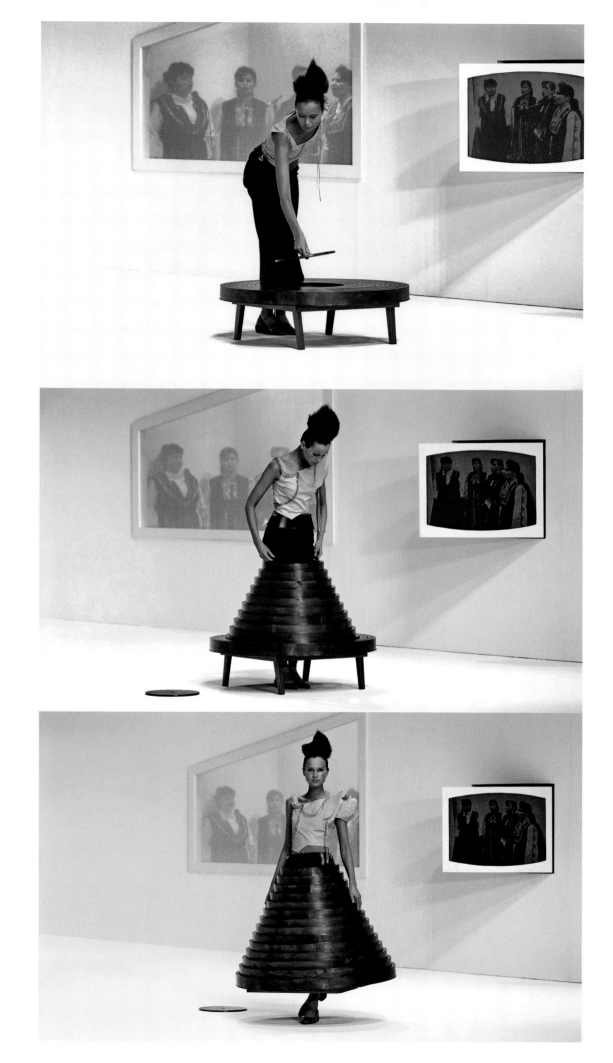

off like suitcases. Most striking of all, the final model stepped into the center of the round coffee table, which transformed into a skirt.

Chalayan had referenced nomadic existence before, in his Spring–Summer 1999 *Geotropics* collection. That presentation included a completely transportable environment in the form of his Chair Dress, which enabled the model to sit down wherever she wished. Another variation on this theme was his 1994 Airmail Clothing, a series of Tyvek garments in his *Cartesia* collection that could be folded down to the size of a letter and sent through the mail.

Some of his most influential collections have been those focusing on the relationships between clothing, the environment, architecture, and technology. Chalayan integrates clothing with its surroundings not by simply making dresses look architectural but by understanding different environments and the principles that govern them. As he explains, "I think of modular systems where clothes are like small parts of an interior, the interiors are part of the architecture, which is then a part of an urban environment."[4] In *Echoform* (Fall–Winter 1999–2000), he joined this

Chalayan designed the Chair Dress, for Spring–Summer 1999, as a transportable personal environment that allowed the model to sit down anywhere.

The Fall–Winter 1998–99 *Panoramic* collection used identity-concealing hoods and multiple mirrors to create a dreamlike reality in which the individual blended in with the environment.

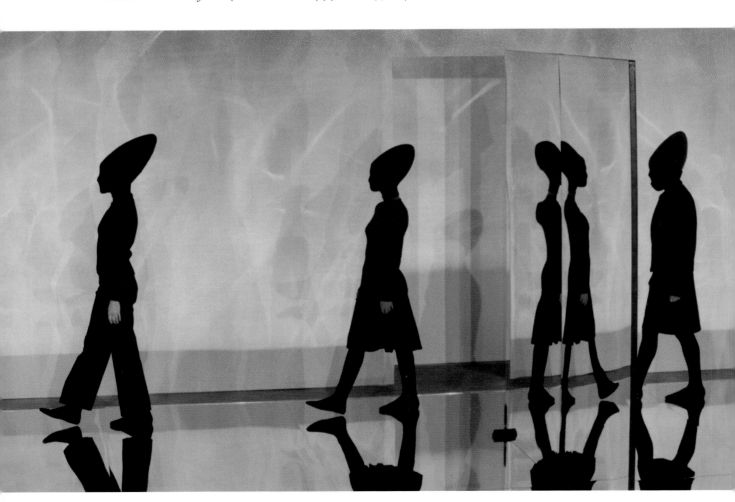

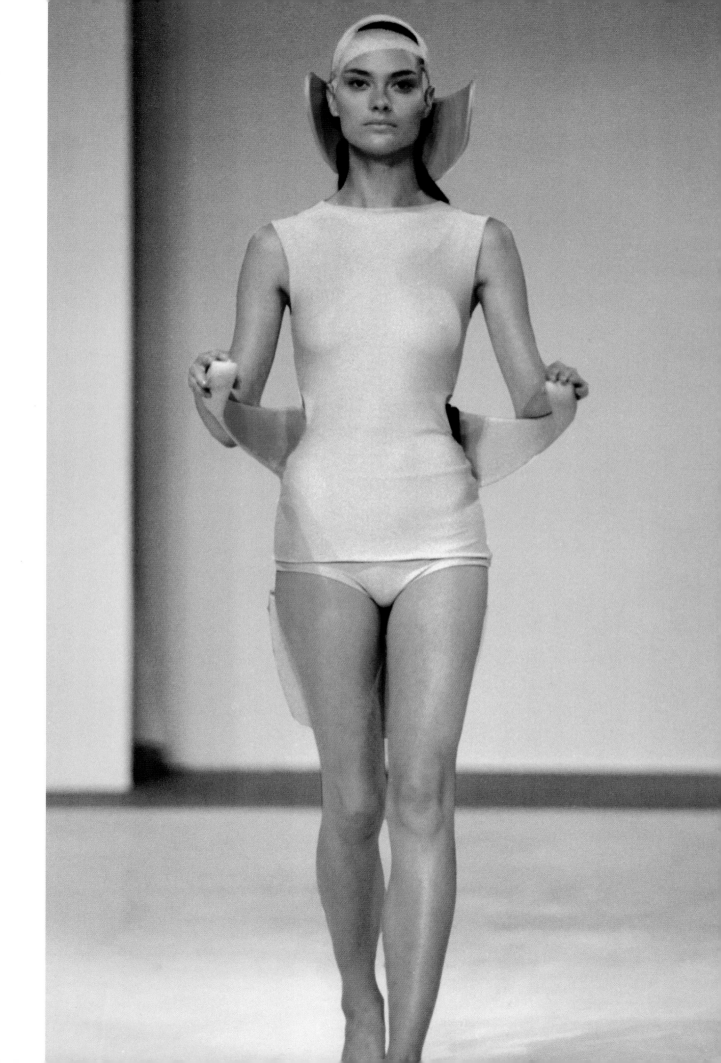

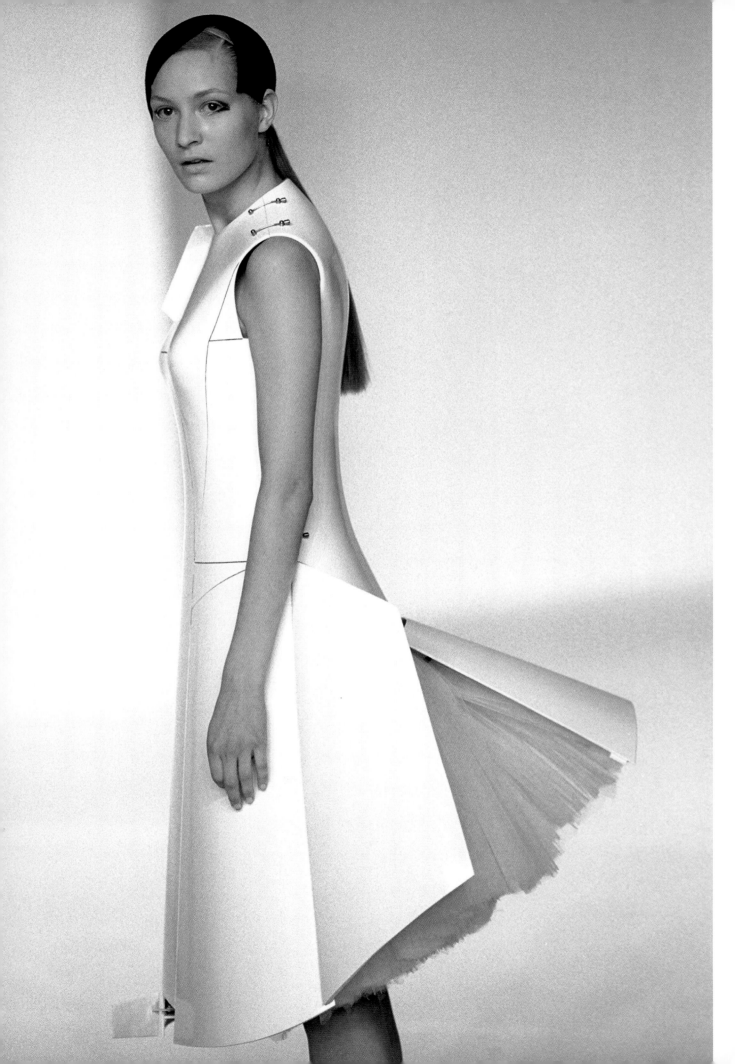

concern with interior environments to an examination of the body's inherent capacity for speed and its enhancement by technology. Inspired by the interiors of cars and airplanes, he attached padded collars or "headrests" to the shoulders of black leather dresses, thereby "externalizing speed and putting it back on the body."[5] The highlight of the *Echoform* collection was the Aeroplane Dress, a fiberglass construction fastened with chrome automobile catches. Incorporating technology used in the aircraft industry, and powered by a hidden battery, the dress had sections that could slide down and extend out like the moving flaps of airplane wings. He presented another variation of the dress in *Before Minus Now* (Spring–Summer 2000), this time with moving flaps that were controlled during the show by a small boy with a remote control.

In 2001, Hussein Chalayan signed a licensing agreement with the Italian manufacturing company Gibo Co. Spa for his ready-to-wear line and moved his collection showings from London to Paris. From 2000 to 2004, he also designed a ready-to-wear line for the British luxury retailer Asprey. He launched a new, lower-priced women's line called *Chalayan* in 2004 and opened his first shop, a Cyprus-themed environment designed in collaboration with a London architecture firm, in Tokyo the same year.

Although Chalayan's collections have continued to be experimental and idea-driven, in recent years he has gained wider recognition in the mainstream fashion world. His clothes, with their luxurious fabrics, masterful cut and tailoring, and simple, clean lines, have won praise in the fashion press for being both intelligent and commercial. The clothing inspired by car interiors, for example, though starting with the abstract concept of speed, also consciously incorporates the comfort and sleekness of padded leather seats, resulting in beautiful and wearable garments that can easily be appreciated on their own merits. — s w

In a lighthearted comment on man's exaggerated expectations of technology, this dress's motorized aircraft-like flaps were operated on the runway by a young boy with a remote control.

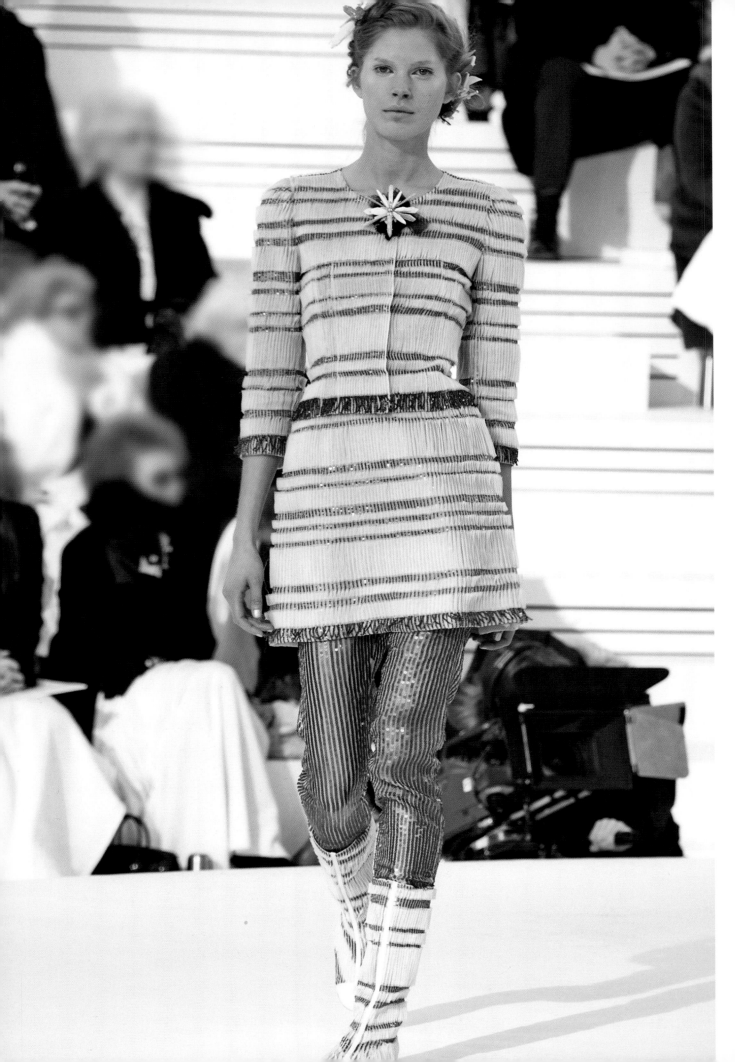

Chanel

The house of Chanel was founded by Gabrielle "Coco" Chanel, an extraordinary woman who was as famous for her unconventional personality and life story as for her revolutionary contributions to twentieth-century fashion. The image of the house evolved from her own distinctive style, a simplified and informal elegance ideally suited to the modern, independent "new woman" of the twentieth century. Over her long career, she created an enduring and instantly recognizable "Chanel look," characterized by signature elements like the little black dress, the tweed cardigan suit, multiple strands of oversized fake pearls, the quilted shoulder bag, the camellia, and the two-tone shoe. After Coco Chanel's death in 1971, the house was faced with the problem of staying true to the spirit of its founder while updating the Chanel look for the contemporary market. Since 1983, artistic director Karl Lagerfeld has returned Chanel to the forefront of fashion, balancing a thorough knowledge and understanding of Coco Chanel's work with a keen sense for when to move the house style in new directions.

Born in 1883, Coco Chanel began her fashion career in 1909 when she opened a millinery business in Paris. In 1910, she moved to a new shop, Chanel Modes, at 21, rue Cambon. Her simple hats, modeled by leading actresses of the day and by Chanel herself, soon appeared in the popular press. In 1913 and 1915, Chanel opened boutiques in the fashionable resort towns of Deauville and Biarritz. There, she presented her first clothing collections, based on the neat tailored suits, simple chemise dresses, and sporty styles that she herself wore.

Chanel dispensed with corsets, heavy linings, and excessive ornamentation, taking her inspiration from the practical, loose-

Karl Lagerfeld's Spring–Summer 2006 couture collection for Chanel is a youthful, refined, and delicate reinvention of the classic house style.

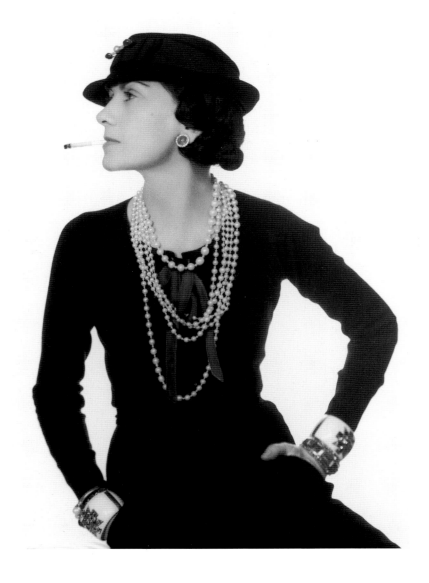

The signature elements of the Chanel look evolved from the audacious and innovative personal style of the house's founder, Gabrielle "Coco" Chanel.

fitting garments worn by men and from traditional work clothes such as fishermen's sweaters and waterproof driving coats. Her first full couture collection, shown in 1916, included clean-lined and comfortable cardigan suits in wool jersey, a fabric previously used primarily for hosiery and men's underwear. Chanel's clothes, although plain and unassuming in appearance, were luxurious in the subtle details of their linings and finishing, prompting the couturier Paul Poiret to describe her style as *le misérabilisme du luxe* (luxurious poverty). Her simple, modern designs profoundly influenced the direction of fashion after World War I and established Chanel's worldwide reputation as a style innovator.

Chanel continued to lead fashion in the 1920s, as the most prominent exponent of the youthful, androgynous "garçonne" look and as the ideal model for her own designs. She was one of the first

In the 1920s, Chanel made the simple little black dress a wardrobe staple for both day and evening wear.

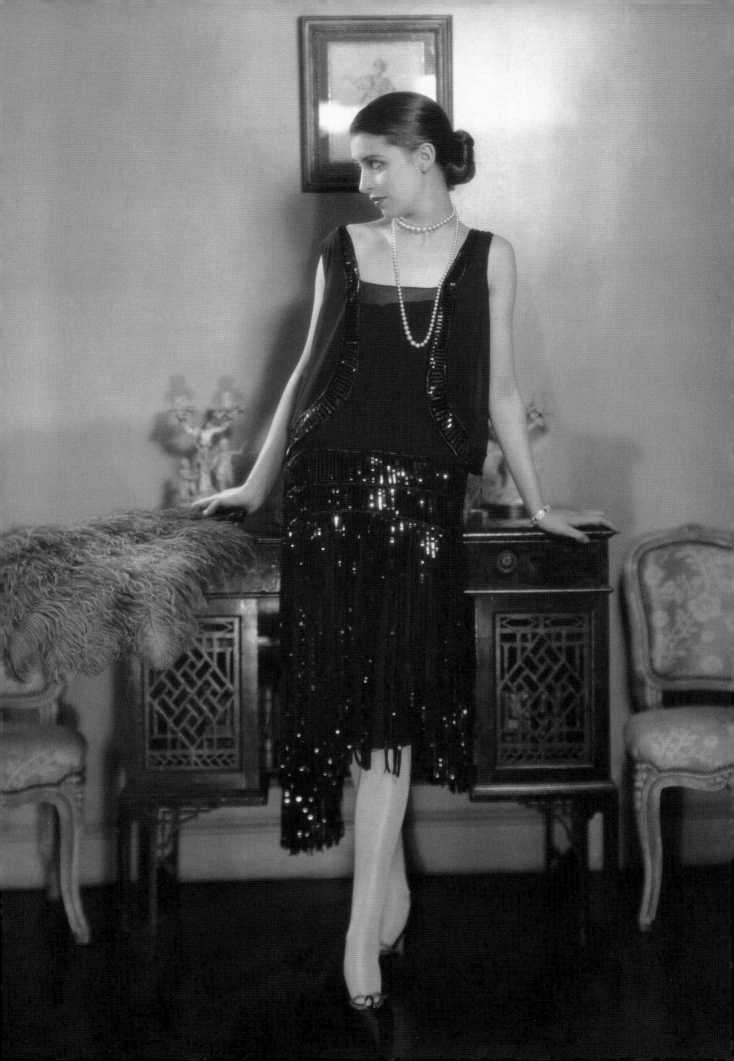

to show trousers and beach pajamas for women, and she found a new source of inspiration in the tweeds, Fair Isle knitwear, and shirts with cufflinks worn by the duke of Westminster, an Englishman with whom she was romantically involved between 1923 and 1930. In 1921 she introduced her first perfume, Chanel No. 5, which was influential both for its fragrance and for its monochrome, clinical-looking packaging. In 1926, *Vogue* magazine published one of her black day dresses as "The Chanel 'Ford' — the frock that all the world will wear."[1] Perhaps her most dramatic innovation of the 1920s was her lavish use of costume jewelry, formerly not considered respectable, for day and evening. Chanel's bold pairing of simple, unadorned clothes with multiple strands of huge fake pearls, colored glass stones, and Byzantine crosses became one of the most recognizable features of the Chanel look and changed the way jewelry was worn.

Her designs continued to evolve through the 1930s, with simple, sophisticated sportswear and crisp tailored suits for day wear, and increasingly dramatic and feminine styles for evening wear. Chanel closed her couture house at the outbreak of World War II, and in 1944 the controversy over her wartime relationship with a German officer led to a self-imposed exile in Switzerland, where she stayed for almost a decade.

In 1953, at the age of seventy, Chanel started working again, in part to boost the sales of her perfumes. She presented her first postwar collection on February 5, 1954. This comeback collection, which reinterpreted and modernized the shapes she had pioneered in the 1920s, was not an immediate success, but within a few years the Chanel look was embraced as a modern and practical alternative to Christian Dior's New Look, particularly in the United States.

Over the next two decades, Chanel refined her basic formula, producing classic cardigan suits in nubby wools, tweeds, and jersey, often trimmed with contrasting braid, and elevating her suit jackets — with sleeves and armholes cut to allow the arms to move freely, multiple functional pockets, hems weighted with gilt chains to hang properly, and quilted linings matched to the dress or blouse fabric — to iconic status. Other signature elements she added in the 1950s were large hair bows of grosgrain ribbon, white camellias, quilted shoulder bags with straps of leather plaited with gilt chain, and slingback shoes with toe caps of a contrasting color, designed to make the foot look shorter. Through the 1960s, while resisting the miniskirt and many of the other changes sweeping through the fashion world, Chanel continued to rework her classic suits each season for her faithful clientele.

After her comeback in 1954, Chanel refined and modernized her classic cardigan suits, raising them to iconic status. This 1959 example was photographed outside the Chanel boutique in the rue Cambon.

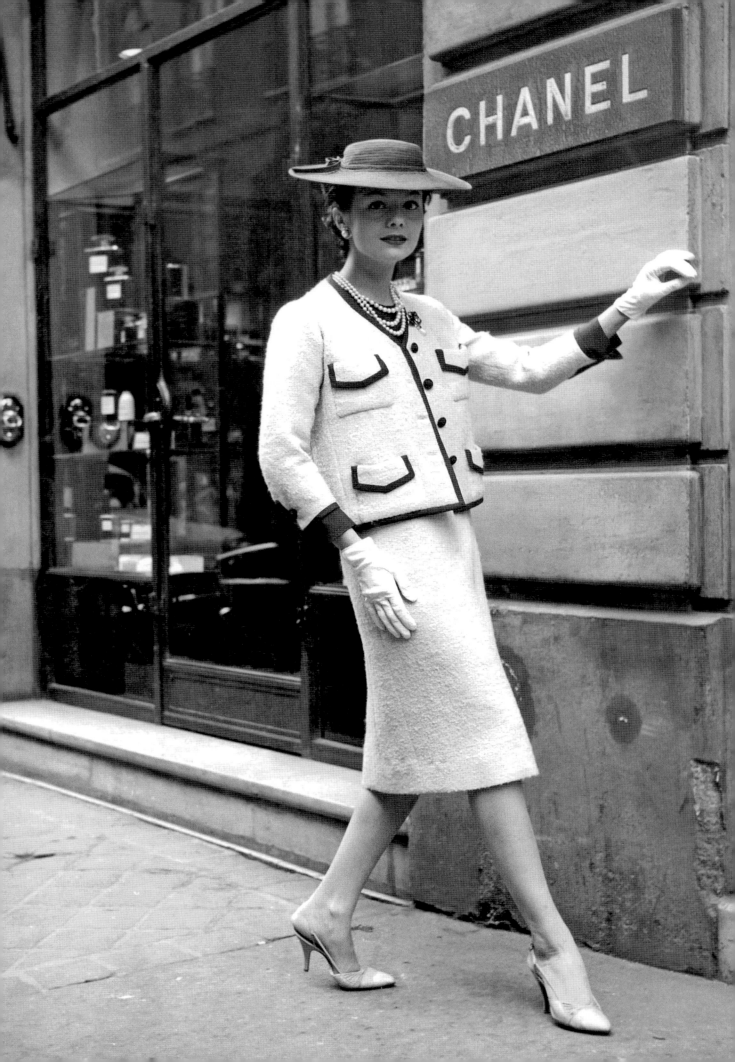

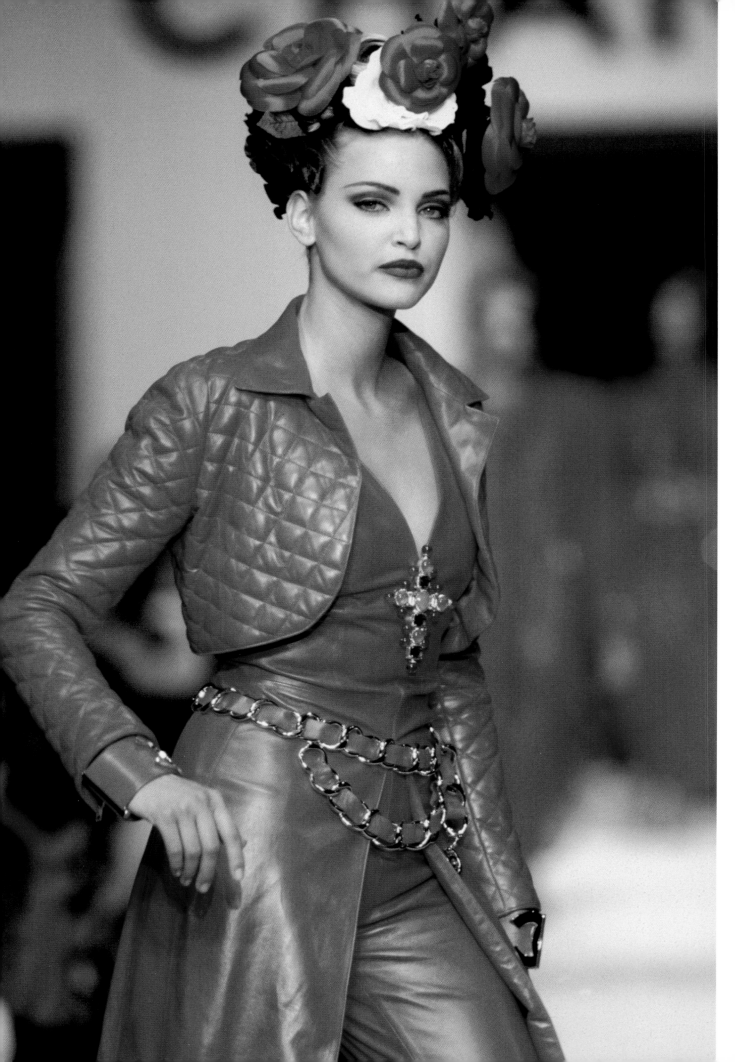

Karl Lagerfeld's ready-to-wear collection for Fall–Winter 1992–93 was inspired by motorcycle gear but also included witty references to Chanel's famous quilted leather shoulder bag.

Since 1983, Lagerfeld has updated the Chanel look for the contemporary market, reinterpreting house signatures such as the tweed suit for a younger, more adventurous clientele.

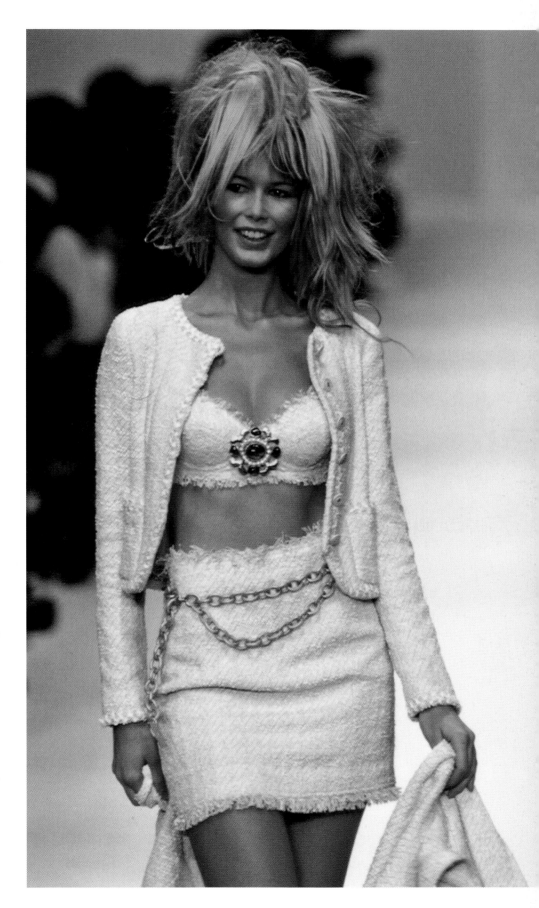

During the decade following Chanel's death in 1971, collections of classic garments in the Chanel style were presented by a number of different designers, but the house did not regain its position in the vanguard of fashion until 1983, when Karl Lagerfeld was appointed artistic director. Born in Hamburg, Germany, in 1938, Lagerfeld moved to Paris in 1952. In 1955, he was one of two winners (the other was Yves Saint Laurent) of a competition sponsored by the International Wool Secretariat, and he was subsequently hired as a design assistant by the couture house of Pierre Balmain. He designed for the house of Patou from 1958 to 1962 and then worked as a freelance designer for a variety of companies, including Krizia, Chloe, Fendi, and a ready-to-wear company founded under his own name in 1984. His ability to design simultaneously for several different houses, often requiring him to work in several different styles at once, made him ideally qualified to take on the challenge of modernizing the Chanel look.

Since his first couture collection for Chanel, presented in January 1983, Lagerfeld has looked beyond the static image associated with Coco Chanel's last years and drawn from many different aspects of her career. He has consistently referenced Chanel icons such as the quilted bag, tweed suit, and double-C logo, at times designing classic interpretations, and at other times deconstructing them to make witty or ironic statements. Lagerfeld has also expanded the range of the house style, introducing new ideas and influences into the Chanel vocabulary while convincingly connecting them to the house's heritage. Just as Coco Chanel borrowed from sportswear and working dress, he has at times taken inspiration from contemporary subcultures and street style, introducing luxe versions of leather motorcycle jackets and boots, and using Chanel's famous gold chains to refer to the jewelry worn by hip-hop musicians.

By constantly revisiting and renewing the elements of the Chanel style in this way, Karl Lagerfeld has succeeded in making the house relevant to the contemporary market, while at the same time strengthening its distinctive identity. In doing so, he is following the model laid out by Chanel herself: "Fashion passes, style remains. *La mode* is made of a few amusing ideas, which are used in order to be used up and replaced by others in a new collection. A style should be preserved even as it is renewed and evolved."[2] — s w

Although this ensemble from Spring–Summer 2006 is unmistakably modern, its frothy tulle ruffles and sequined trousers recall Coco Chanel's romantic evening-wear designs of the 1930s.

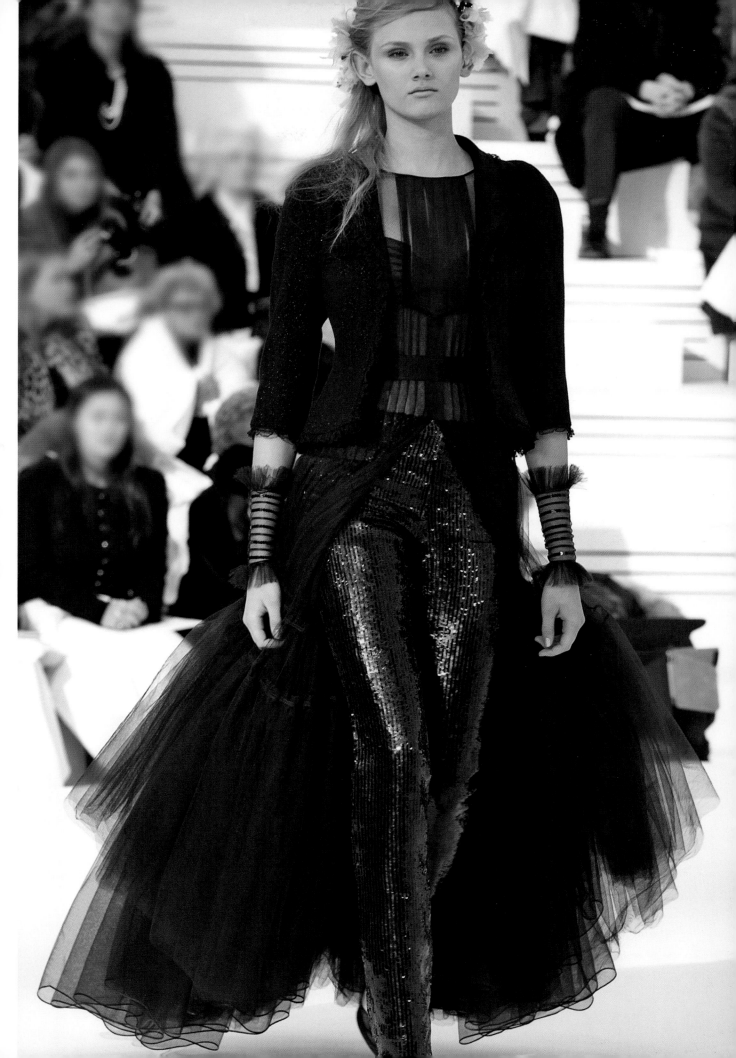

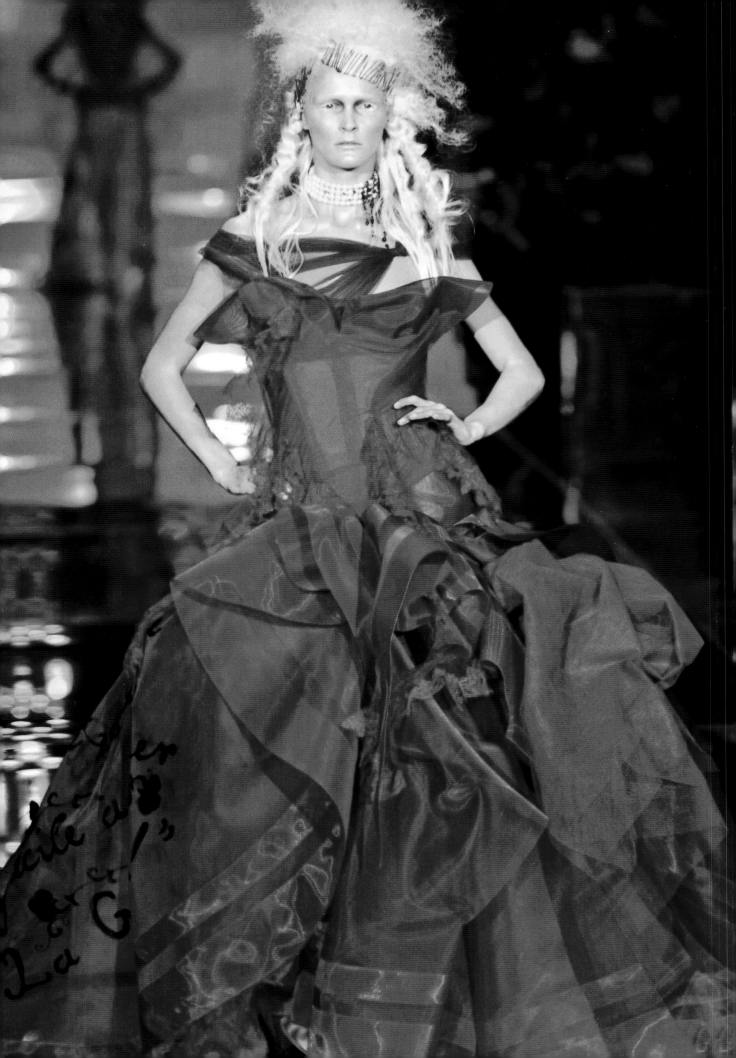

Christian Dior

The house of Christian Dior is one of the oldest and most prominent couture houses in Paris. Its longstanding reputation as a fashion leader commenced during the decade following the landmark 1947 New Look collection, when the shapes, hemlines, and fashion directions presented in Dior's couture collections assumed unprecedented influence over the fashion world. Under the leadership of its founder, Christian Dior, the house set a standard for classical elegance and technical perfection, carefully constructing each collection to express a new ideal of feminine grace. After Dior's death in 1957, his successors — Yves Saint Laurent, followed by Marc Bohan and Gianfranco Ferré — continued to work in the tradition of the founder, creating couture collections that won critical praise and maintained the house's prestige. In 1996, John Galliano was appointed principal designer and charged with updating the house and its image. His spectacular, theatrical fashion shows, combining references to Dior's history and traditional tailoring with a kaleidoscopic range of historic, thematic, and cultural influences, have generated both praise and controversy and have redefined the Christian Dior brand for the twenty-first century.

Born in 1905, Christian Dior did not launch his career in fashion until the age of thirty, when the failure of the art gallery where he had been working forced him to find a new source of income. Encouraged by a friend, he began to study fashion sketches and to make some of his own. He was able to sell his drawings to couture houses and newspapers. In 1938, he was offered a position in couturier Robert Piguet's design studio, where he stayed until the outbreak of war in 1939. In the fall of 1941, Dior went to work for the house of Lucien Lelong, where he learned his craft while dealing with wartime restrictions.

The house of Dior's Spring–Summer 2006 couture show was a dramatic and macabre spectacle inspired by the violence of the French Revolution, the passion of the bullfight, and the libertinism of the Marquis de Sade.

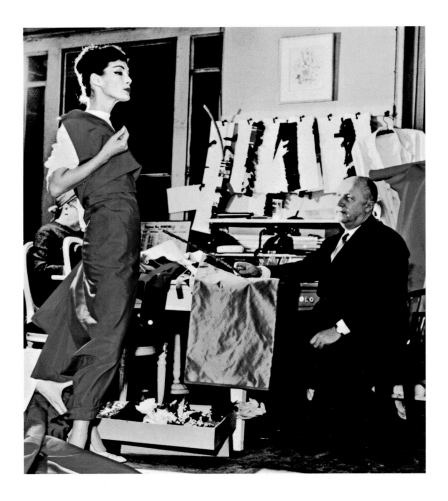

In 1946, the textile millionaire Marcel Boussac offered him the
chance to resurrect the small and aging couture house of Philippe
et Gaston. Dior instead proposed opening an entirely new house
under his own name, "in which every single thing will be new:
from the *ambiance* and the staff, down to the furniture and even
the address."[1] Impressed by Dior's vision for the new house, which
included the character of the clothes (apparently simple, but made
with elaborate workmanship) and the "clientele of really elegant
women" they would target, Boussac provided the financial backing
for the house of Christian Dior, which opened on October 8, 1946.

Dior's first collection, the *Corolle* and *En Huit* lines, was based
on a highly structured hourglass silhouette, with nipped-in waists
and calf-length, widely flaring skirts, some of which required up
to twenty-five yards of fabric to create. Although this style was in
many ways a return to a pre-1920s image of femininity, it came as a
welcome change from the short skirts and broad shoulders of wartime
fashions. Christened the "New Look" by *Harper's Bazaar* editor
Carmel Snow, it was a spectacular success for Dior and for the Paris
couture, and it caused a fundamental shift in the direction of fashion.

Dior's debut collection,
presented on February 12,
1947, changed the direction
of fashion. His *Bar* suit
epitomized the highly
structured hourglass
silhouette that became
known as the New Look.

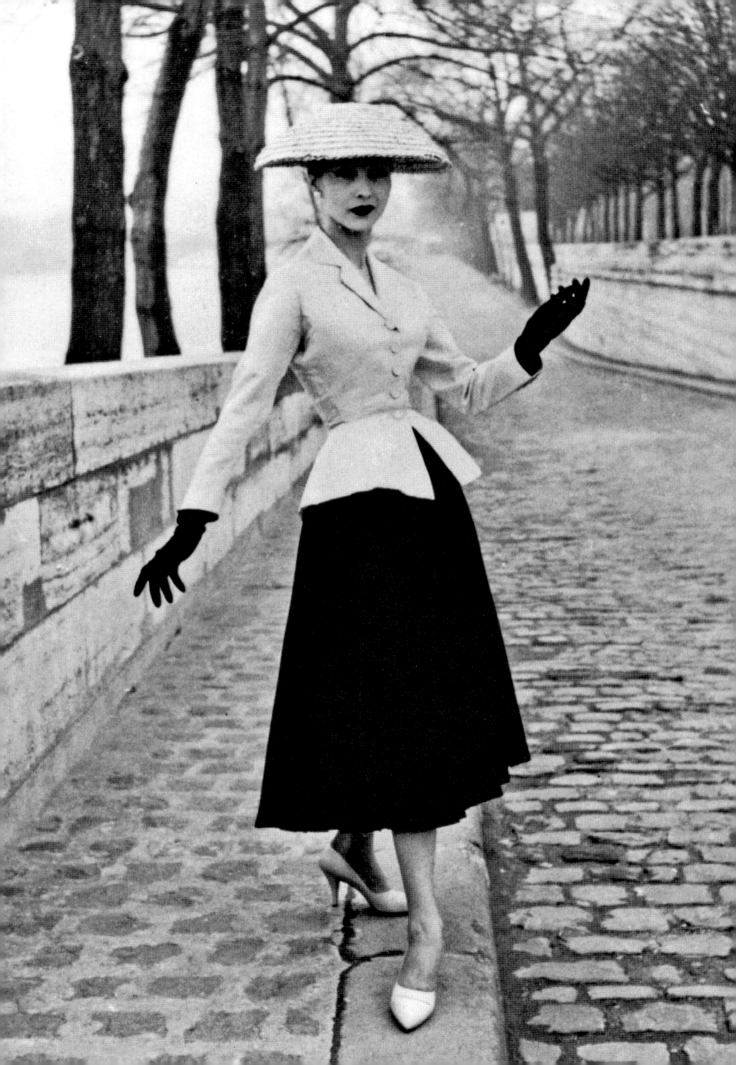

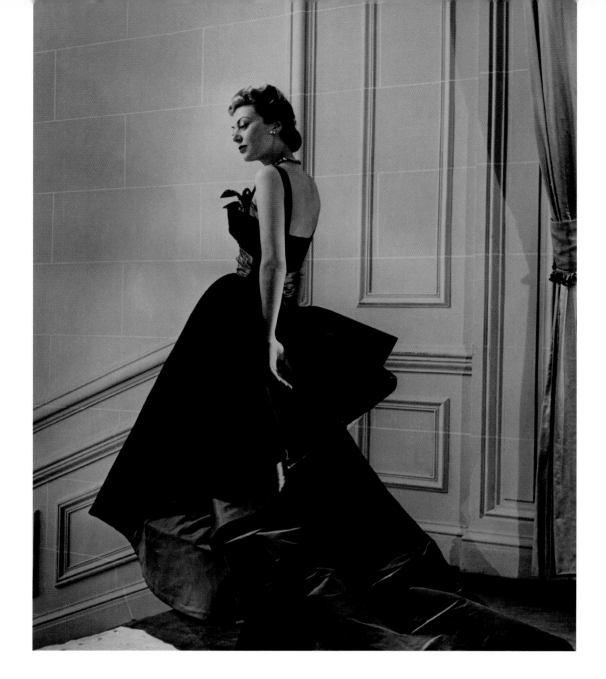

Dior organized each of his subsequent collections around a particular shape or "line" — for example, the *Tulip*, *Zig Zag*, or *A* line — which would inspire the look of every ensemble, from tailored suits to ball gowns. Though the new line was often quite different from the one that had preceded it, Dior's sure hand and impeccable taste made certain that each was quickly adopted by the fashion world. He soon became an international celebrity, and the house of Christian Dior, the most influential house in Paris, became the basis of a multimillion-dollar fashion empire.

When Christian Dior died suddenly in 1957, the responsibility for the couture collections fell to the twenty-one-year-old Yves Saint Laurent, an Algerian-born designer who had worked as Dior's assistant since 1955. In the spring of 1958, Saint Laurent presented his first collection for Dior, the *Trapeze* line, to great

Dior was particularly noted for his dramatic and opulent ball gowns. This example, *La Dame en Bleu*, was part of the Fall–Winter 1948–49 *Zig Zag* line.

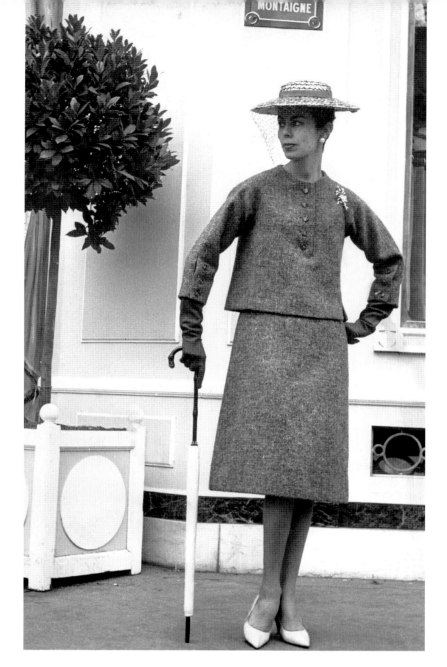

Following Christian Dior's death in 1957, the success of Yves Saint Laurent's Spring–Summer 1958 *Trapeze* line for Dior ensured the house's survival.

critical and public acclaim. He was hailed as the savior of the house and designed for Dior until he was drafted for military service shortly after presenting the Fall–Winter 1960–61 collection. Saint Laurent would go on to start his own couture house in 1962.

Marc Bohan took over as Dior's chief designer in 1960. Born in 1926, he had worked in the couture for over a decade before coming to Dior in 1958. He soon established himself as a success-ful couturier, staying true to the established Dior style while adding softer and more youthful lines. He also designed Dior's ready-to-wear line, which was introduced in 1967. Bohan led Dior for twenty-nine years, attracting a faithful and prominent clientele with his classic and wearable designs. In 1989, he was replaced by the Italian designer Gianfranco Ferré (born in 1944), who brought an architectural sensibility and bolder color sense to the house style.

When Ferré returned to working exclusively for his own company in 1996, Bernard Arnault, the chairman of LVMH, which owns Dior, offered his position to the British designer John Galliano, with the idea of bringing a new sense of excitement to the Dior brand.

Galliano was born in 1960 in Gibraltar and moved with his family to South London in 1966. While studying fashion design at St. Martin's School of Art in the early 1980s, he briefly worked for the Savile Row tailor Tommy Nutter and as a dresser at the National Theatre, where he learned to appreciate the dramatic potential of clothes. He studied the cut and construction of historical garments and experimented with alternative, and sometimes revolutionary, methods of cutting. The thriving London club scene, which at the time revolved around the creation and display of eccentric, historically inspired costumes, also strongly influenced him. Galliano's degree show in 1984, based on the fantastic clothing worn by young Incroyables after the French Revolution, immediately earned him a cult following in London fashion circles. He launched his own label that same year, and over the next several years he produced a number of critically acclaimed collections. Commercial success proved elusive, however, and in 1990, hoping for better work prospects, he moved to Paris.

In the early 1990s, Galliano found increasing support for his work, which mixes a rigorous attention to cut, fabric, and traditional glamour with a dizzying array of references to other times, people, and places, organized around an imaginary, and often hallucinatory, story line. His spectacular and theatrical method of showing his clothes, in which the models act out the parts of historical or fictional characters as if on a film set, was also very influential. In 1995, Galliano was appointed head designer at the house of Givenchy, where he presented two successful couture collections before moving to Christian Dior in October 1996.

After extensive research in the Dior archives, Galliano presented his first Dior collection, conceived as a fiftieth-anniversary tribute to Christian Dior's New Look, in January 1997. In his usual eclectic fashion, he mixed house trademarks, such as gray flannel and hound's-tooth checks, with liquid, bias-cut gowns and exotic makeup evoking Chinese opium dens in the 1920s. Tailored jackets appeared in leather cutwork imitating lace, and voluminous organza ball gowns were overlaid with Masai beadwork collars and corsets from Africa.

Since 1997, Galliano has continued to mount his eclectic, inventive, and provocative couture shows, sometimes concocting amusing and unlikely themes such as "Barbie Goes to Tibet" (his description

One highlight of John Galliano's eclectic first collection for Dior was this modern version of a Dior ball gown in silk organza and Masai beadwork.

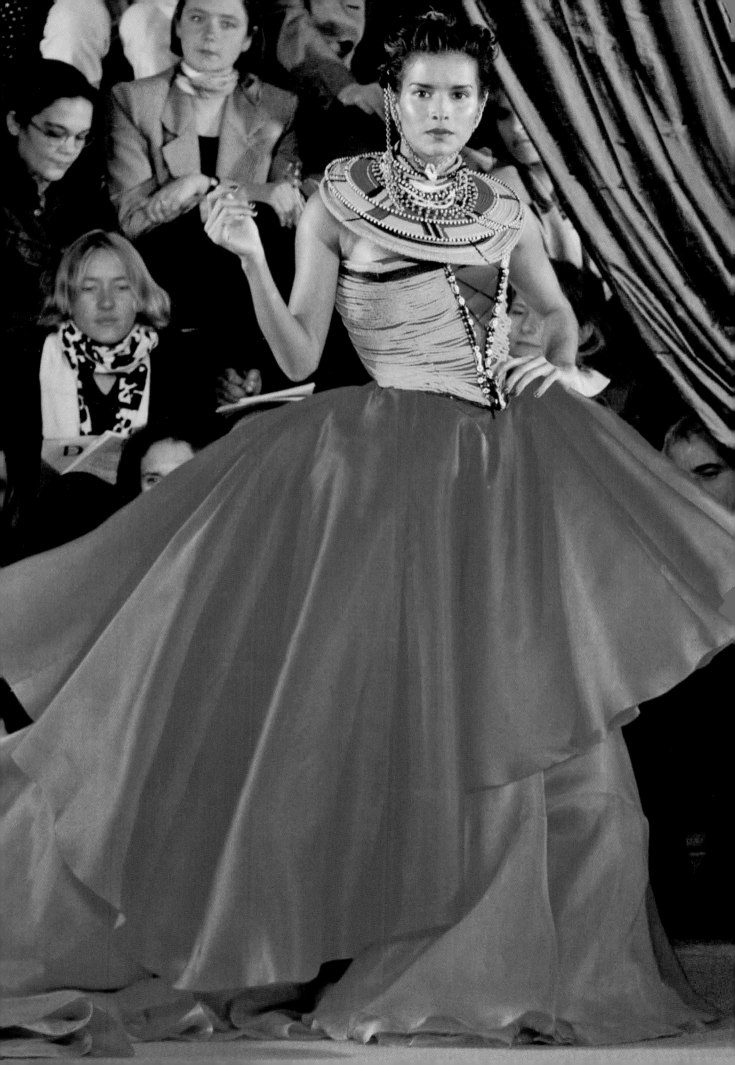

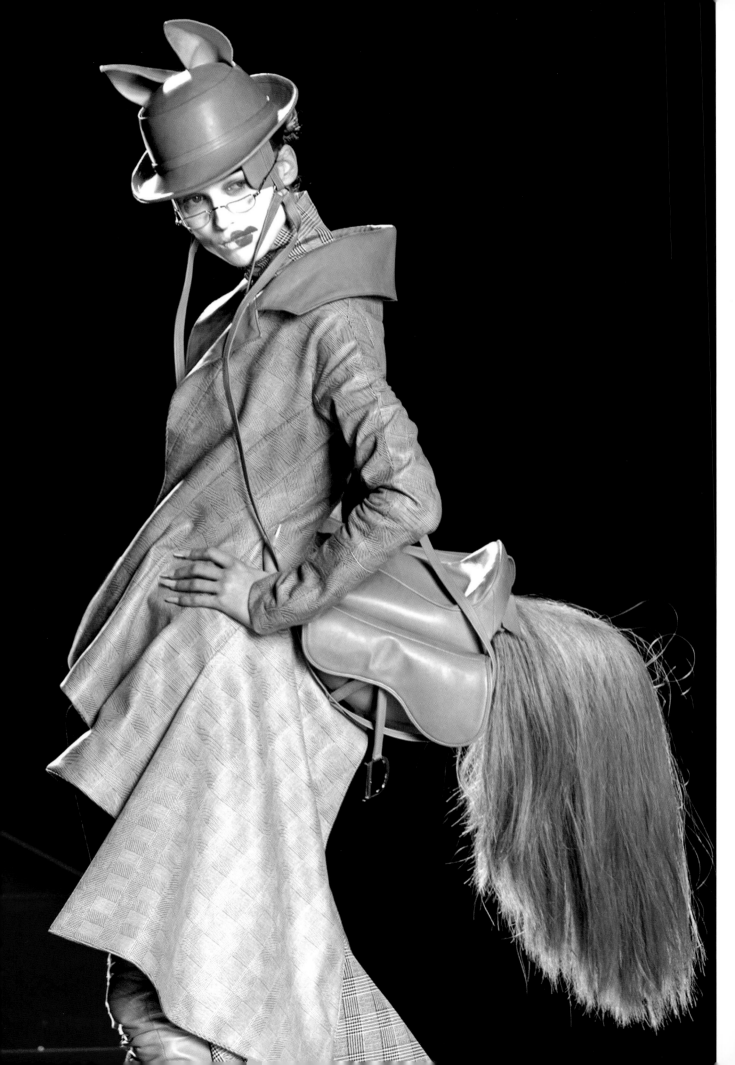

of the finale of his Fall–Winter 2001–2 couture show).[2] He alternately pays homage to Dior's tradition of elegance by combining his sources of inspiration in a romantic and poetic manner, and deliberately subverts that tradition by letting his influences collide violently or jolting his audiences with offensive and disturbing elements. These attention-getting shows and garments, together with Galliano's success at creating more wearable adaptations for Dior's lines of ready-to-wear and accessories, have given the house of Christian Dior a new identity: that of a luxury brand on the cutting edge. — sw

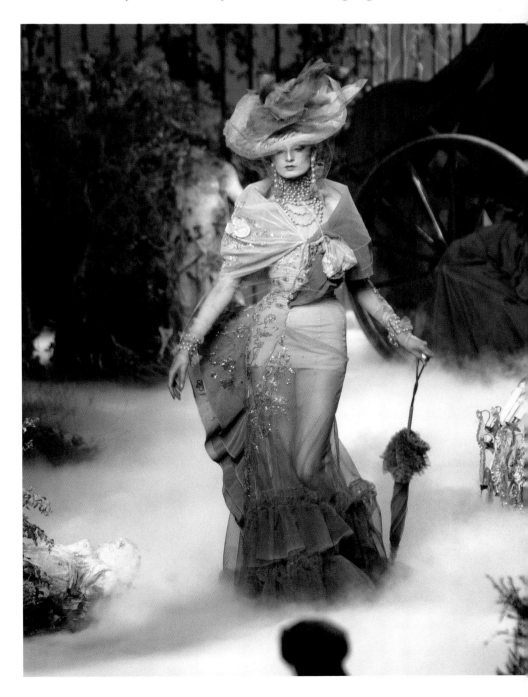

Galliano's deliberately provocative Fall–Winter 2000–2001 collection, inspired by fetishism and bondage gear, was shown to a soundtrack of whips and heavy breathing.

For the Fall–Winter 2005–6 collection, Galliano paid homage to Christian Dior on the hundredth anniversary of his birth. The show opened with an atmospheric tableau evocative of Dior's belle-époque childhood.

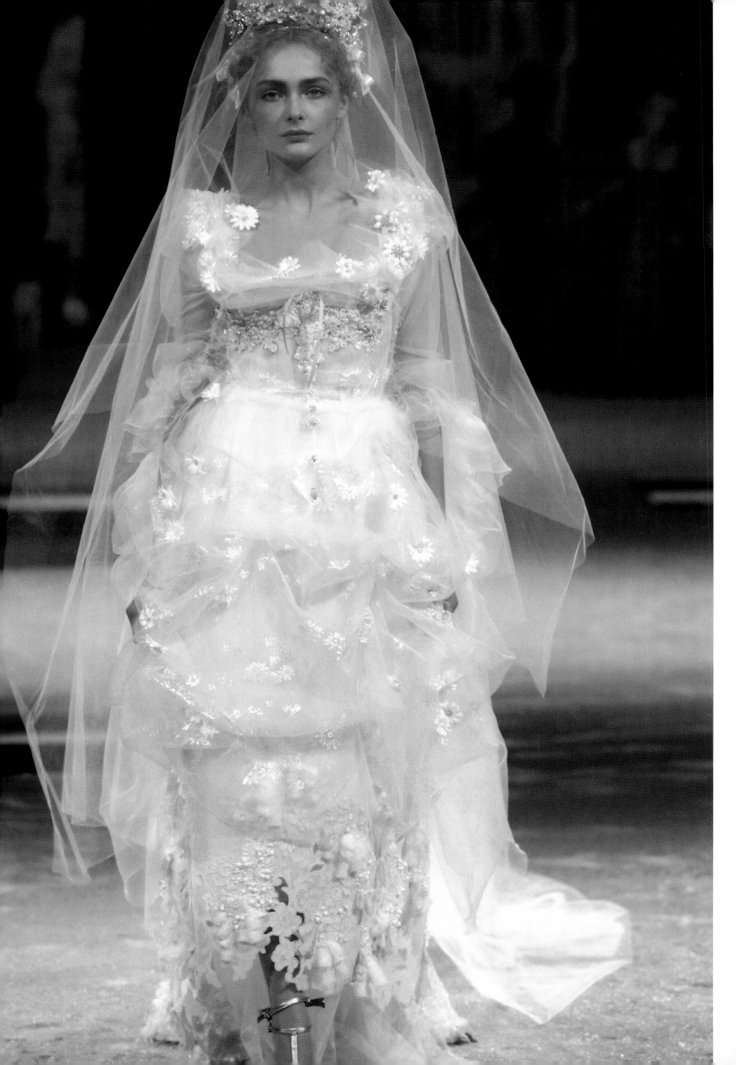

Christian Lacroix

Since his dramatic debut in the 1980s, Christian Lacroix has been among the most original and influential talents working in haute couture. His work is a lively and sometimes chaotic blend of elements and influences drawn from his Provençal upbringing, historic costume, the operatic stage, 1960s street fashion, and the clutter of the flea market. Combining disparate shapes, colors, textures, and ornaments, his designs breathe new life into familiar forms through inspired and unexpected juxtapositions. Although he first became famous for capturing the ostentatious mood and taste for conspicuous consumption of the 1980s, Lacroix has since demonstrated his range and versatility, adding new ideas and reexamining old ones, while maintaining his distinctive artistic identity. He described his evolution as a couturier in his 1992 book, *Pieces of a Pattern*: "I believe that we often have only one thing to say — just as it is said that a great novelist always writes the same book — but that this one thing is constantly evolving. It is this constancy within change which determines a style." [1]

Lacroix was born in Arles, France, in 1951 and became interested in costume and design at an early age, trying out designs for theater costumes on small cardboard figures and assembling albums of images he found inspiring. He has always taken inspiration from his youth in Arles and the Camargue region. Recurring themes in his work include the pleated lace fichus, cross pendants, and patterned cottons of the region's traditional folk costumes; the pageantry of religious festivals, operas, and bullfights; and the exotic allure of gypsy encampments and the circus.

He left Arles to study art history in Montpellier, then enrolled at the Sorbonne in Paris in 1973 with the intention of becoming a

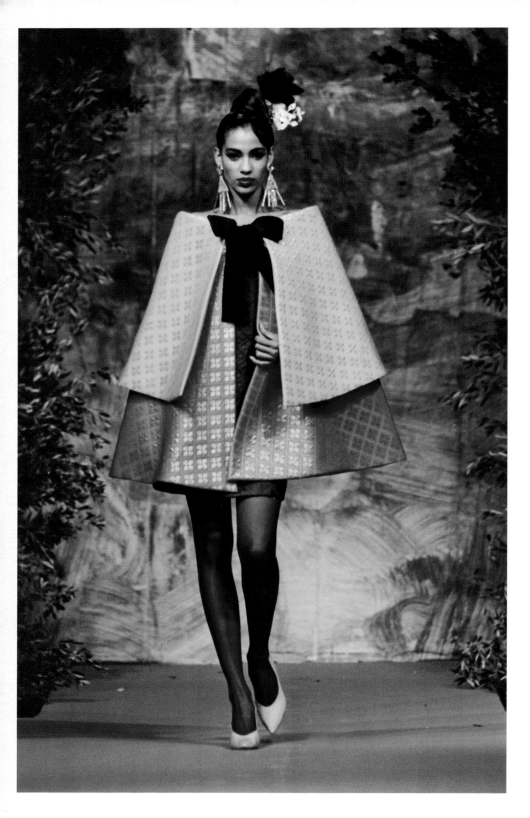

For Spring–Summer 1991, Lacroix emphasized volume, structure, and construction, while still expressing his fondness for bold and contrasting colors.

The Spring–Summer 1994 collection, loosely based on eighteenth-century silhouettes, was a high-spirited celebration of decoration and excess.

museum curator. While working on a master's thesis on costume in seventeenth-century French painting, Lacroix met his future wife, Françoise Rosensthiel, who encouraged him to pursue his interest in fashion design. In 1978, he went to work for the luxury house Hermès, where he learned the technical side of the business. He later worked as an accessory designer for Guy Paulin, before succeeding Roy Gonzales as designer for the venerable couture house of Jean Patou in 1981.

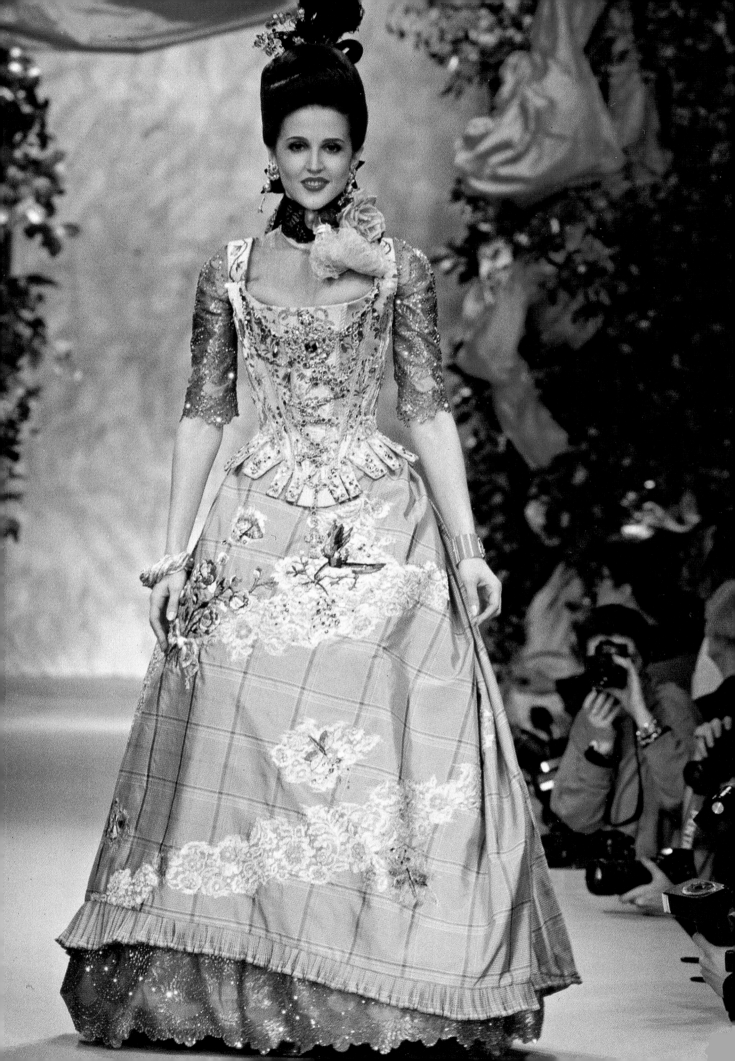

Over the next several years, while gaining firsthand experience of the rituals, technical restrictions, and requirements involved in the world of couture, Lacroix began to build a reputation for his theatrical, witty, and imaginative designs. The most famous style he created for Patou was the "pouf," an exuberant, miniskirted version of the bustled gowns of the 1880s. By the mid-1980s, he was credited with bringing new vigor to the couture, which at the time was seen to be losing creative ground to the growing field of ready-to-wear. His bold shapes and colors, baby-doll dresses with ruffled petticoats, and exaggerated accessories brought him worldwide press attention, along with a Dé d'Or (Golden Thimble) award in 1986. The following year, with financial support from LVMH, he was able to open his own haute couture house.

Christian Lacroix's first collection under his own name, presented in July 1987, was a spectacular success, a watershed fashion moment whose impact is often compared with that of Christian Dior's New Look debut forty years earlier. Its importance was perhaps best expressed by the headline of a review in the *New York Times*: "For Lacroix, a Triumph; For Couture, a Future." [2] Inspired by Provençal and Spanish folk costumes, the new collection was more controlled and balanced than the sometimes zany styles he had designed for Patou. Critics praised its verve, its youthful air, and its sophisticated combinations of bright colors, stripes, and floral patterns. The dramatic flamenco-inspired and balloon skirts, bolero and matador jackets with heavy gold embroidery, and romantic fichu and portrait necklines were particularly influential.

Lacroix's debut, which coincided with an economic boom and a reaction against the muted, casual fashions of the 1970s, was perfectly timed to fulfill the widespread desire for a revival of luxury and extravagance in fashion. The success of his first collection quickly made him an international star and led to the launch of a successful ready-to-wear line and licensing agreements. From Lacroix's point of view, however, his most significant accomplishment was returning the couture to its former role in guiding the direction of fashion. As he said before the presentation of his first collection, "I want to get back to the position where the couture becomes a kind of laboratory of ideas, the way it was with Schiaparelli 40 years ago." [3]

Over the ensuing decades, through shifting economic conditions and dramatic changes in the mood of fashion, Lacroix has persisted in exploring and reworking the sources that most inspire him, while developing and refining the technical aspects of his craft. He has also continued to explore design interests outside the world of fashion.

Lacroix's opulent and witty debut collection, featuring many variations on his trademark "pouf," brought new life to haute couture and made him an international star.

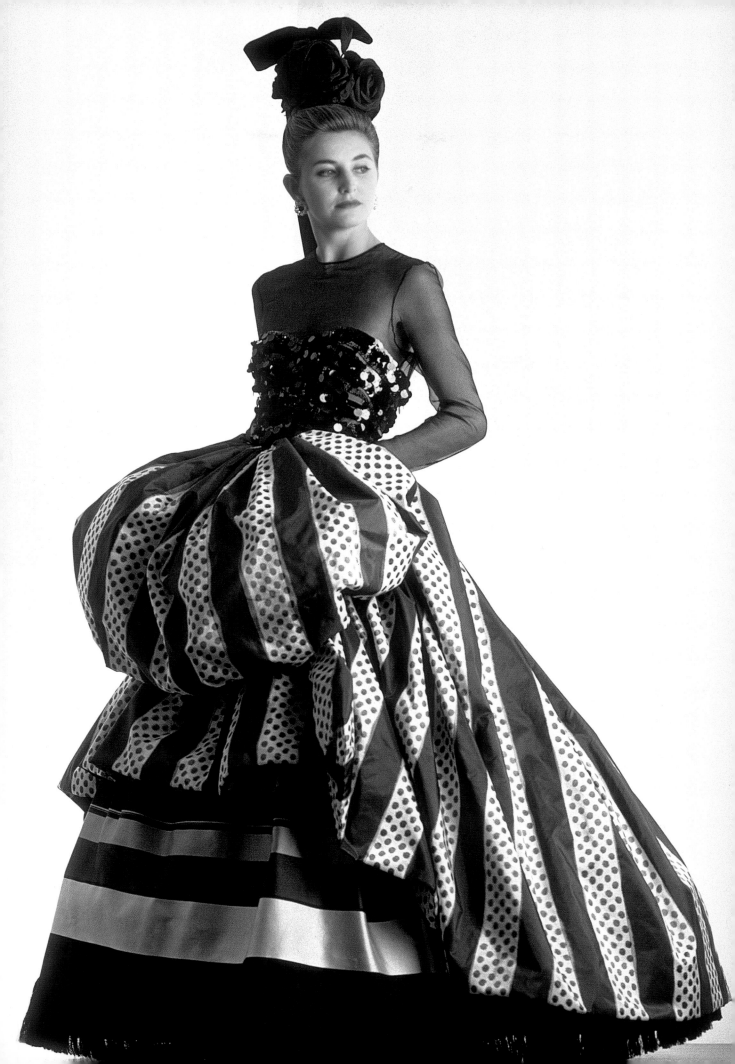

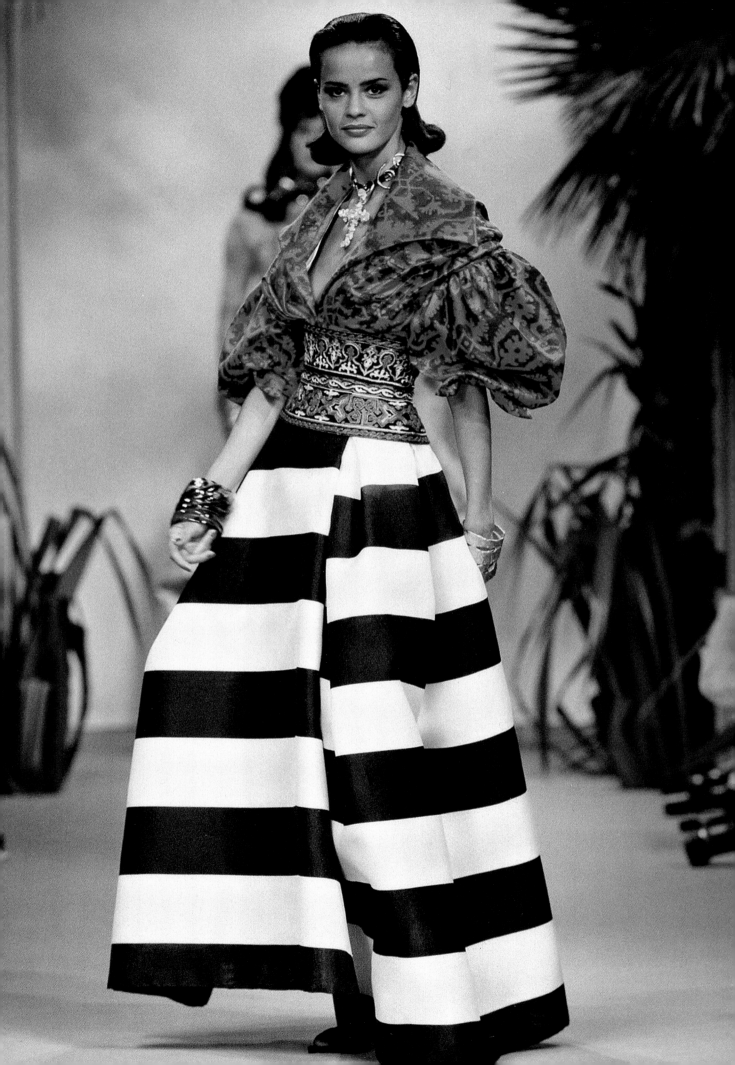

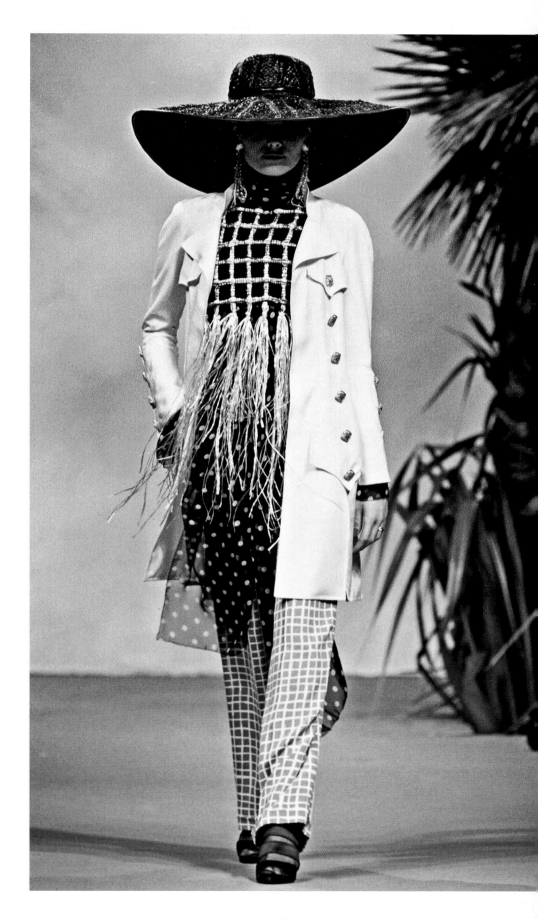

These two ensembles from Spring–Summer 1993 demonstrate Lacroix's range and versatility as a designer. While best known for bold combinations of colors, patterns, and folkloric references from around the world, he is also comfortable working in a more subdued and classical idiom.

Recent projects have included theater costumes (among them, a corset for Madonna's "ReInvention World Tour" in 2004); new uniforms for Air France in 2005; and collaborative exhibitions at the Paris Opera and the Musée des Beaux-Arts et de la Dentelle in Alençon.

Lacroix still looks to historical costumes for ideas, but he prefers to consider them analytically rather than simply copying them, "as you might turn a complex garment inside out in order to understand the idea behind it and the way it has been put together."[4] He also finds it more interesting to view historical costume through the filter of earlier revivals; in his costumes for a 1988 production of the ballet *La Gaîté parisienne*, for example, he tried to imagine not the authentic fin-de-siècle world of Toulouse Lautrec, but how that world would appear in a Technicolor musical film of the 1950s. The historical fashions that most fascinate him are those that arose at times of crisis, such as the improvised and outlandish hats worn by Frenchwomen during the World War II German occupation of Paris.

He also continues to look to Arles for inspiration, both for specific design elements and for the model of mixtures and contrasts it represents for him: "sacred and pagan, civilized and primitive, sophisticated and instinctive, reserved and loquacious, classical and baroque, elegant and trivial, light and dark, theatrical and simple, elaborate and austere."[5] His latest work, in particular, has mixed diverse influences, materials, and textures — assembling hand-painted fabrics, lace, and folk embroidery as patchwork, or painstakingly layering them over each other, working them together and re-embroidering them. As Lacroix's approach has lightened and refined, his work has become more responsive to general trends in fashion, yet without losing its individuality. In a review of his Fall–Winter 2003–4 couture collection, Sarah Mower concluded, "After 20 years, Christian Lacroix has perfected what he does. It's a singular vision that makes a spectacular contribution to the vitality of haute couture."[6] — s w

Lacroix's inventiveness, sophisticated color sense, and theatrical flair have done much to ensure the survival of haute couture as a laboratory for fashion ideas.

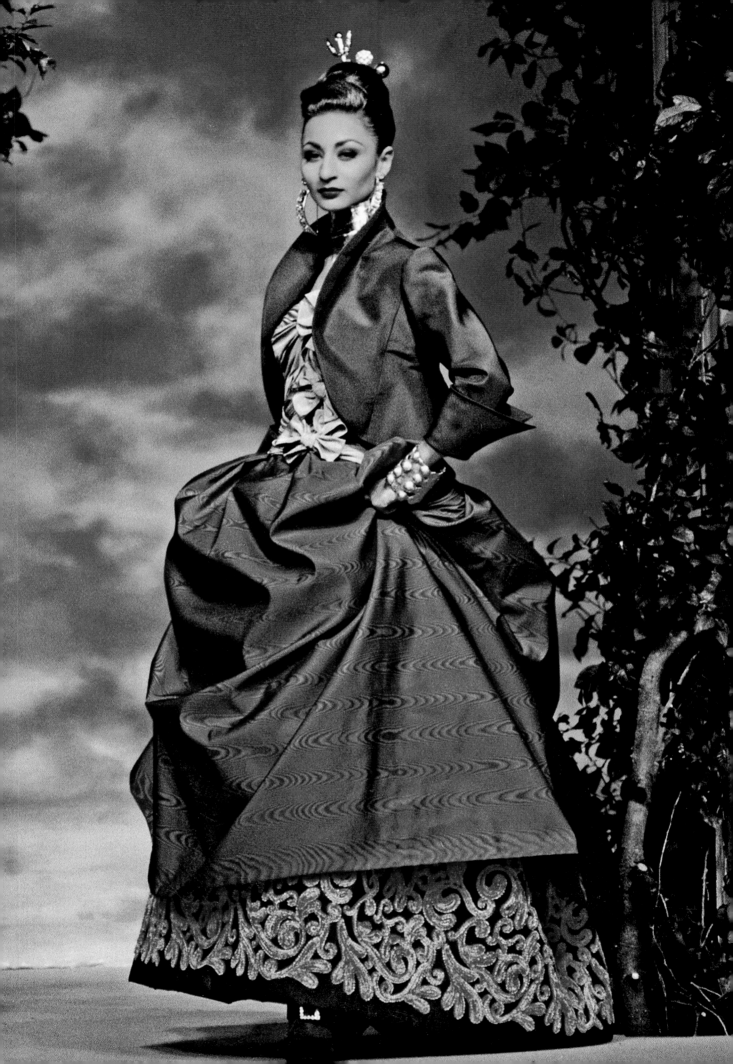

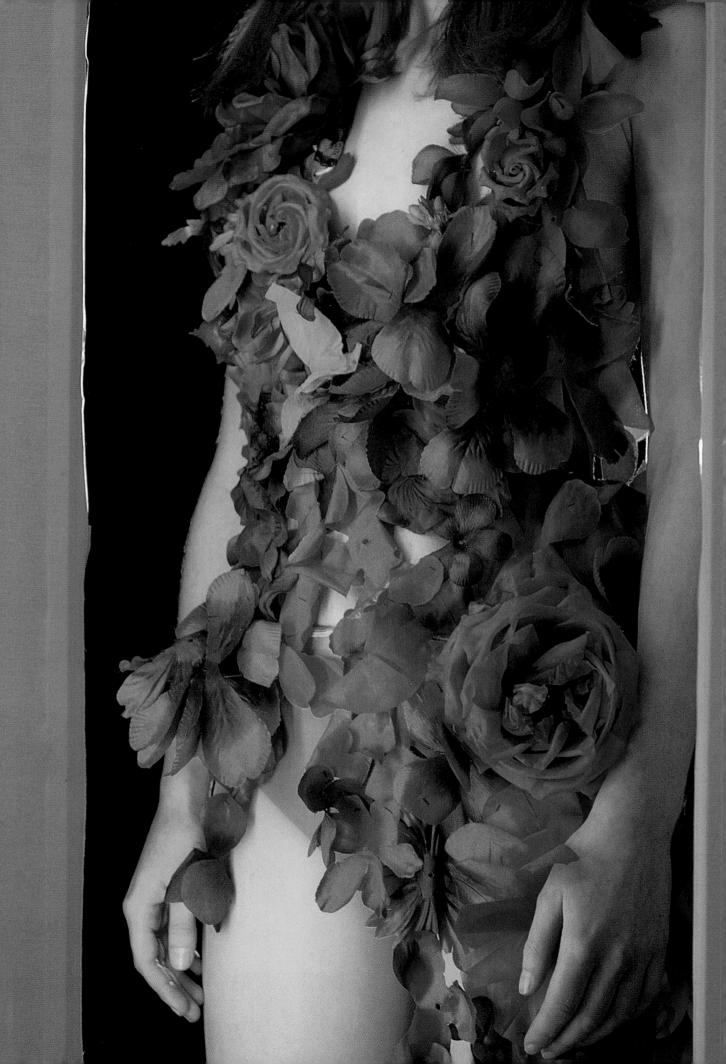

Maison Martin Margiela

Martin Margiela, working through the Maison Martin Margiela, first rose to fame in the late 1980s as the leading proponent of a radical new kind of fashion that became known as deconstructionism. Reacting against the commercialism and opulence of the eighties, Margiela approached fashion analytically. He began taking existing garments apart to make them into new ones and exposing details of clothing construction that are normally hidden from view. Valuing creativity and authenticity above all, the Maison Martin Margiela has taken a similarly analytical approach to the whole fashion system, inventing alternative and idiosyncratic conventions for labeling and showing its clothes, and doing business in a manner that challenges conventional assumptions about fashion and the role of the designer. Over the last decade, the Maison has expanded and diversified its production to reach a wider audience, while preserving its founding principles. In doing so, it has earned the respect of designers and critics alike and has profoundly influenced the direction of fashion.

Born in 1957, Martin Margiela studied fashion design at the Royal Academy of Fine Arts in Antwerp, Belgium, from 1977 to 1980. He was one of a group of young, avant-garde Belgian designers — along with fellow Royal Academy graduates Ann Demeulemeester and Dries Van Noten — who appeared on the fashion scene in the early 1980s, just as the Belgian government was making efforts to promote the country's fashion and textile industry. While his contemporaries decided to stay in Antwerp, Margiela moved to Paris; he worked as a design assistant for Jean Paul Gaultier from 1984 to 1987. In 1988, he and Jenny Meirens founded the Maison Martin Margiela, which presented its first collection in October of that year and soon attracted an enthusiastic following in avant-garde fashion circles.

For the Spring–Summer 2006 *Artisanal* collection, the Maison Martin Margiela painstakingly reworked flea-market garments and materials such as artificial flowers into new clothing.

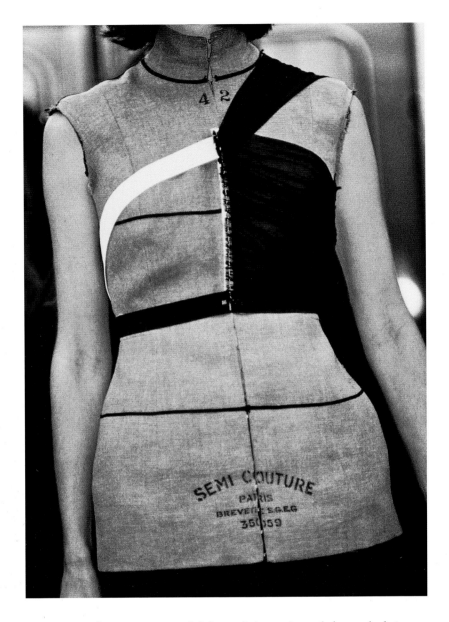

The Spring–Summer 1997 collection took an analytical approach to the tailoring process, starting with a series of sleeveless linen jackets based on an old Stockman dress form. Some had marking tapes, shoulder pads, and parts of garments attached to them, as if in the process of being draped on the form.

From the outset, Margiela's work investigated the underlying structure, materials, and techniques involved in creating an article of clothing. Finding beauty in the hidden details of tailoring, he started to turn seams, darts, and shoulder pads to the outside of garments and to make beautifully tailored and finished jackets with the sleeves left unattached, showing the raw edges of the fabric and linings. One famous series consisted of sleeveless jackets in rough linen reproducing an old Stockman dress form, complete with the printed size and patent numbers; some had parts of dresses or skirts pinned to them, as though in the process of being draped on the form.

Margiela also used recycled materials and secondhand clothes extensively. He cut and unraveled old socks, for example, to make them into sweaters, and he transformed used blue jeans

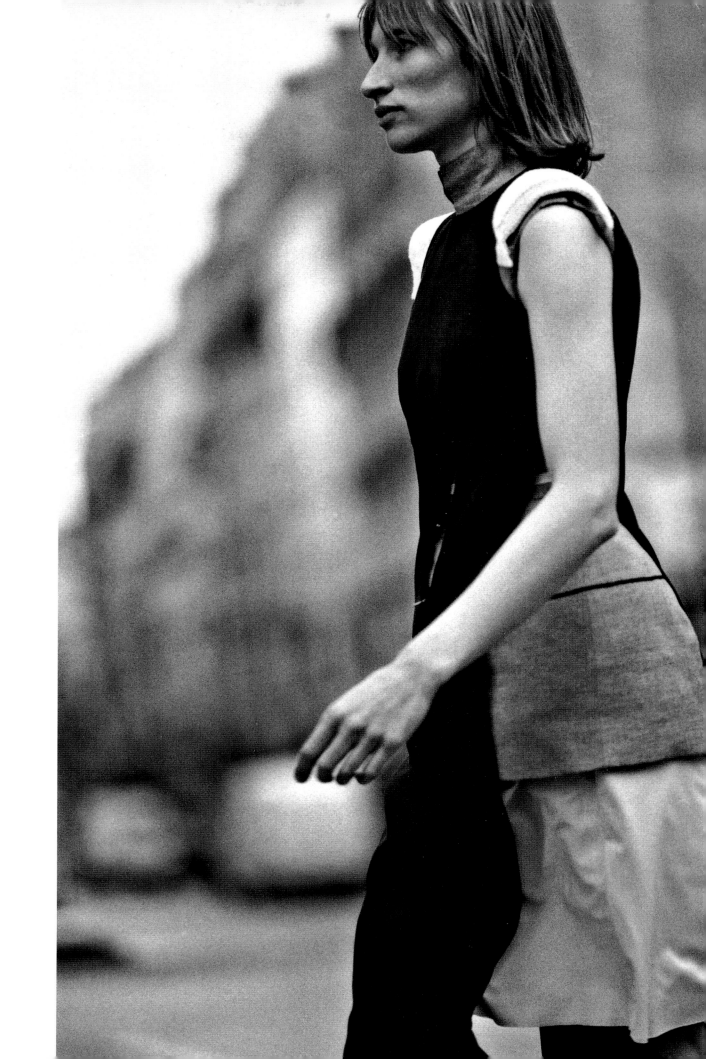

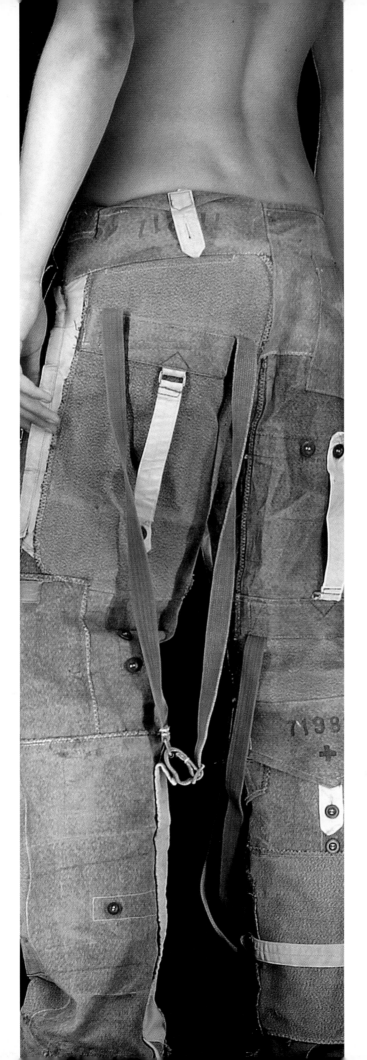

The Maison used a wide range of materials for the Spring–Summer 2006 *Artisanal* lines. For men, Swiss army satchels were softened, overdyed, and opened flat to become the fabric for jackets and trousers. For women, the tops of vintage leather sandals were modeled directly on a dress form into jackets and waistcoats.

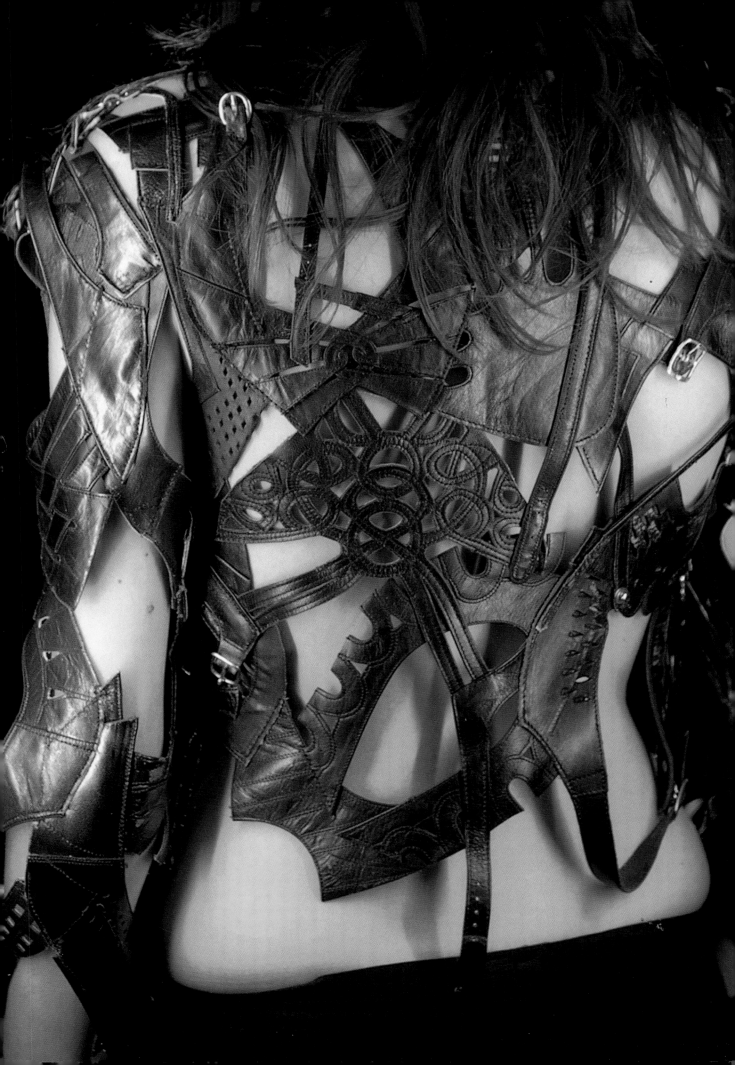

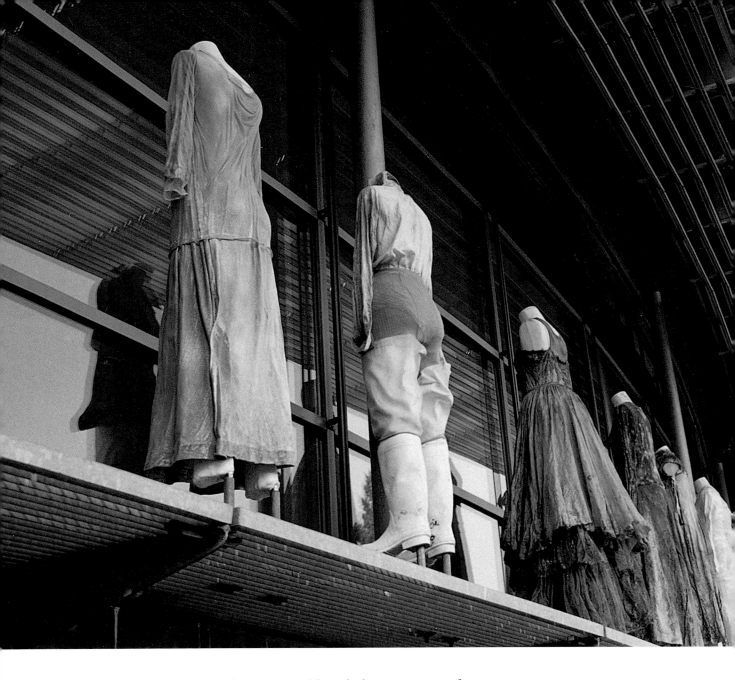

and jean jackets into long coats. Although the appearance of raw and raveling edges and garments clearly made from other garments caused the French fashion press to call Margiela's clothes *la mode destroy*, Margiela did not consider his method destructive. On the contrary, he believes that remaking old clothes is a way of giving new life to discarded objects, while allowing them to retain traces of their original form and function.

Just as its work has defied conventions of design and construction, the Maison Martin Margiela has called into question many of the traditional rituals of the fashion system. While numerous designers have become major celebrities, Martin Margiela has always declined to be photographed or to make appearances at his fashion shows. He turns down requests for interviews, explaining that he prefers the focus to be on the clothes. He also

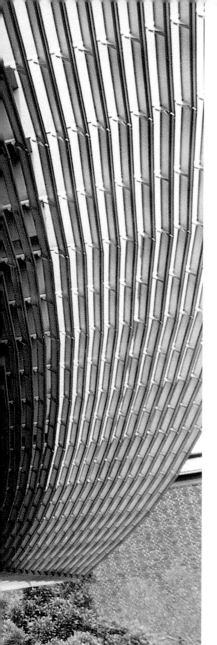

takes pains to emphasize that the creations of the Maison are a team effort rather than the product of an individual "genius" designer; all work is credited to the Maison Martin Margiela, and faxed questions from the press are answered in the third person plural, with the explanation, "our answers to your questions have been reached as a team with the input of Mr. Margiela."[1]

In a similar vein, the Maison has rejected the trend-conscious seasonal cycle of fashion design, which requires each season's collection to have a new theme or inspiration. The house instead prefers to develop the same ideas over several seasons, and successful items often reappear in later collections. For example, Margiela's distinctive cloven-toed Tabi boots, based on the footwear worn by Japanese workmen, appeared in his first collection, and variations have since become a house trademark.

For a 1997 exhibition at the Museum Boijmans van Beuningen, Rotterdam, the Maison collaborated with a prominent Dutch microbiologist. They treated white cotton garments with various strains of bacteria, yeast, and mold, selected to produce different colors and textures. Once the organisms had developed, the garments were arranged outside a long glass wall of the museum.

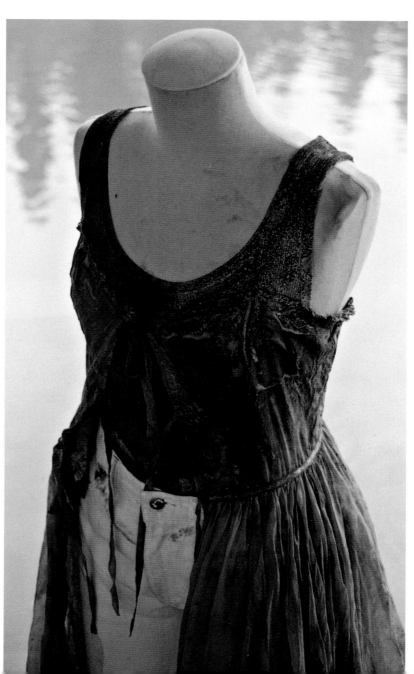

Another, more famous trademark of the Maison is its system for labeling its garments, which challenges assumptions about authorship, authenticity, and conspicuous "designer" branding. The label it used for its first several years, and still uses for the main line of women's garments (now called '1'), is a large blank piece of white twill tape, affixed at each corner with oversized white stitches visible on the outside of the garment. This conspicuous but consciously blank label is an ironic reference to the status conferred by designer clothing, but it has itself become a status symbol among fashion insiders. In 1997, when the Maison introduced a line of basic garments for women (called MM6), it created a second white label, this time printed with the numbers 0 to 23; the collection number (for example, 6) was circled on each garment's label. Over the next several years, the house launched additional lines, including '10', a wardrobe for men; '22', shoes for women; and '13', publications and objects. The *Artisanal* collection, consisting of one-of-a-kind garments reworked (or "transformed") by hand from used materials, became a separate line called '0' for women and '0''10' for men.

The Maison early became famous for fashion shows that confounded the press's expectations. Preferring to work and present its clothes in well-used places with character, the house has held shows in such unusual and out-of-the-way locations as a Salvation Army depot, an abandoned subway station, a disused parking garage, and a rubble-strewn lot on the outskirts of Paris (where neighborhood children were invited to join the models on the runway). One season, two versions of the collection — one all white and one all black — were shown simultaneously in two separate locations. Other lines have been introduced on giant puppets, on film, in almost total darkness, or on hangers held up in front of the audience by men in white work coats (the Maison staff wear these coats, associated with haute couture workrooms, as an unofficial uniform).

Although the Maison Martin Margiela is best known for its avant-garde and experimental work, it has always included wearable and well-cut garments in its collections. As author Valerie Steele has written, "Margiela is an excellent tailor who really knows how to sew, and his clothes, although undeniably strange, are beautifully (de)constructed."[2] From 1998 until 2004, Martin Margiela also designed for the French luxury house Hermès, creating ready-to-wear collections praised for their minimalist refinement and flawless finishing.

During the same period, a more classical strain emerged in the work of the Maison, which added two new lines of timeless, beautifully tailored garments in 2004: '4', a wardrobe for women,

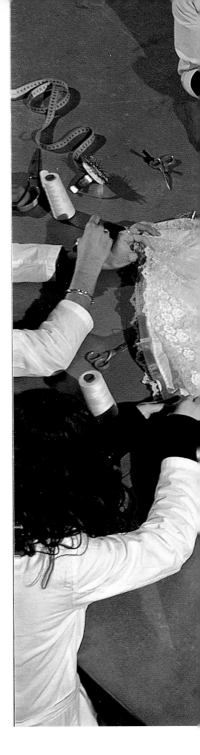

The Maison Martin Margiela values the authenticity of hand labor and used garments, and emphasizes the cooperative nature of the creative process. Here, members of the staff combine three vintage wedding dresses to make a new ball gown.

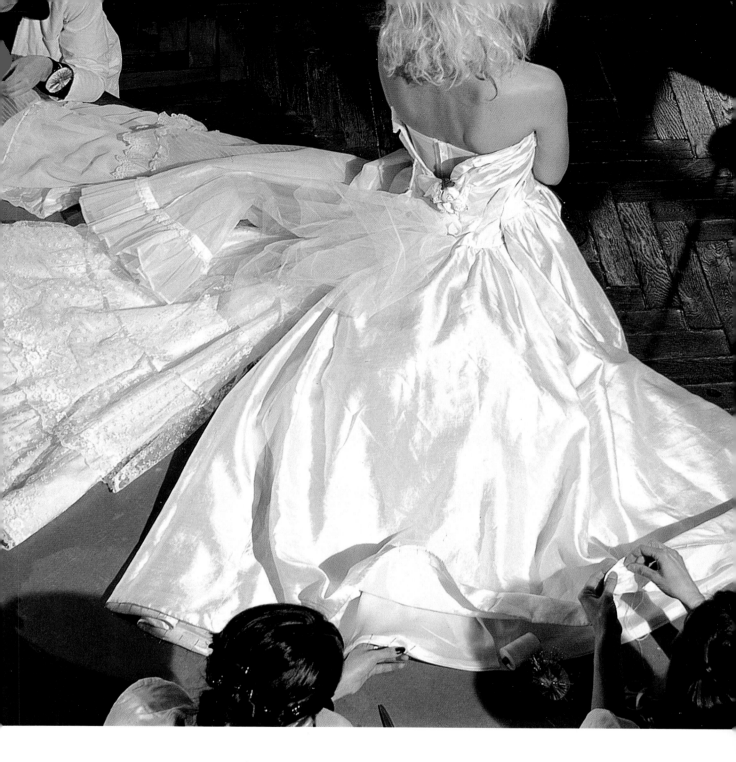

and '14', a wardrobe for men. These collections included a reprise of the 1994 *Replica* series, in which archetypal found garments such as a 1960s American trench coat, representing "pieces of the collective memory of clothing,"[3] were faithfully reproduced for modern wearers. While adding more lines to its range and opening new shops worldwide, the house has also returned to its roots by reinvigorating the *Artisanal* collections for men and women. Operating from its new headquarters, a former industrial design college in Paris, the Maison continues to develop its unique take on the fashion system for an increasingly global audience. — s w

MAISON MARTIN MARGIELA

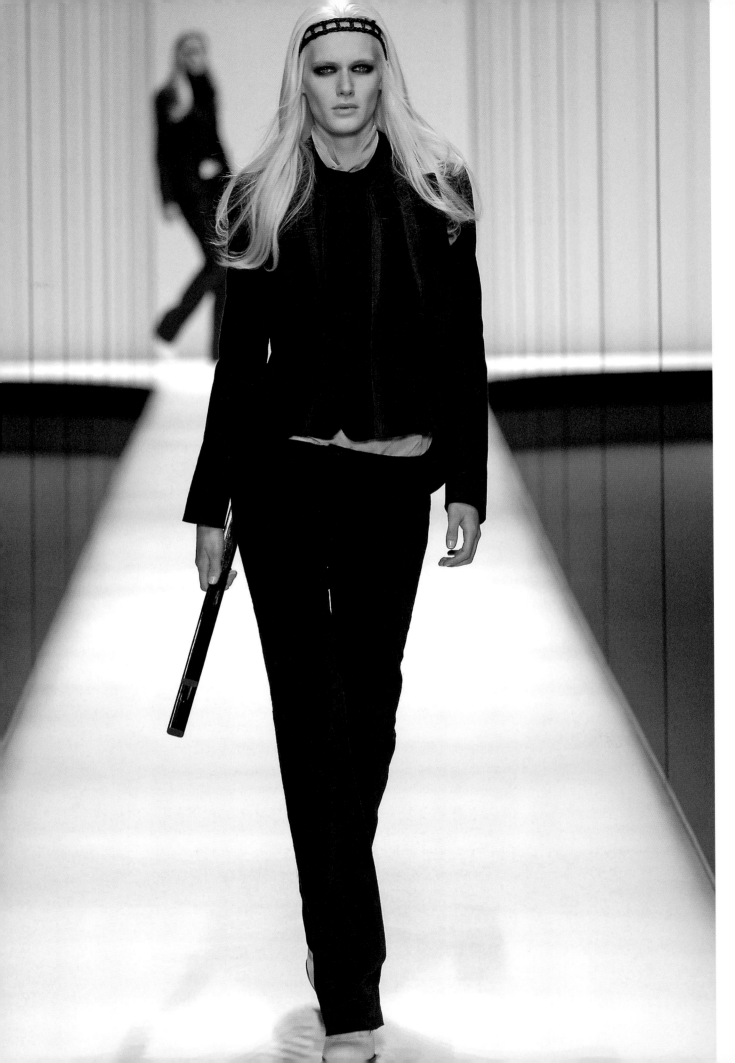

Rochas

The house of Rochas has recently reemerged as one of the most influential fashion houses in Paris. For many years, the name had all but vanished from the clothing industry. Marcel Rochas established the house in 1925 with the motto "Jeunesse, Simplicité, et Personnalité" (Youth, Simplicity, Personality),[1] and during the 1930s and 1940s, Rochas built a reputation for chic, feminine, and youthful clothing supplemented by accessories and perfumes. After the closing of the fashion house in 1953 and Marcel's death in 1955, however, the Rochas name became associated primarily with its perfumes. The house of Rochas was not fully revived until the arrival of current artistic director Olivier Theyskens in 2002. Since then, Theyskens has breathed new life into the venerable house's fashions, presenting ready-to-wear collections that combine elegance and technical sophistication with a skill that is reminiscent of the house's founder.

Born in 1902 in Paris, Marcel Rochas trained initially as a lawyer and left his law career in 1925 to open his own couture house so he could keep his young wife well dressed.[2] He was one of the youngest designers working in Paris in the 1920s, and he quickly gained recognition for his smart and youthful sports clothes. Rochas established a name for himself as an elegant innovator, as well. In an age when women wore pants only for recreation or casual events, he launched gray flannel trouser suits, as well as cleverly cut beach pajamas. He even claimed to have coined the word "slacks."[3] By 1931, Rochas was successful enough to move to 12, avenue Matignon, where he continued to expand his clientele. The Rochas woman was stylish and relaxed, and the designer counted among his clients notable celebrities such as

For Rochas's Fall–Winter 2006–7 collection, Olivier Theyskens paired long, lean trousers with snug, tailored jackets in a dark palette inspired by chimney sweeps — a point underscored by the tiny ladder this model holds.

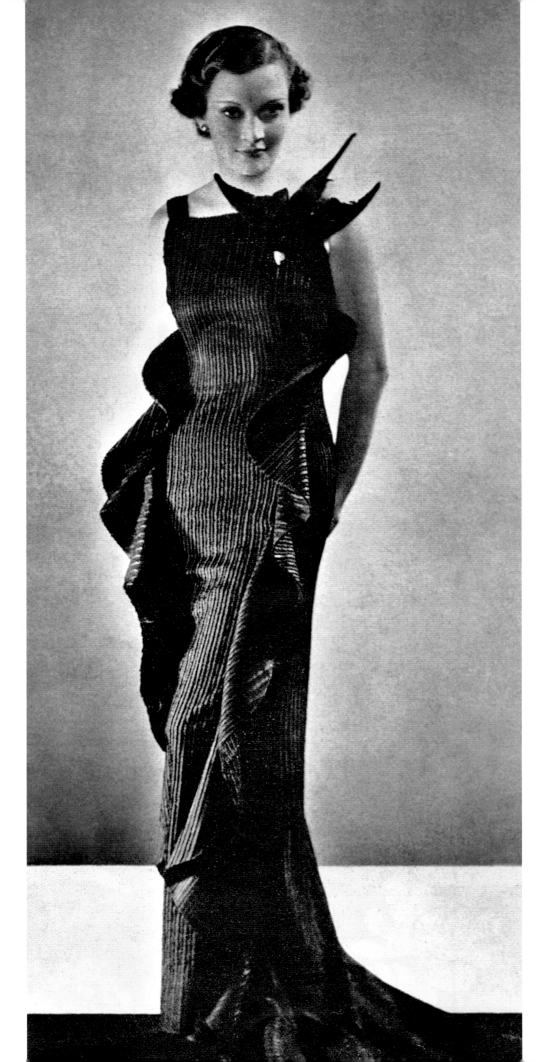

Marcel Rochas frequently arranged striking three-dimensional details such as pleats, oversized flowers, and birds — often at the neckline — on dresses noted for their drama.

By 1951, when this photograph was snapped backstage between fashion shows, Rochas had long established an international reputation for elegance and innovation.

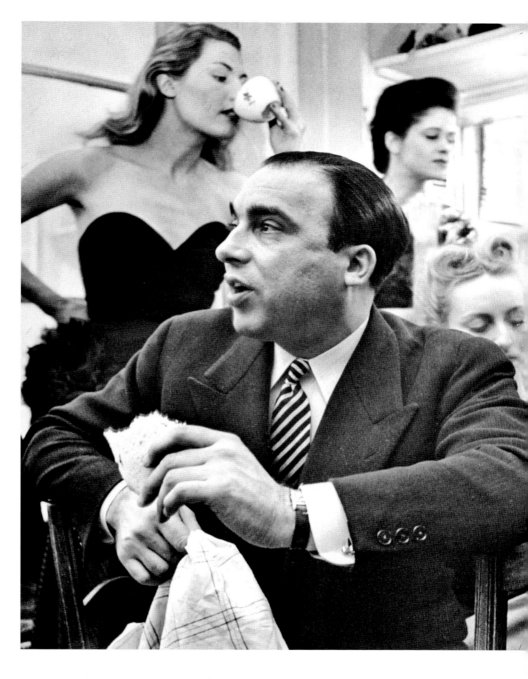

Joan Crawford, Marlene Dietrich, Jean Harlow, and Mae West.

Rochas's most important years of creativity began in the 1930s. Along with his contemporaries Gilbert Adrian and Elsa Schiaparelli, he introduced a wider shoulder line. Unlike the other two, however, Rochas professed that he was inspired by the costumes in a Balinese dance performance at the 1931 Exposition Coloniale.[4] His designs often possessed a sense of drama. He was known to add oversized flowers, colorful bird feathers, and three-dimensional pleats to necklines, and to cleverly manipulate geometric patterns on wool suits for maximum graphic appeal.

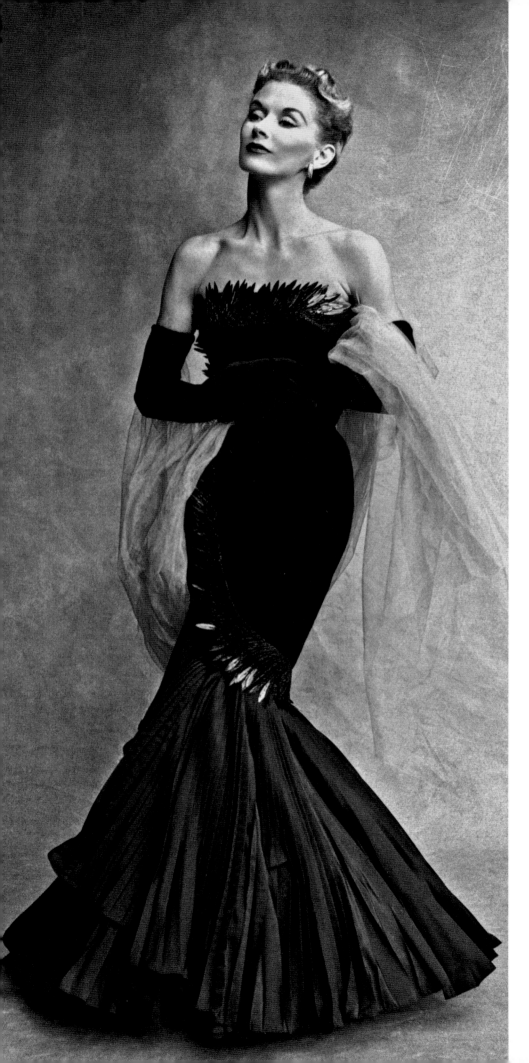

The new feminine shape
Rochas introduced in 1942
with his "guêpiere" corset
became a hallmark of his
1950 *Sirène* dress, worn
here by Lisa Fonssagrives in
a photograph shot by Irving
Penn for *Vogue*.

Irving Penn also photo-
graphed Nicole Kidman
in a dramatic evening dress
that Olivier Theyskens
designed in 2003 as part of
his debut collection for the
house of Rochas.

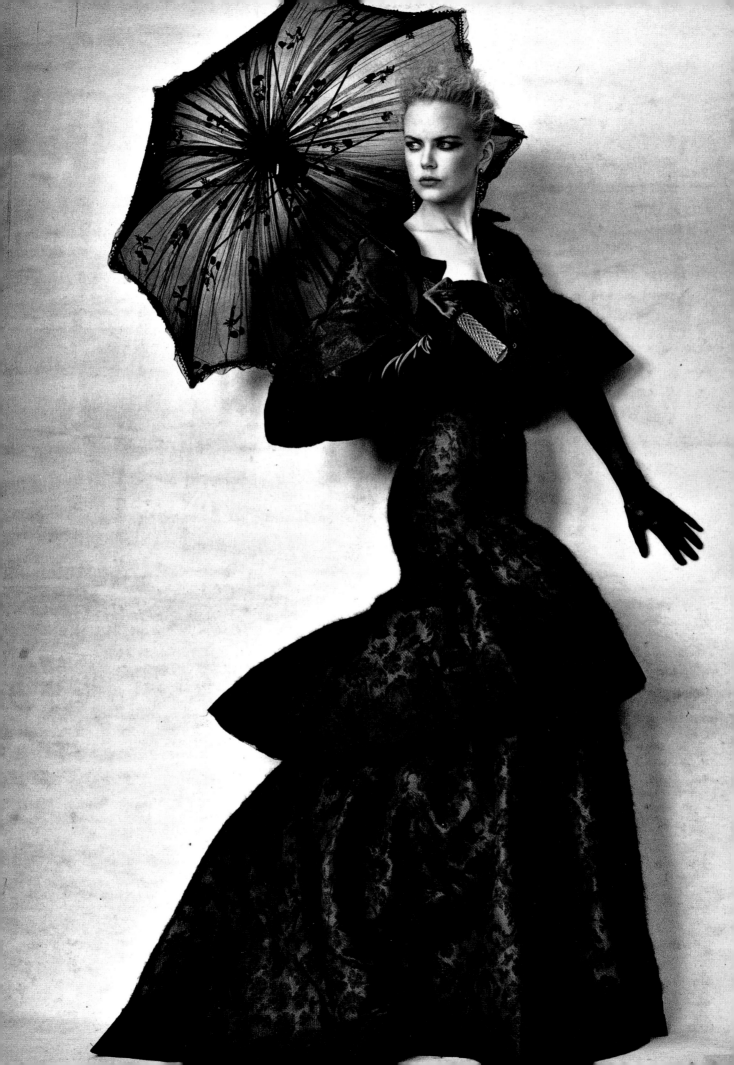

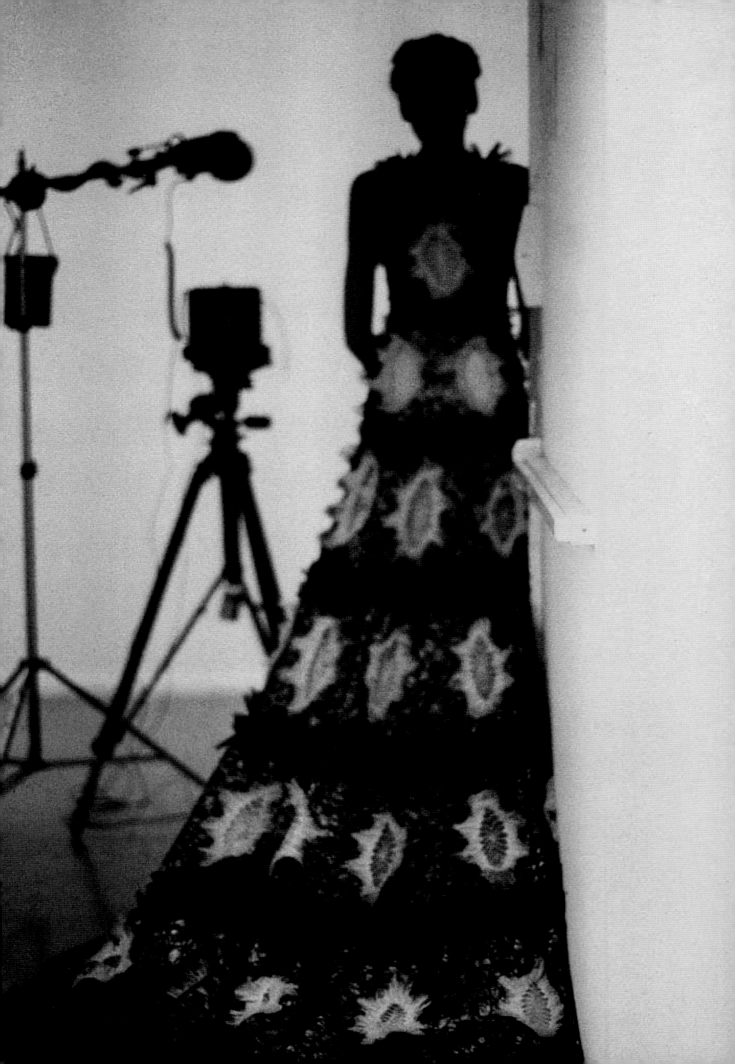

Rochas's calculated originality extended into the 1940s. In 1942, he introduced a corset called the "guêpiere" (after the French word for wasp), anticipating Dior's feminine wasp-waisted New Look silhouette by several years. In 1944, Rochas added a line of perfumes to his fashion business. Femmes, dedicated to his third wife, Hélène, was the first of six created by 1949.

Marcel Rochas died in 1955. Under the supervision of Hélène and several subsequent directors, the house of Rochas continued to produce mainly accessories and perfumes, eventually adding twenty-three more scents to its roster. The clothing line was licensed to Irishman Peter O'Brien in 1990.

In 2002, the torch was passed to Olivier Theyskens, whose ready-to-wear lines reestablished the house of Rochas, expanding upon the house's tradition of innovative elegance. Theyskens, born in Belgium in 1977, was only twenty-six when he joined Rochas, making him one of the youngest artistic directors of a major fashion house. He was not the first Belgian to take Paris by storm. In the early 1980s, a wave of talented young Belgian designers introduced a radical new aesthetic into ready-to-wear fashion. Among them was Martin Margiela, who apprenticed with Jean Paul Gaultier for three years before establishing Maison Martin Margiela in 1988. Dries Van Noten, Ann Demeulemeester, Walter Van Beirendonck, Dirk Van Saene, Marina Yee, and Dirk Bikkembergs became known as the "Antwerp 6." Together, these Belgian designers established a conceptual vision of fashion that lauded "the backside, the recycled, throwaway fashions, the underdog; not so extroverted as English fashion, not so sexy as Italian, not so cerebral as Japanese fashion."[5]

Theyskens is part of the second influx of Belgians to arrive on the fashion scene. Unlike his compatriots, however, he is not a product of the influential Royal Academy in Antwerp. He trained for two years in Brussels at the Ecole Nationale Supérieure des Arts Visuele de la Cambre but quit before his final year. Instead of finishing, he launched his first collection in Paris in 1997. Theyskens caught the attention of the fashion world in 1998, when Madonna wore one of his dramatic black satin dresses to the Oscars.

Theyskens joined the house of Rochas in 2002. When asked about this decision, he commented: "to me Rochas seemed instinctively right. It's still contemporary. Even the name, Rochas, has a modern ring to it."[6] And Theyskens is nothing if not modern. His first collection, shown in a mansion in Paris, was widely acclaimed. Its vision was dark, almost gothic, and the tone was somber. But it was also resolutely feminine, featuring long dresses in black

Theyskens's Spring–Summer 2004 collection incorporated black lace in complex embroidered and layered arrangements over *lamé* fabrics, building on his early vision of long, dark, feminine silhouettes.

Chantilly lace. More importantly, Theyskens's unique look was impeccably crafted and technically accomplished, reviving an attention to methods and details traditionally reserved for haute couture.

Long, lean, dark, and feminine are words that are frequently associated with Theyskens's designs. Asserting that his aim was to dress a "goddess from another world,"[7] he employed black lace once again in the Spring–Summer 2004 collection, embroidered and layered over *lamé*. For Fall–Winter 2004–5, his rigid bustiers trimmed with soft satin and velvet roses and his pencil skirts and bolero jackets edged with flounces all evoked "a notion of femininity that embraces neither girlish modesty nor matronly ascent."[8] This new femininity was at the heart of Theyskens's Spring–Summer 2005 collection, which featured lighter fabrics and a fresh palette in aquas and blues.

An insistence on perfection of construction led to his Fall–Winter 2005–6 creations in bias-cut silks, soft wools, and mohairs. In addition to the new cut of fabrics, this collection was noted for super-long skirts with ruffles, high necklines, and frilled blouses that were almost Edwardian in their unabashed romanticism. Theyskens has continued to plumb a feminine vision enriched by his impeccable dressmaking skills, while firmly establishing a modern outlook. Long gray linen skirts, with plain white cotton voile blouses, delicate lace dresses, and pared-down pantsuits in tones of gray, blue, and white reinforced his more minimalist tack in the Spring–Summer 2006 Claude Monet–inspired collections.

Theyskens's line for Fall–Winter 2006–7 was inspired by chimney sweeps, expressed in the palette of charcoal grays, sooty blacks, and silvers. His black silk pantsuits with Victorian snug vests, schoolboy short outfits, and billowing evening dresses — clouds of shimmering silver silk — have led some critics to praise him as a poet, or "a Belgian poet to be specific,"[9] acknowledging his deftness in combining dark edginess with romanticism. Typical of Belgian designers, Theyskens remains untheatrical in his approach. He is daring, yet modest and, above all else, committed to a level of professionalism in his craft. His highly structured and perfectly detailed garments may approach haute couture in construction, but he is utterly practical in his philosophy of making clothes. He is "just thinking of the woman in the streets. What will appeal to her? That is the only thing that matters."[10] — LDW

The chimney-sweep theme of the Fall–Winter 2006–7 collection also inspired billowing evening dresses in smoky hues, skillfully combining dark edginess and romanticism.

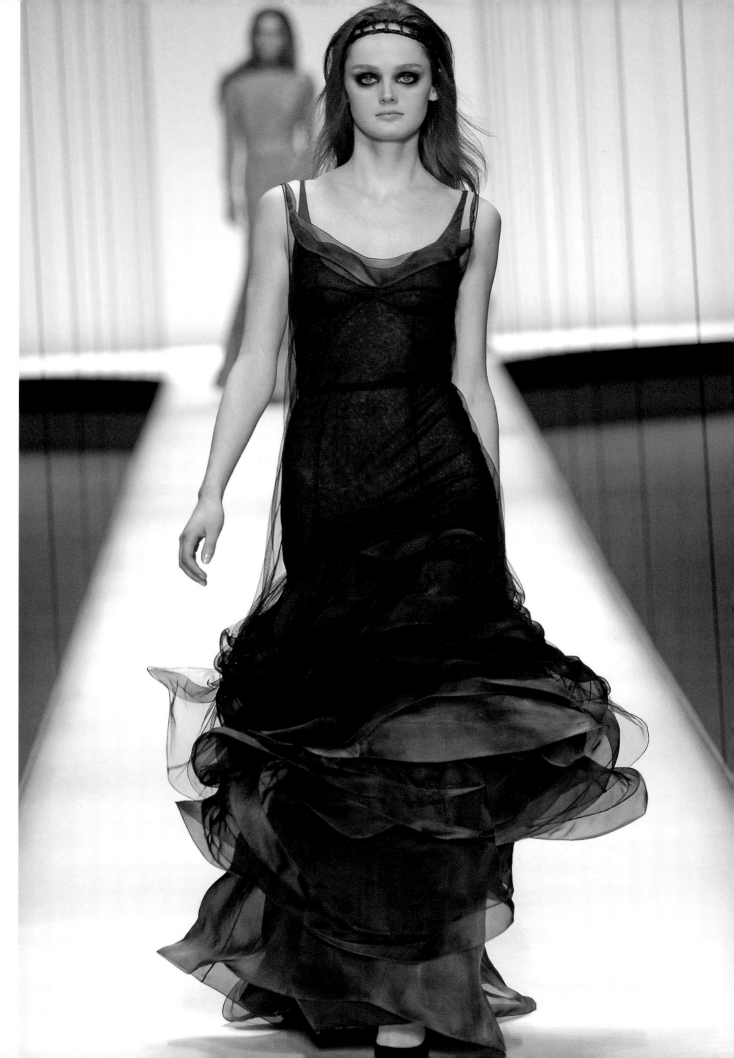

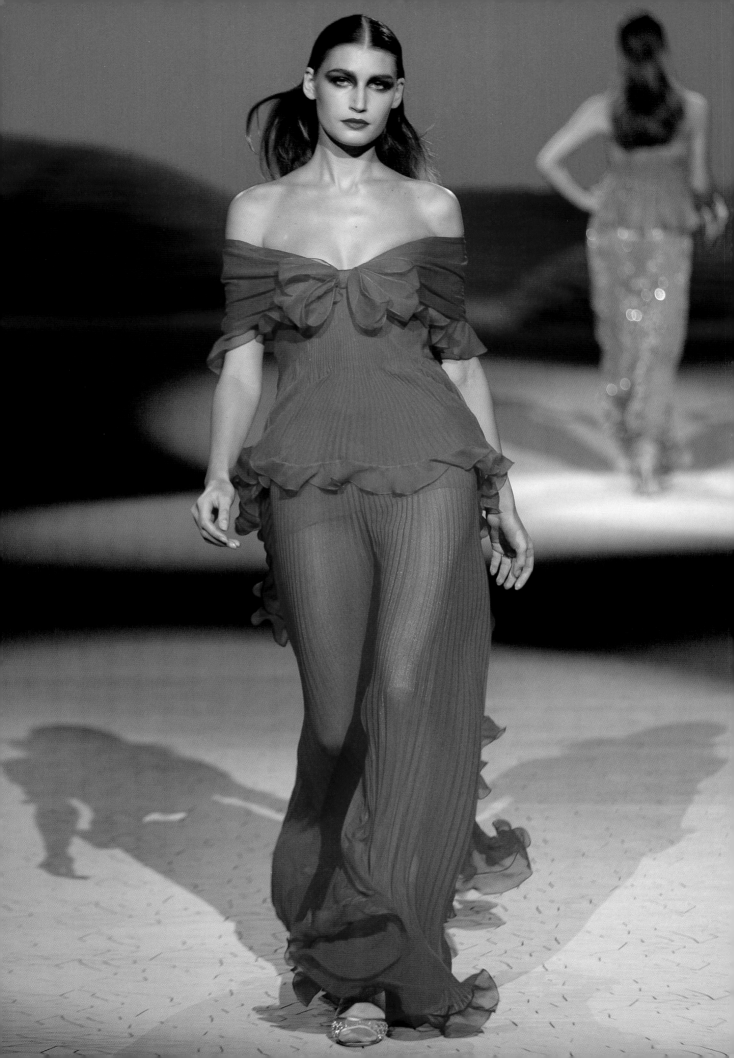

Valentino

Valentino has been one of the most important names in international fashion for over forty years. Working in the tradition of the great postwar couturiers, he has consistently created clothes that are beautiful, sophisticated, and perfect in craftsmanship and detail. Although he has kept pace with general trends in fashion, he is renowned for inventing and cultivating a recognizable personal style rooted in idealized femininity, timeless elegance, and understated luxury. Whether classically simple or extravagantly ornamented, Valentino's clothes are designed to beautify the wearers and surround them with the finest materials and finishing. In a 1990 interview, he explained, "I want my customer to look at a dress and say, 'I have to have it.' . . . And when she tries it on, she should say, 'It feels wonderful.'"[1] Although some consider his commitment to tradition and elegance too conservative, his technical mastery, inventiveness, and openness to fresh ideas have earned him many devoted long-term customers and the enduring respect of the fashion world.

Valentino has worked primarily in Rome, but Paris has always played an important role in his career. Born Valentino Garavani in Voghera, Italy, he moved to Paris in 1950 to study fashion design at the school run by the Chambre Syndicale. In 1952, he won a fashion design competition sponsored by the International Wool Secretariat, leading to a position at the couture house of Jean Dessès. He spent five years working in Dessès's atelier, an experience he later likened to being "at university."[2] One of the most prominent Parisian couturiers in the early 1950s, Dessès was known for masterful draped and pleated gowns in delicate fabrics such as chiffon, inspired by the costume of his native Greece, and for the fluid, feminine lines of his designs, which often featured

The lightness of wind-blown desert sand inspired Valentino's fluid and seemingly effortless Spring–Summer 2006 couture collection.

floating handkerchief panels and scarves with long trailing ends. The perfection of Dessès's draping made a strong impression on Valentino. So did the couturier's preference for working in his own style rather than seeking to set or follow new fashion trends. Valentino spent two more years in Paris working for fellow Dessès protegé Guy Laroche, who opened his own salon in 1957.

Valentino returned to Rome to open his first salon in 1959, on the Via Condotti, and presented his first collection in November of that year. His decision to move back to Rome was in part a practical one, as the Paris couture establishment at the time made it very difficult for foreign designers to show there. He always maintained a connection to Paris, however, choosing the city for the site of his first boutique, opened in 1968, and showing his ready-to-wear collections there regularly beginning in 1975. In 1989, by which time the French fashion industry was more welcoming to non-French houses, he also began to show his couture collections in Paris and was immediately hailed as one of the top Parisian couturiers.

Right from the beginning, Valentino found devoted clients among the Roman aristocracy and attracted the attention of film

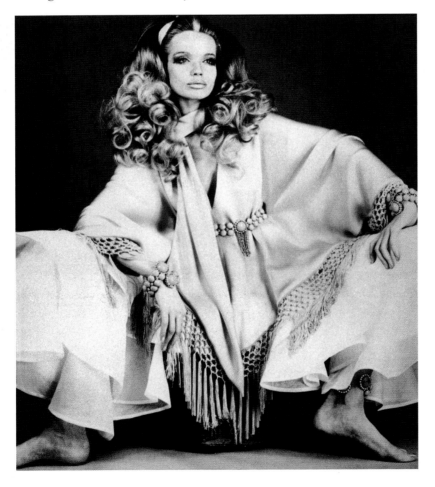

In the late 1960s, varied cultural influences appeared in Valentino's romantic evening ensembles, such as this fringed satin poncho and ruffled organdy trousers from 1969.

The Spring–Summer 1968 collection, which included this silk organza dress densely embroidered with lace flowers, explored the expressive possibilities of pure white.

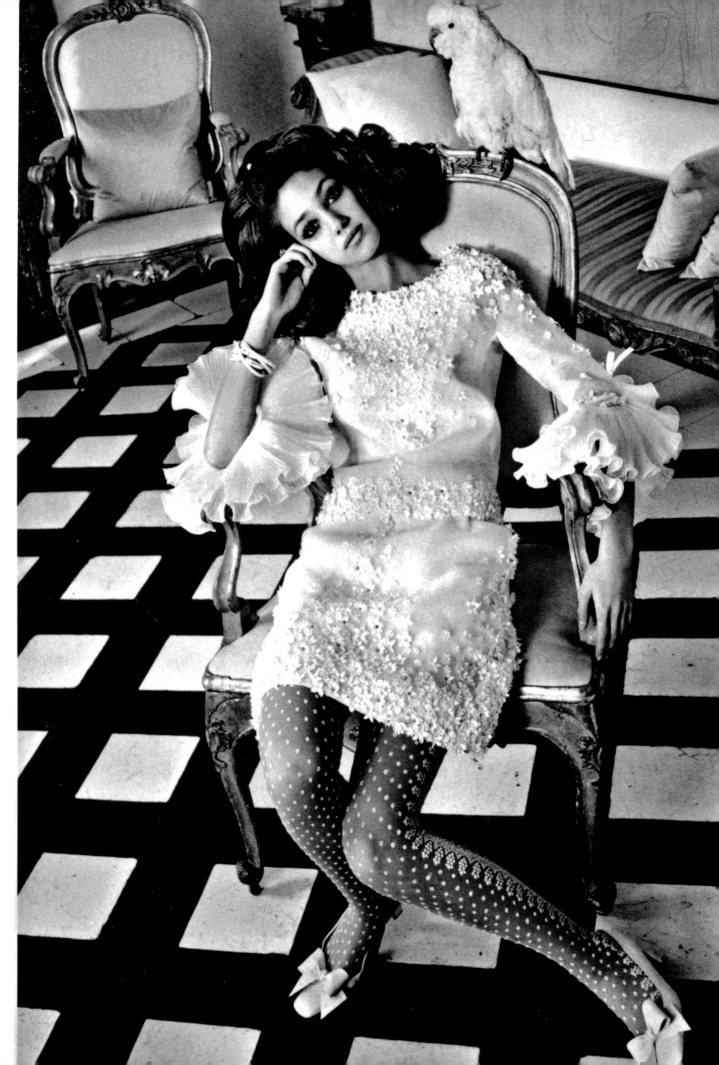

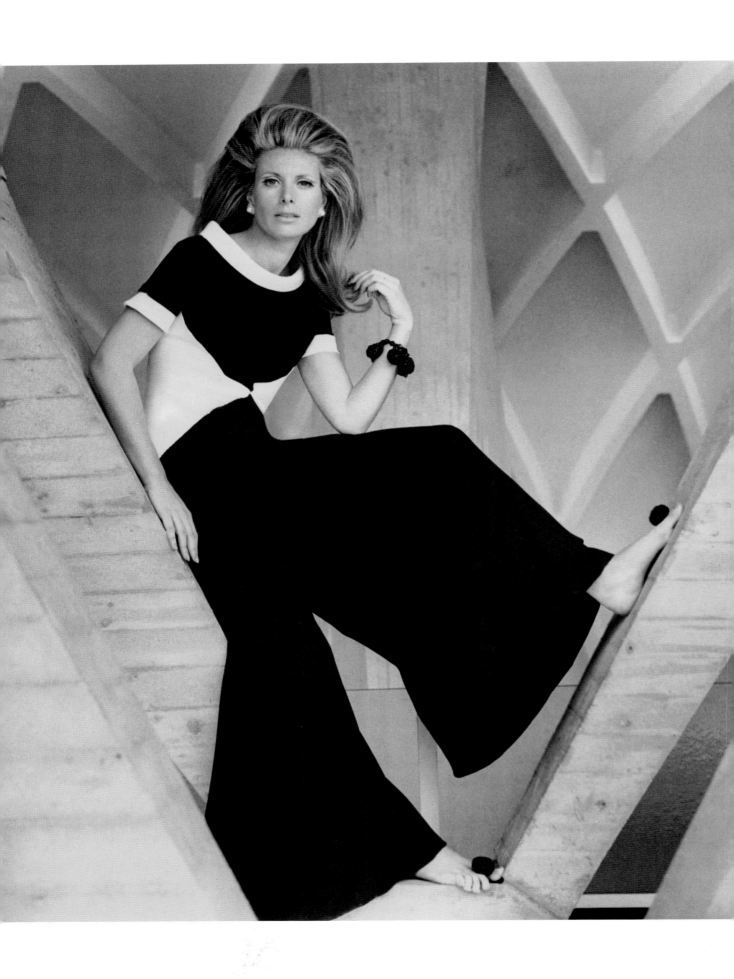

stars — both Italians, such as Monica Vitti, and international stars such as Elizabeth Taylor, who discovered Valentino's clothes when she was in Rome filming *Cleopatra*. In 1960, he met Giancarlo Giammetti, who became his managing director, and made his first venture into ready-to-wear, signing an agreement with a British firm to reproduce some of his couture designs. The true beginning of his international success, however, came in 1962, when he moved his couture showings to the Sala Bianca at the Pitti Palace in Florence, then the most prominent showcase for the flourishing Italian fashion industry. The collection he introduced there in July 1962 caught the eye of foreign buyers and editors, and he became the first Italian designer to have his clothes featured on the cover of French *Vogue*.[3] He moved his showings back to Rome in the mid-1960s, by which time the *New York Times* declared, "Valentino's brilliance is firmly established."[4] Additional celebrity clients, including Jacqueline Kennedy, Mrs. Gianni Agnelli, and the film stars Virna Lisi and Claudia Cardinale, strengthened his international reputation.

Since then, Valentino has been responsible for many fashion trends and innovations, including the use of a monogram as a decorative pattern on clothing and accessories (beginning with his "V" in 1965), and the return in the early 1970s to longer "midi" skirts, which he anticipated with his Spring–Summer 1970 collection. His designs have also responded to fashion trends, emphasizing ethnic influences in the 1970s; exuberant volumes and decorations in the 1980s; and sleeker, more subdued lines in the 1990s. In discussing Valentino's work, however, chronology is less important than the recurring themes that have become part of his recognizable "look" and personal style.

The themes he explores include a number of signature colors and decorative motifs. He is best known for his iconic dresses in "Valentino red," a brilliant shade that has become his trademark. On a visit to the Barcelona opera in the early 1950s, Valentino was so impressed by a beautiful woman in the audience dressed entirely in red that he decided to feature the color in his work. As he says, "I think a woman dressed in red is always magnificent."[5] The combination of black and white — in stripes, large-scale optical patterns, hound's-tooth checks, or polka dots — is another color theme Valentino favors. Pure white was the focus of his famous Spring–Summer 1968 collection, in which he used the color for crisply tailored ensembles, stockings embroidered with lace patterns, and dresses and suits heavily textured and trimmed with re-embroidered lace, soutache braid, pearls, and ostrich

Valentino's sense of line, proportion, and drama have won him many devoted celebrity clients. Here, Princess Luciana Pignatelli models black-and-white evening pajamas in silk crêpe.

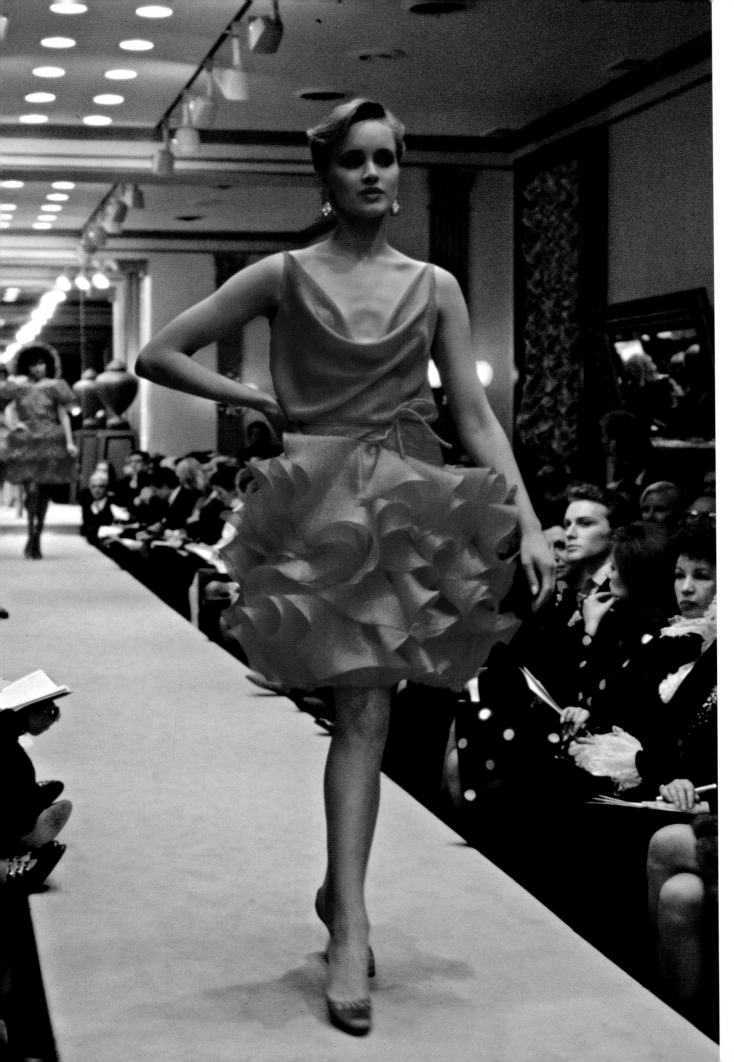

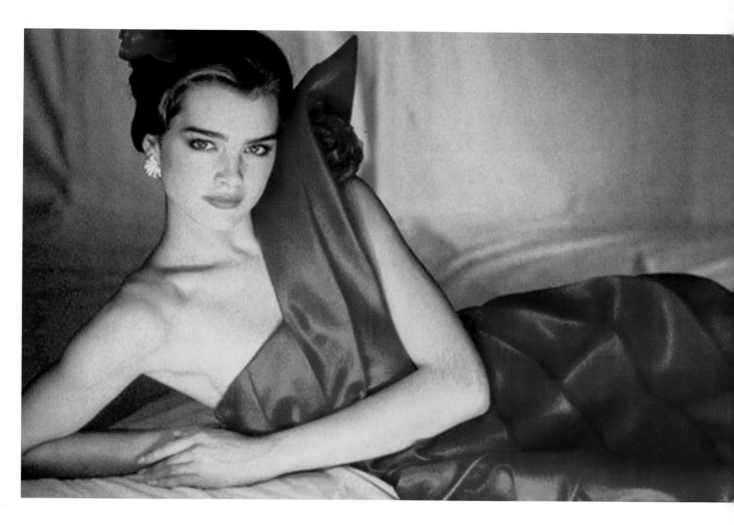

Valentino's collections always include at least one dress in his signature "Valentino red." The sculptural 1981 design above, with pleats that spiral around the body, is also a tour de force of draping.

feathers. Wild animals have also inspired his designs, appearing as leopard, giraffe, and crocodile patterns printed and embroidered on dresses, coats, and pantsuits, as well as faux zebra effects created in pleated chiffon and leather appliqué. Flowers also appear frequently in Valentino's designs, in the form of printed chiffon, sequin and bead embroidery, and entire skirts covered in tulle roses.

Many of the most characteristic features of Valentino's work are technical devices that for him symbolize femininity and of which he is the undisputed master. He employs draping expertly to produce fluid lines and graceful movement, particularly in delicate fabrics such as chiffon. Valentino is also a master of bows, which he frequently adds as an accent, or "exclamation point," and of scalloped edges, which he uses to soften the impact of tailored garments. Ruffles of all kinds, often combined with fine, complex pleating and lace insets, form large massed volumes and delicate frilled edges.

In recent years, Valentino has continued to create variations on his favorite themes and to emphasize luxury and quality, but his work has become ever more relaxed, light, and subtle. Today, he is

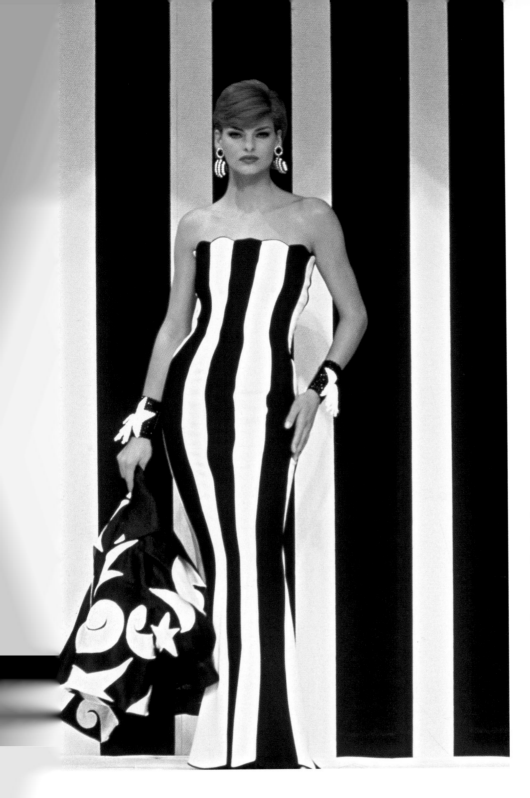

The combination of black and white, often in bold, graphic patterns inspired by the Wiener Werkstätte, has become another Valentino signature.

Valentino is the undisputed master of delicate fabrics, floral prints, ruffles, and bows, which he uses to express his vision of ideal-ized femininity.

inspired by the liveliness, independent spirit, and modern glamour of the women who wear his clothes, including such celebrities as Julia Roberts and Halle Berry. In a 2001 interview, he articulated his current approach in the context of his long career: "Of course, I refer to my own designs but, with my eyes of today, everything can be even more beautiful . . . I am not trendy . . . What I try to do is a young collection — glamorous, sexy, extremely feminine — but not clothes that only last for a short, short season."[6] — s w

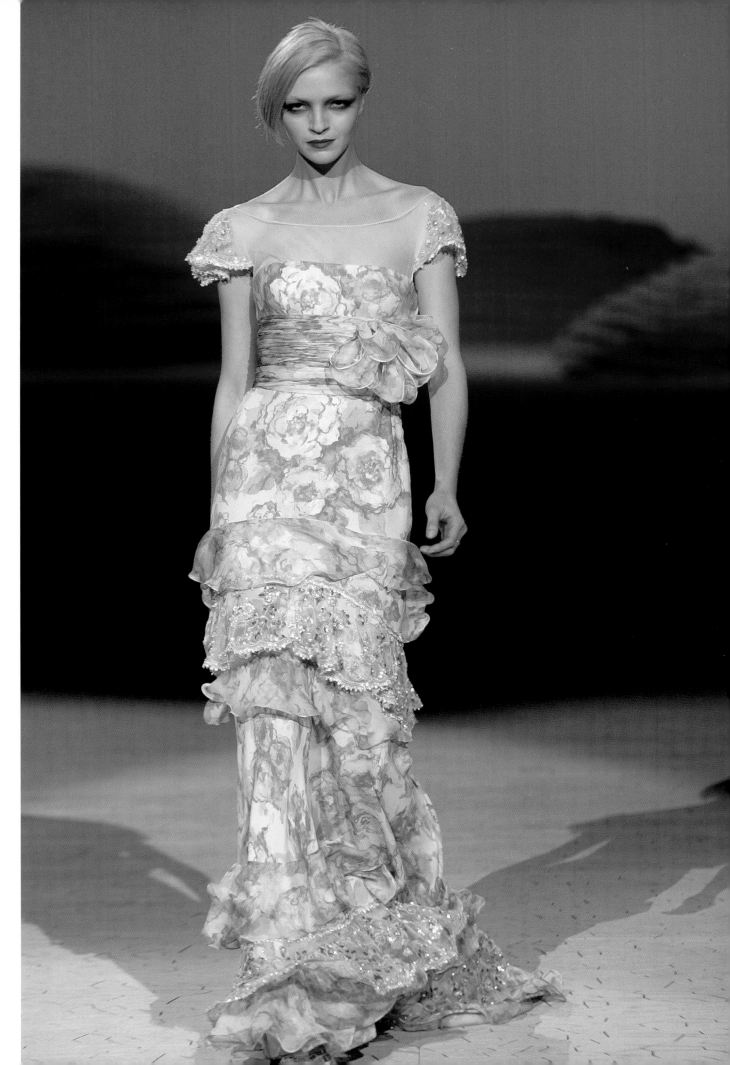

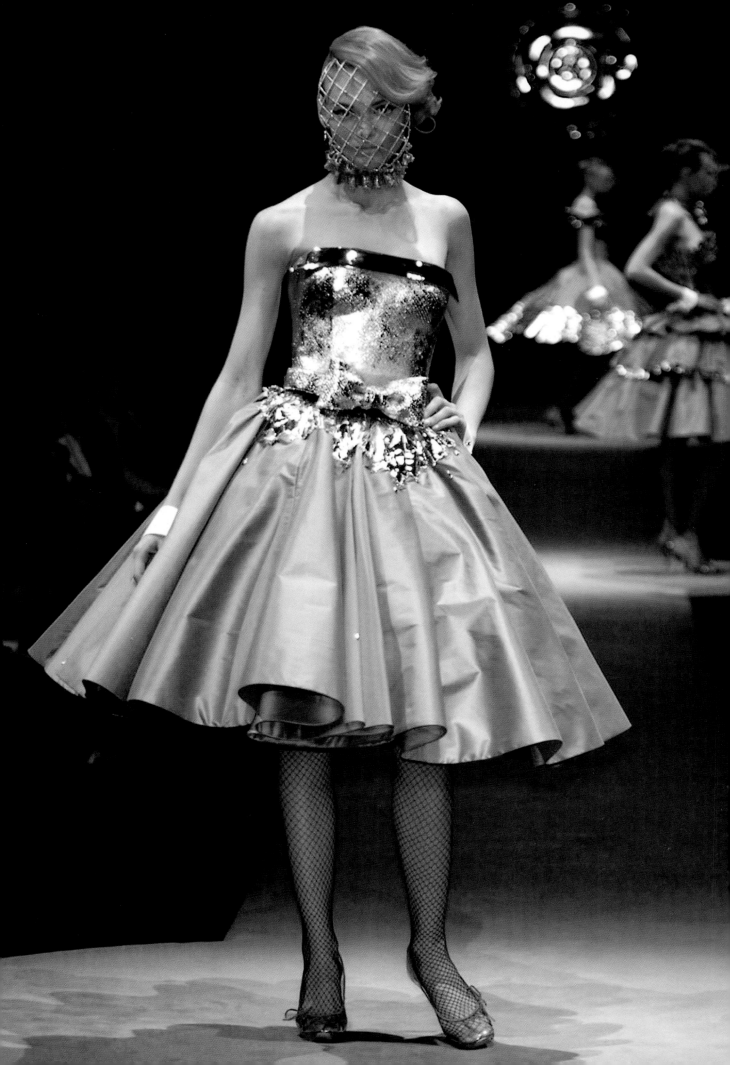

Viktor & Rolf

Viktor & Rolf's unconventional, conceptual approach to fashion has often prompted critics to ask if their work should be considered fashion or art. The designers themselves resist such distinctions; while they often critique the stereotypes and excesses of the fashion system, they remain unabashedly enthusiastic about fashion and its possibilities. The pair first became known for experimental haute couture collections that took ideas to unwearable extremes and for theatrical runway presentations, usually including the designers themselves as part of the performance. In recent years, they have brought their unique sensibility to the field of ready-to-wear, using their mastery of cut and construction to create clothes that are wearable and commercial, but still idea-driven and strikingly original.

Both born in 1969, Viktor Horsting and Rolf Snoeren met in 1988, when both were fashion students at the Arnhem Academy of Art in the Netherlands. After graduating in 1992, they collaborated on their first collection, a group of experimental garments reconstructed from existing elements, such as men's button-down shirts. The collection won the grand prize at the 1993 Salon Européen des Jeunes Stylistes, a prestigious fashion competition held in the southern French city of Hyères. For several years, the designers lived in Paris and continued to work on highly conceptual collections, which they called "experiments." Notable were the gallery installations *l'Apparence du Vide*, of 1994, in which ostentatious gold garments suspended from the ceiling cast wearable black "shadows" on the floor, and *Launch*, a couture collection presented in 1996 on doll-size mannequins.

Launch was emblematic of the designers' ambitions. A small-scale, dreamlike presentation of the entire fashion process — with a miniature runway, sketching and draping session, and photo-shoot

Viktor & Rolf's Fall–Winter 2006–7 collection was inspired by the rigorous and tightly controlled elegance of the 1950s. Some of the clothes, like baby shoes, were electroplated with silver, emphasizing their timeless, armorlike quality.

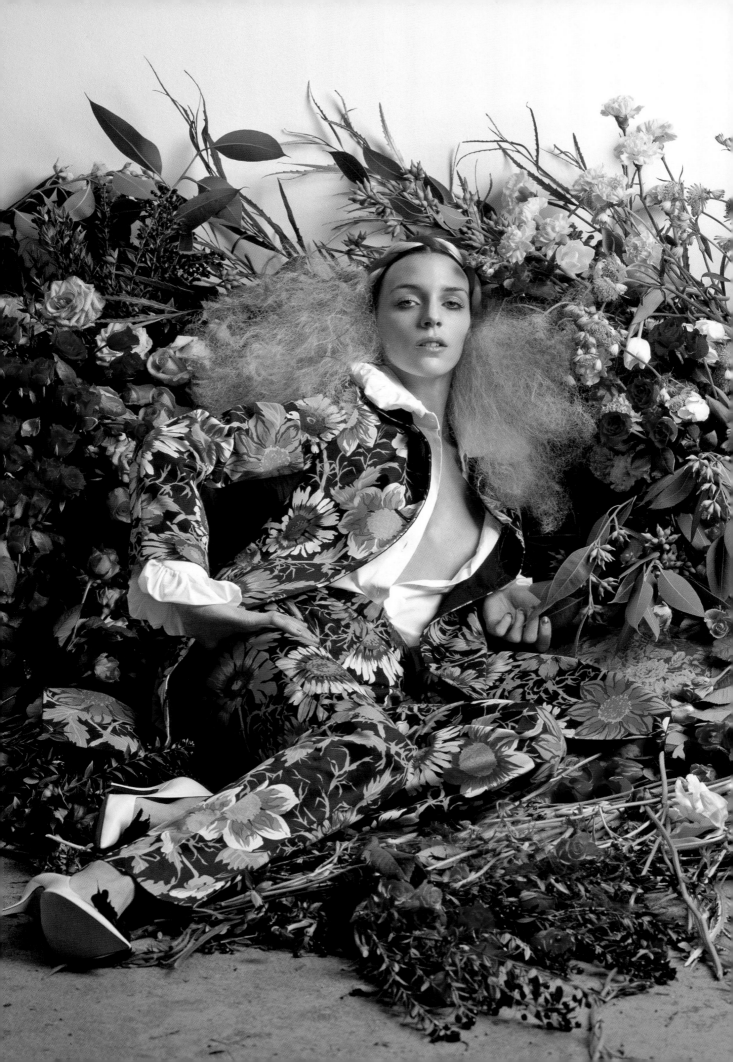

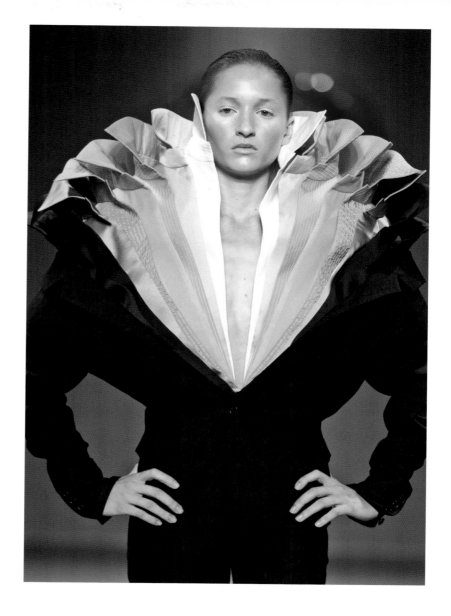

The Fall–Winter 2003–4 collection used layering, repetition, and altered proportions to take basic tailored garments in new directions.

While working on their perfume Flowerbomb, Viktor & Rolf designed their Spring–Summer 2003 collection as an exuberant celebration of flower power and 1970s decadence.

setup — it represented a fashion world they could not yet afford to create in reality and shrewdly distilled fashion's fantasy, glamour, excesses, and clichés. An important feature of this collection, and part of its exploration of the idea of designer branding and image, was the introduction of Viktor & Rolf, le Parfum. As an ironic statement on the name-dependent fantasy attached to designer fragrances, this limited-edition perfume was launched with a seductively photographed ad campaign, but it had no scent and was sold in bottles deliberately designed so they could not be opened.

Determined to make their mark in the fashion world, Viktor & Rolf decided to start with haute couture, which they considered "the most sublime form of fashion."[1] With the support of the Dutch government and the Groninger Museum in the Netherlands, they presented their first haute couture collections in 1998. For Fall–Winter 1998–99, they translated uncertainty about the coming millennium into the Atomic Bomb silhouette, skinny on the bottom and exaggerated on top. Fit for either the end of the

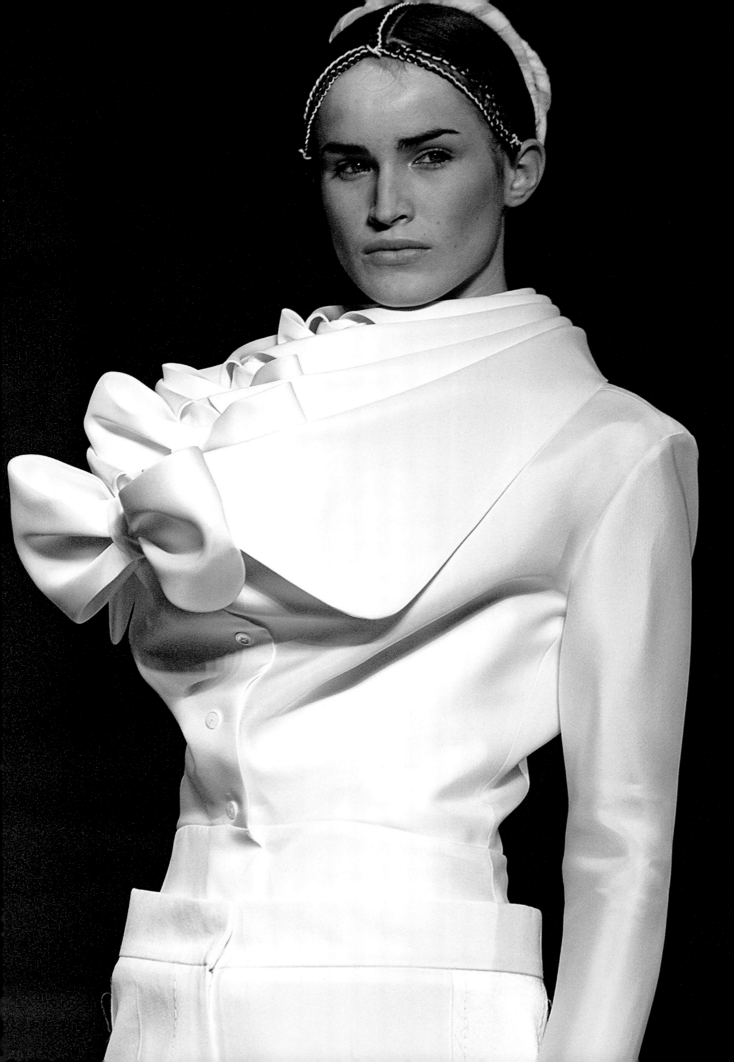

world or the biggest party ever, the clothes were deformed into mushroom-cloud shapes by colorful balloons and party streamers. The somewhat bizarre results gained the designers a great deal of press and critical attention. What won Viktor & Rolf the respect of fashion insiders, however, was the second part of the show, when they presented the same outfits without the balloons and stuffing, revealing them to be well-cut, wearable clothes.

Following this collection, although Viktor & Rolf still did not conform to the usual rules and guidelines, the Chambre Syndicale recognized their label. Over the next several years, their collections were presented on the official couture calendar. Support from the Netherlands removed the commercial pressures common to young designers, so Viktor & Rolf were free to express themselves creatively and to take the idea behind each collection to its logical (or illogical) conclusion; as they explained in a 1994 interview, "We will go very far to express ourselves properly."[2]

In their Fall–Winter 1999–2000 show, for example, they presented the entire collection — nine carefully engineered garments encrusted with Swarovski crystals — on one model. As she stood on a revolving platform, the designers layered the garments one over another, like a Russian doll in reverse. The final layer, an enormous conical cape, covered all but the model's face. This ceremony expressed the notion of couture as an unattainable jewel, something that everyone can enjoy but no one can purchase. Once again, the designers stated that the extreme final silhouette was necessary to fully communicate their idea; it also received widespread attention in the press. As Viktor & Rolf told *Elle* in 2001, "Exaggeration has always played a major role in our work. An exaggerated detail can make you see the familiar in a new light."[3]

In a similar vein, their other couture collections used the theatrical possibilities of the runway show as a means of reinforcing the concepts expressed in their designs and an effective method of conveying their vision to the audience. The Spring–Summer 1999 *Screams and Whispers* collection, a group of simple, crisply tailored garments in black and white silk gazar, was first presented in virtual darkness, with only the white details visible under black light. The garments were then shown again under normal light, so that the entire silhouette could be appreciated. This idea — that garments are changeable, not fixed, and can be seen in many different ways — is a recurring theme in Viktor & Rolf's work.

In 2000, the designers turned their attention to ready-to-wear, taking on the challenge of creating "real," wearable clothes

Viktor & Rolf frequently use exaggeration to shed new light on familiar forms. The bows and ruffles of their all-white Spring–Summer 2002 collection also demonstrated their mastery of cut and construction.

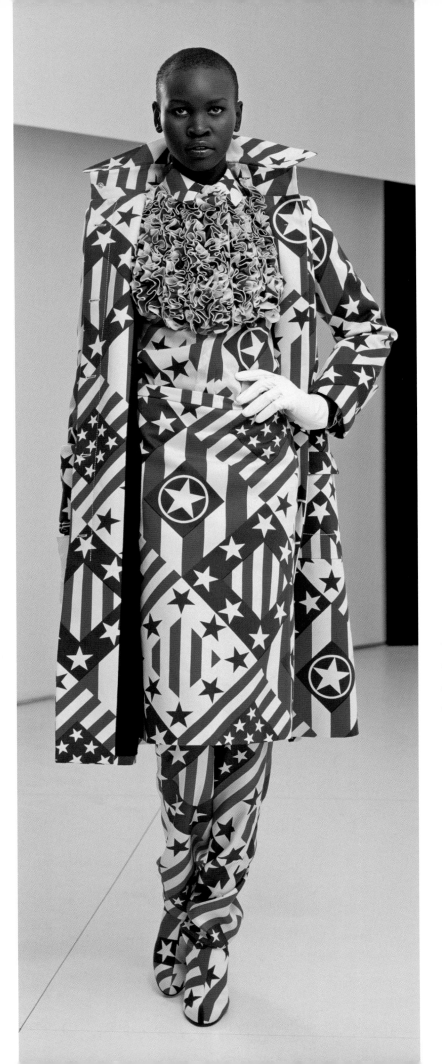

The designers' first ready-to-wear collection applied their conceptual approach to the idea of "classic" separates and explored the struggle between the personal and the commercial.

The dramatic *Black Hole* collection was shown on models with black hair and makeup, focusing attention on silhouettes and on the light-absorbing qualities of the fabrics.

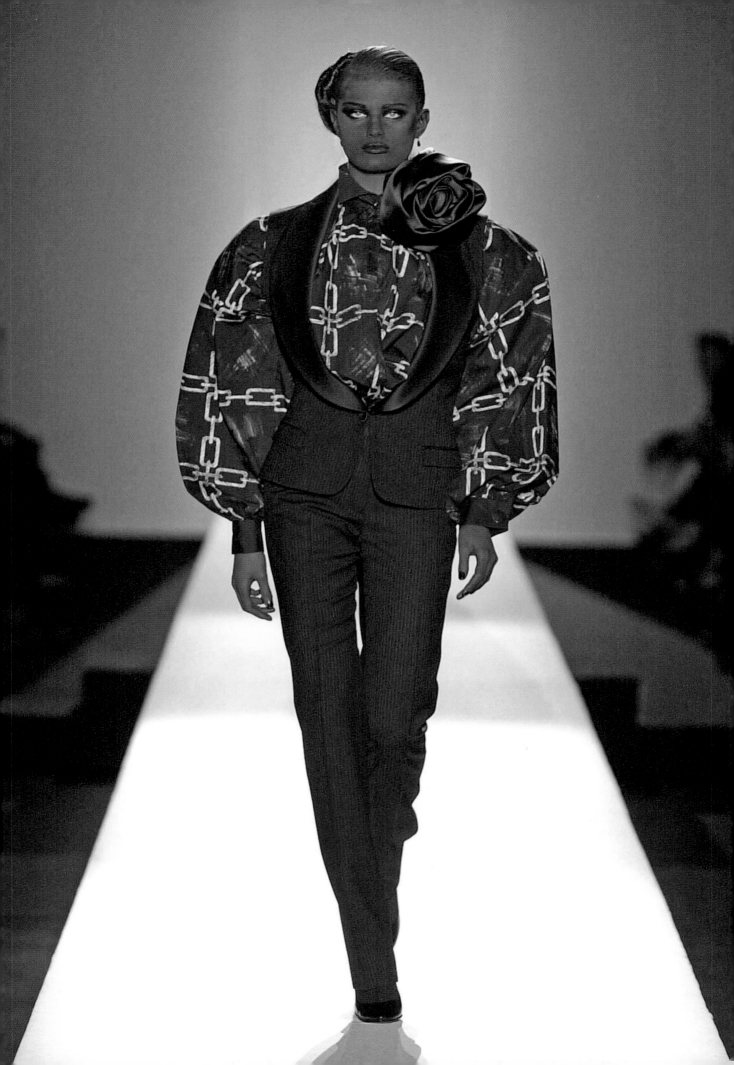

while adapting their conceptual approach to concepts such as globalism, commercialism, and the notion of "classic" separates. Their first ready-to-wear collection was an American-themed exploration of the struggle between the personal and the commercial, featuring garments printed with a stars-and-stripes pattern partially wrapped with black cloth, gray sweatpants emblazoned with a large "wax" seal of the house logo, and many variations on the ruffled tuxedo shirt. As Rolf Snoeren described it, "We wanted to look at stereotypes like polo shirts, jeans and *le smoking*, then reinterpret them with our sense of shape and cut."[4]

Subsequent ready-to-wear collections, while still intended to be wearable, have continued to demonstrate Viktor & Rolf's rigorous, analytical approach to fashion and their skillful use of fabric, texture, cut, and construction to express abstract concepts. The runway show for the Fall–Winter 2001–2 *Black Hole* ready-to-wear collection featured all-black garments shown on models with black hair and makeup, focusing attention on each ensemble's silhouette and on the cut and light-absorbing qualities of the fabrics. For Viktor & Rolf, the idea of a black hole was also a means of dealing with negative emotions by using them creatively, reflecting the designers' deeply personal approach to their work. Another memorable show presented the Fall–Winter 2002–3 *Long Live the Immaterial* collection, using blue-screen technology to project video images onto strategically colored garments and accessories.

Over the past few years, Viktor & Rolf have added new lines to their brand, fulfilling their ambition to be more commercially successful and to spread their vision of "conceptual glamour," while retaining their artistic independence. In 2003, they launched their men's wear line, *"Monsieur,"* a wearable collection of reinterpreted men's wear basics, such as denim dinner jackets, which they modeled themselves at its introduction in Florence. In the spring of 2005, they released their first real perfume, Flowerbomb, for L'Oréal, and later that year they opened their first boutique, in Milan. This boutique was designed as a traditional French salon turned upside-down, with chandeliers sprouting from the floor and urns of flowers hanging from the ceiling, introducing a theme they continued in a collection of upside-down garments for Spring–Summer 2006. Viktor & Rolf have also collaborated with several museums, presenting a ten-year retrospective of their work at the Musée de la Mode et du Textile in Paris in 2003, and acting as guest curators for the 2004 "Fashion in Colors" exhibition at the National Museum of Modern Art, Kyoto. — sw

For the Fall–Winter 2002–3 *Long Live the Immaterial* collection, Viktor & Rolf used video blue-screen technology to project still and moving images onto strategically colored garments and accessories.

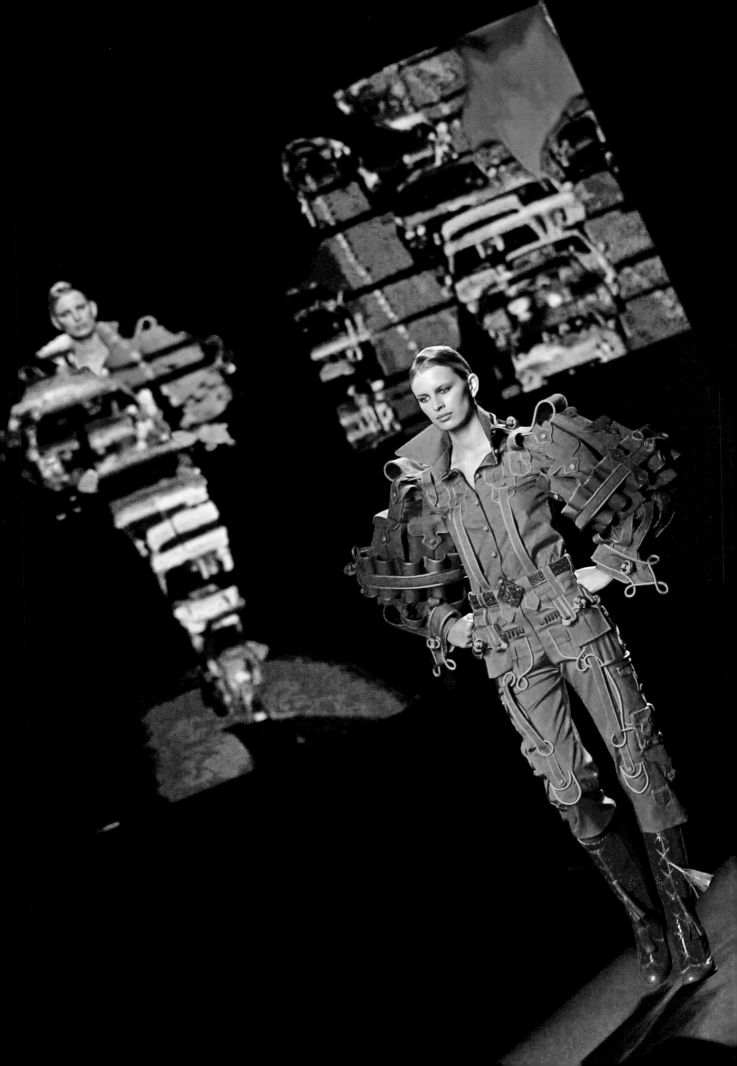

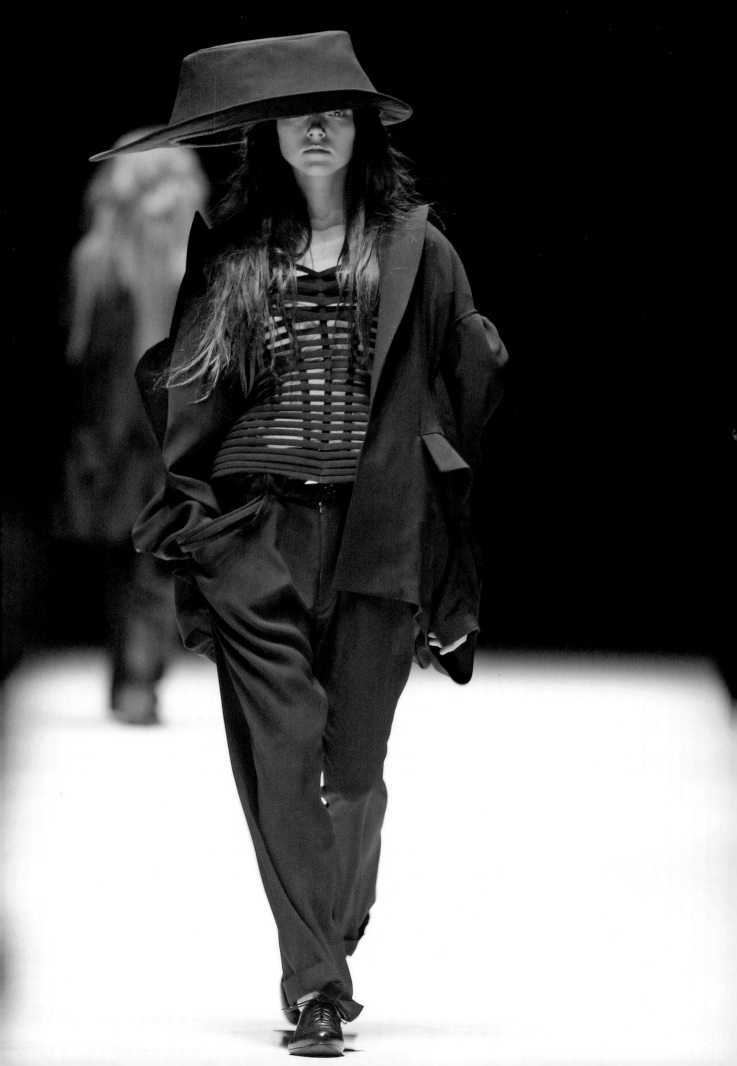

Yohji Yamamoto

Yohji Yamamoto has been called many things — poetic, visionary, antifashion, and avant-garde. An uncompromising nontraditionalist, he was at the forefront of the Japanese revolution in fashion in the early 1980s. Along with Rei Kawakubo and Issey Miyake, he introduced an entirely new way of dressing that melded Japanese design ideas with Western dressmaking traditions. He has continued to champion his unique vision of beauty since then, through strong textures and deconstructed forms. Yohji Yamamoto's complex layered silhouettes made with contrasting fabrics and his reconfigurations of classic tailored garments into unexpected shapes have contributed to a new understanding of the relationship between clothing and the body. Today, he is widely regarded as one of the giants of contemporary fashion.

Yohji Yamamoto did not start out in couture. Born in Japan in 1943, he was raised by his seamstress mother and never knew his father, who was killed in World War II. He enrolled at Keio University and received a law degree in 1966, but he never pursued practice. Instead, he entered the well-known Bunka College of Fashion, where he took a two-year general course in design. In 1968, he won a scholarship to study fashion in Paris. He stayed in the city until 1970, when he returned to Japan. Yohji Yamamoto established his own ready-to-wear company under the label *Y's* in 1972. In 1977, he showed his first *Y's* collection in Tokyo.

The first high-end ready-to-wear collection he presented in Paris, in 1981, astonished the audience. His garments were neither glamorous nor flattering, and they presented an entirely different vision of clothing, defined by seemingly unfinished and haphazard construction. Relentlessly black and fashioned from carefully distressed fabrics, they featured asymmetrical shapes with odd

For his Fall–Winter 2006–7 collection, Yohji Yamamoto reworked his signature black suits in outsized proportions.

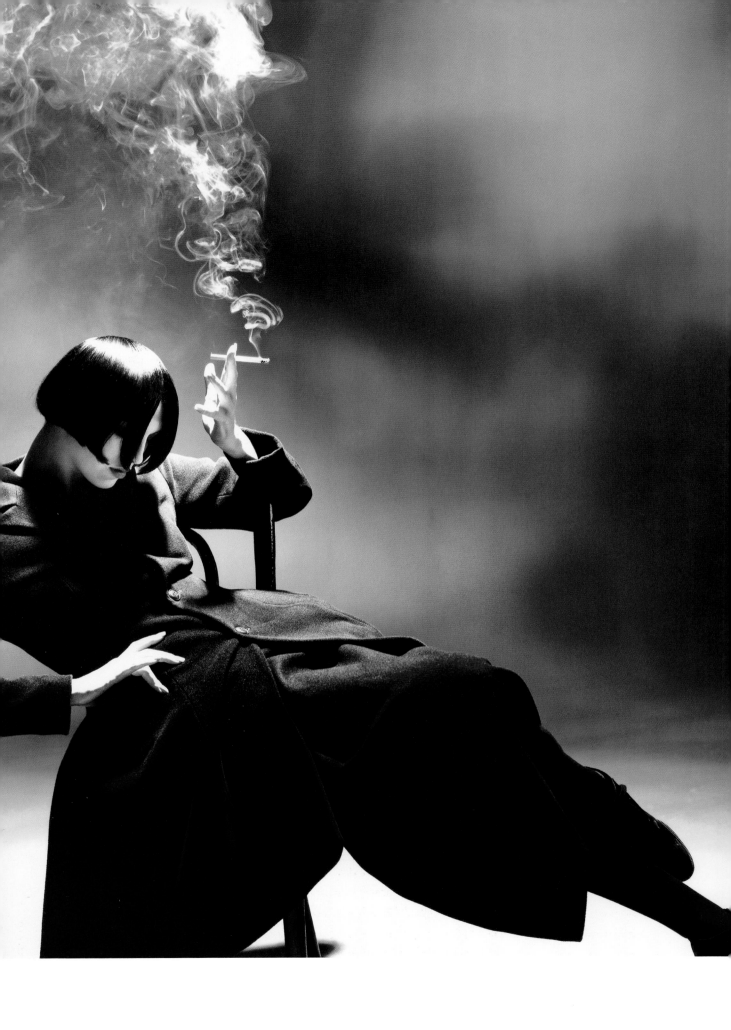

flaps and pockets, voluminous layers, lopsided collars, and uneven hems that took on new life as the wearers moved. Perhaps even more unusual, Yohji Yamamoto's models wore flat, practical shoes, a visual contrast to the usual high-heeled feminine look.

These strange and powerful silhouettes shocked and impressed the international fashion world but quickly caught on within artistic circles. Yohji Yamamoto's earliest patrons included architects, artists, and writers, for whom his dark, urban aesthetic held much appeal, especially after he started his men's wear line in 1984. Filmmaker Wim Wenders, one of his early admirers, went so far as to make an eighty-minute documentary on the inscrutable designer in 1989, titling it *Notebook on Cities and Clothes*. The film, however, did little to reveal the complex vision that drives Yohji Yamamoto's designs. At the core of his approach is a unique notion of beauty derived in part from traditional Japanese aesthetics. He rejects Western ideas of glamour defined by figure-hugging female display, instead preferring to drape, and thereby disguise, the body in unstructured garments, keeping air between the body and the garments.

Fabric has always been the starting point for Yohji Yamamoto, a master cutter. As he explains, "I start by finding the heaviest point of the fabric. This point will then be placed on the collarbone; this is the place from which all my clothes begin; what allows the material to remain alive."[1] In his hands, soft materials become complex layered and wrapped shapes, while stiff fabrics evolve into sharp, powerful silhouettes. Yohji Yamamoto has been at the forefront in advocating new materials, as well as employing traditional textiles in novel ways. He often exploits linen and rayon's inherent tendency to crease, using the wrinkles as design elements. He also juxtaposes different textures and weights to achieve unusual dialogues between textiles. Yohji Yamamoto's many knitwear collections consistently incorporate innovative construction, so that "on the body seams curl up at the edges, straight lines distort, insides become outside, pockets appear and disappear in playfully designed but intricately thought-out configurations."[2] In 2001, he even showed a dress that had a built-in sequined bag.

During the 1980s and early 1990s, Yohji Yamamoto continued to develop his avant-garde ideas, refining certain signature elements in his work. He remained devoted to the color black. Wearers of his fashions were nicknamed *karasuzoku*, which translated as "members of the crow tribe."[3] Black was very modern during the 1980s. The color of punks and urban aesthetes, it presented a strong antifashion statement that contrasted with the prevailing taste for bright colors.

In the 1980s, Yohji Yamamoto revolutionized fashion with his androgynous vision of clothing featuring complex layered fabrics and asymmetrical forms.

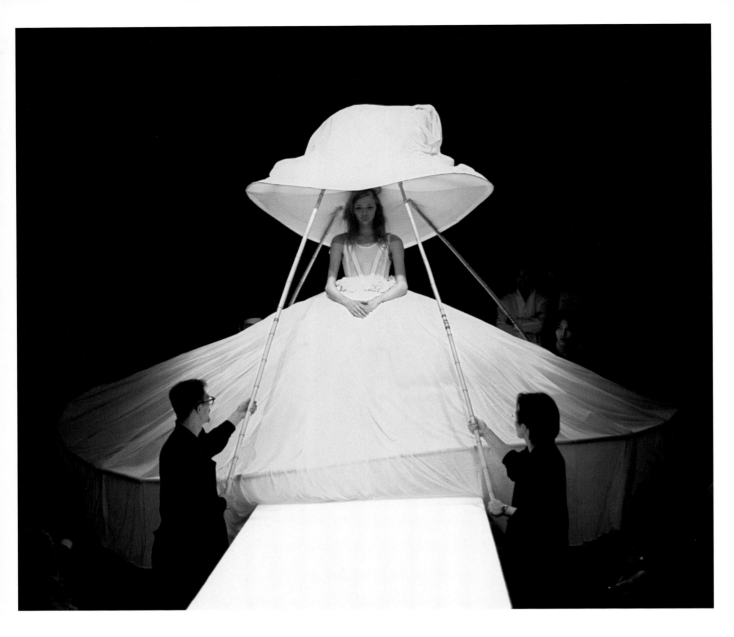

Yohji Yamamoto also expanded his explorations of deconstructed form, working toward an abstract vision of structure that created interaction with the body but was not defined by it. He disrupted directionality and frontality by wrapping voluminous folds around the wearer. Like other avant-garde designers, including compatriot Rei Kawakubo, he cut up and reassembled traditional tailored garments, arriving at some radical and unexpected shapes. As further proof of his intentions, he included labels on his *Y's* collection inscribed with the line "There is nothing so boring as a neat and tidy look."[4]

By denying the traditional feminine silhouette, Yohji Yamamoto allowed for greater gender ambiguity in his fashions. Indeed, some of his best designs have been dark tailored suits and white shirts, icons of power and sexuality for both men and women. He pushed the gender mixing even further by employing female models to show his men's wear collections on several occasions. His Spring–Summer 1999 *Wedding Dress* collection, however, was a turning point in his

The highlight of Yohji Yamamoto's Fall–Winter 1998–99 collection was a gown so large that it spilled over the runway and engulfed several rows of seats.

Nick Knight's iconic photograph of a design from Yohji Yamamoto's Fall–Winter 1986–87 collection reveals the designer's brilliance at manipulating fabrics into sharp, powerful silhouettes.

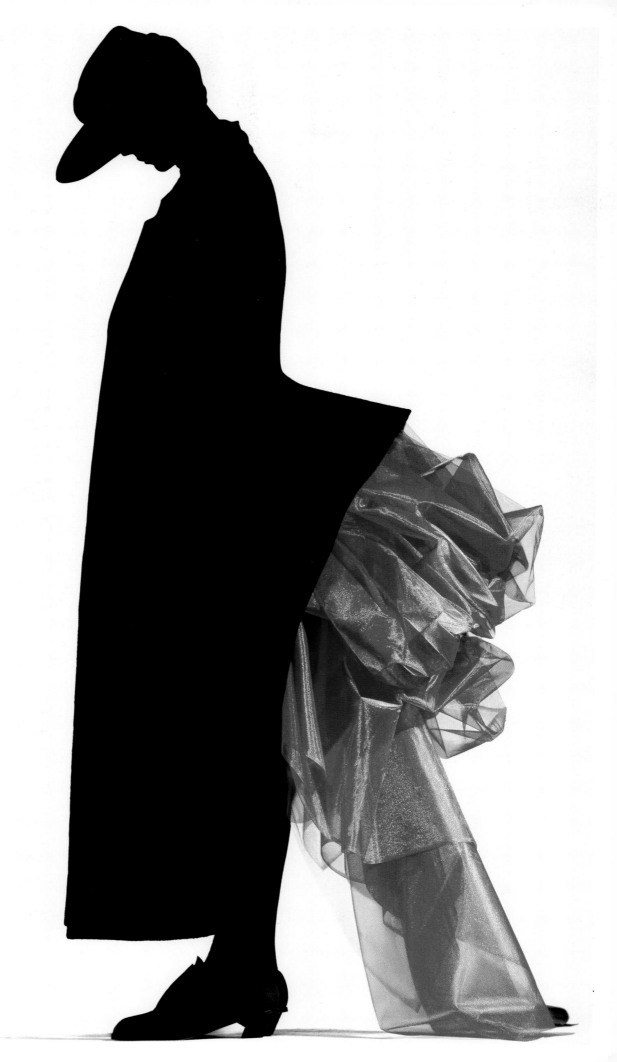

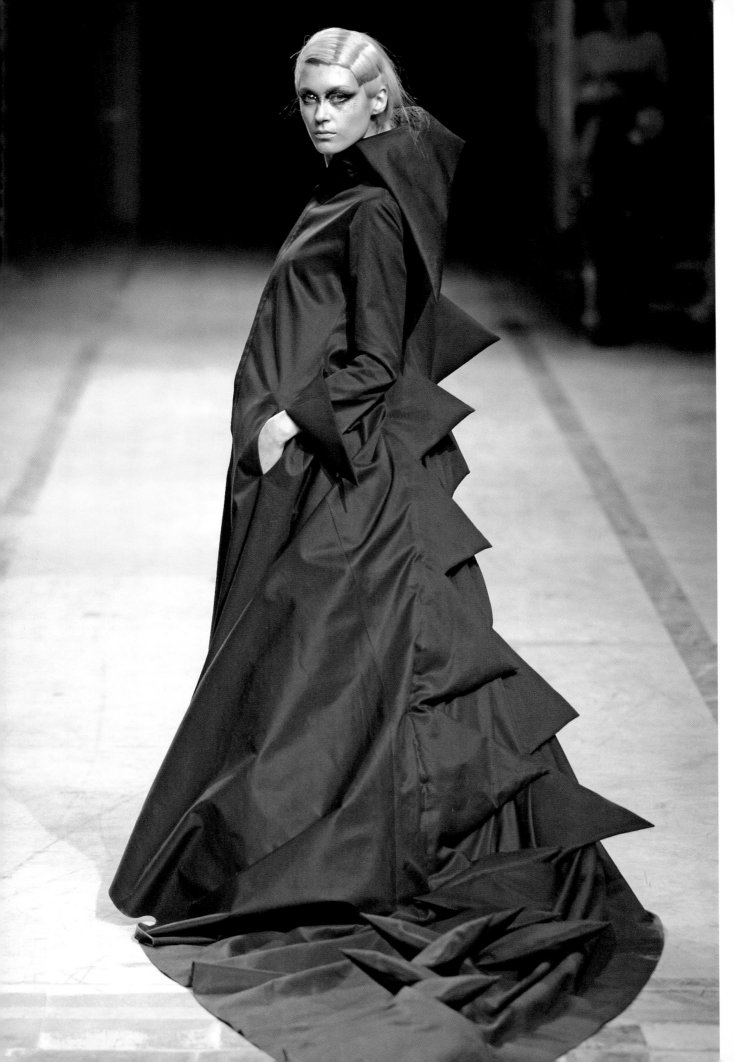

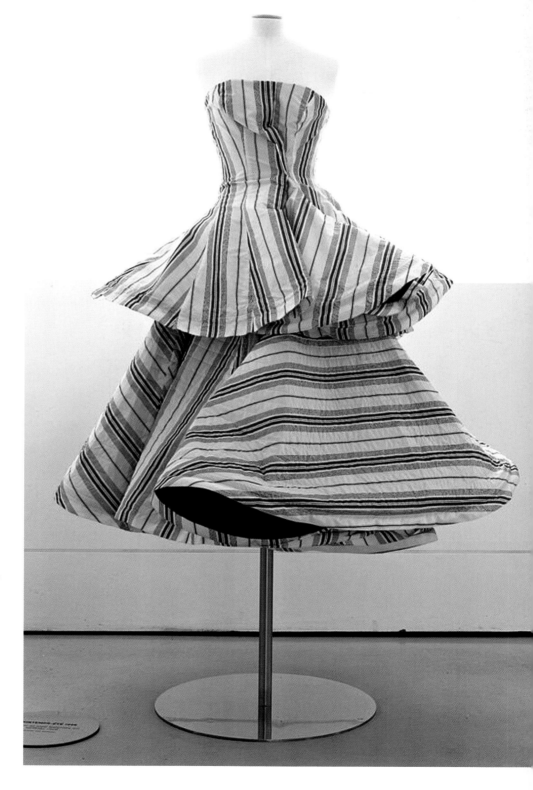

Paying homage to the
"history of the earth from
dinosaurs to humans,"
the Spring–Summer 2006
collection included over-
sized flowing evening gowns
with dragonlike spines
cascading down the back.

While Yohji Yamamoto has
explored more traditionally
feminine silhouettes in
recent years, he has not
abandoned his interest in
complex dress construction.

design development. While it still featured his signature androgynous garments, such as masculine-tailored suits, it also contained magnificent and unabashedly romantic gowns that took inspiration from Western grand couture, rather than the avant-garde. One of his dresses from Fall–Winter 1998–99 was a prelude to this collection and was so enormous it swept away the front rows of the audience.[5] Since 1999, Yohji Yamamoto has continued to develop feminine garments in his utterly modern style. While romantic, these designs reveal his enduring interest in structure; several are "attached to the body by knotted coils of silk," in a feat of technical virtuosity.[6]

For some, Yohji Yamamoto's 2006 collections confirm that of all the designers, his creations come closest to art. Claiming a desire to "play with the history of fashion" and the "history of the earth from dinosaurs to humans,"[7] he showcased an inventive group of garments linked by exaggerated and blown-out proportions in his Spring–Summer 2006 collection. Still present were the signature black suits and white shirts, only this time they incorporated huge collars, cravats, and cuffs, mismatched shirt tails, and lopsided jackets with streaming tails, in what looked like rearranged tuxedos. These were followed by more feminine ensembles in camouflage fabric, often sporting supersized ruffles and floor-length bustles. Even the color was more expansive than his typical black-and-white, adding not only camouflage but also royal blue. Other garments reflected Yohji Yamamoto's enduring interest in construction. Perhaps his most fantastical piece was a wedding dress "with a ball skirt bustling in every direction, atop a rope ring and a corsage of braided tubes."[8]

In his Fall–Winter 2006–7 collection, Yohji Yamamoto has reexamined the classic suit anew, this time achieving a remarkable lyricism in the loose and flowing silhouettes. The suits are characteristically exaggerated in shape; relaxed trousers are paired with jackets and coats that wrap like kimonos and sport oversized cuffs, asymmetrical tab closures, and even false hanging sleeves. Deep tones of navy blue and black are enlivened by surprising additions of brilliant peacock blues and unusually graphic dual-tone bleached fabrics. Despite the outsized proportions, Yohji Yamamoto's suits maintain a tone of chic, urban femininity, as overalls — complete with spiral zippers — zip off to make elegant evening dresses.

These recent, imaginative collections prove that Yohji Yamamoto continues to be at the forefront of fashion innovation, juxtaposing modernity with tradition, East with West, and spirit with sensibility. — LDW

Yohji Yamamoto's suits for Fall–Winter 2006–7 are noted for their relaxed wrapped shapes and soft flowing lines, reinforced by the false hanging sleeves.

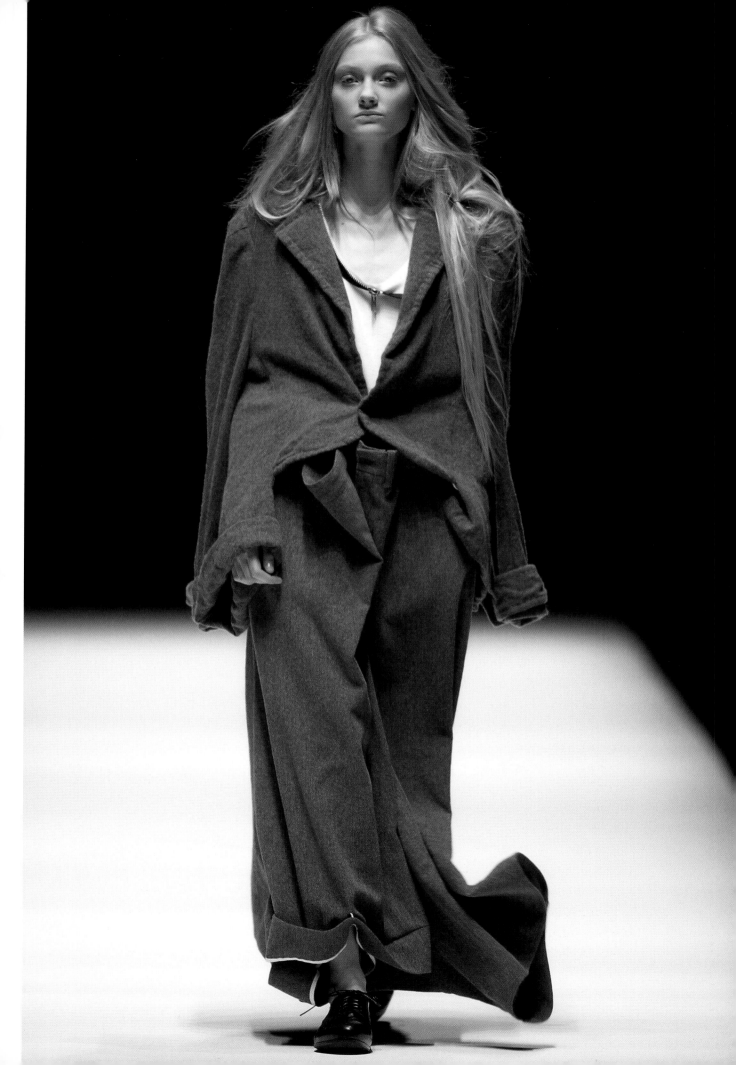

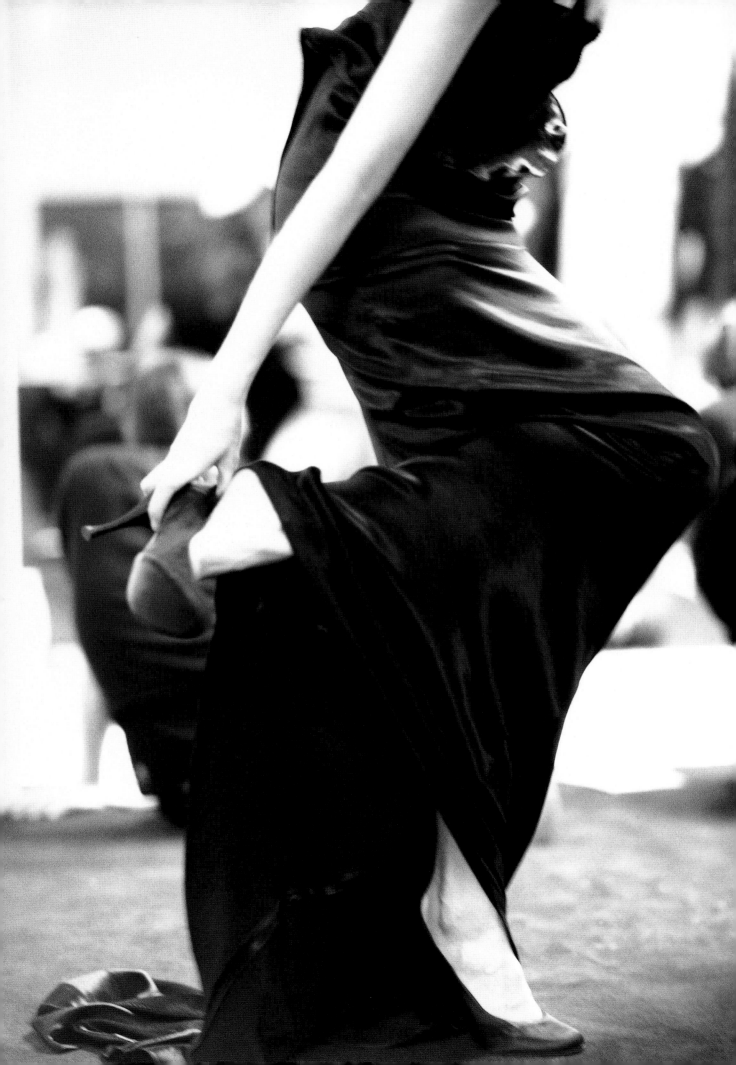

Notes

LA MODE: PARIS AND THE DEVELOPMENT OF THE FRENCH FASHION INDUSTRY

1. Sue Welsh Reed, *French Prints from the Age of the Musketeers* (Boston: Museum of Fine Arts, 1998), 72–74.

2. For a discussion of Colbert's economic policies, see Charles Woolsey Cole, *Colbert and a Century of French Mercantilism*, 2 vols., (Hamden, CT: Archon Books, 1964).

3. See Daniel Roche, "Between a 'moral economy' and a 'consumer economy': clothes and their function in the 17th and 18th centuries," in *Luxury Trades and Consumerism in Ancien Régime Paris*, ed. Robert Fox and Anthony Turner (Aldershot, UK: Ashgate, 1998), 219–29.

4. From S. Locatelli, *Voyage in France* (Paris: A. Picard et fils, 1905), as quoted in Diana de Marly, *Louis XIV and Versailles* (New York: Holmes and Meier, 1987) 35–37.

5. Clare Haru Crowston, *Fabricating Women: The Seamstresses of Old Regime France, 1675–1791* (Durham: Duke University Press, 2001), 29.

6. There is little concrete information on the subject of the fashion dolls, or *les poupées de mode*. Two informative sources are Madeleine Delpierre, *La Mode et ses Métiers du XVIIIe Siècle à nos Jours* (Paris: Musée de la Mode et du Costume, 1981), 32, and Raymond Gaudriault, *La Gravure de Mode Feminine en France* (Paris: les Editions de l'Amateur, 1983), 25.

7. Jean Donneau de Visé, *Extraordinaire du Mercure Galant*, January 15, 1678 (published May 15, 1678), 542.

8. Ibid., 543.

9. Daniel Roche, *The Culture of Clothing: Dress and Fashion in the Ancien Regime*, trans. Jean Birrell (Cambridge: Cambridge University Press, 1996), 347.

10. Sjoukje Colenbrander, "The Roeters Family and the Dutch Silk Industry in the 18th Century," in *18th-Century Silk: The Industries of England and Northern Europe*, Riggisberger Berichte 8 (Riggisberg: Abegg-Stiftung, 2000), 159–61.

11. See Lesley Ellis Miller, "Dialogue in the Design of Luxury Silks," in Fox and Turner, *Luxury Trades and Consumerism*, 139–67.

12. Barbier's correspondence is housed at the Victoria and Albert Museum in London. See Carolyn Sargentson, *Merchants and Luxury Markets: The Marchands Merciers of Eighteenth-Century Paris* (London: Victoria and Albert Museum; Malibu: J. Paul Getty Museum, 1996), 102.

13. Ibid., 97–103.

14. Sjoukje Colenbrander, "Dutch Silks, Narrow or ?," *CIETA Bulletin* 79 (2002): 59–65.

15. Savary des Bruslons, *Dictionnaire Universel de Commerce* (Paris, 1723), as quoted in Sargentson, *Merchants and Luxury Markets*, 12.

16. Roche, *The Culture of Clothing*, 308, and Crowston, *Fabricating Women*, 67.

17. Crowston, *Fabricating Women*, 67.

18. Jeanne Louise Henriette Campan, *Memoirs of the Private Life of Marie Antoinette*, rev. ed. (1823; rev., New York: Tudor Publishing, 1934), 1:87.

19. Michael Sonenscher, "Fashion's Empire: Trade and Power," in Fox and Turner, *Luxury Trades and Consumerism*, 237.

20. *Le Cabinet des Modes, ou les Modes Nouvelles* (Paris: Chez Buisson) 1 (November 15, 1785): 3–4.

21. *The Fashions of London and Paris during the Years 1798, 1799, and 1800* (London: R. Phillips, 1801), 3.

22. Roche, "Between a 'moral economy,'" 222.

23. E. O. Lami, *Dictionnaire de l'Industrie et des Arts Industriels* (Paris, 1883), 3:758.

24. Philippe Perrot, *Fashioning the Bourgeoisie: A History of Clothing in the Nineteenth Century*, trans. Richard Bienvenu (Princeton: Princeton University Press, 1994), 219n60.

25. Pierre Larousse, *Grand Dictionnaire Universel du XIXième siecle* (Paris, 1869), 4:112.

26. Françoise Tétart-Vittu and Piedade da Silveira, *Au Paradis des Dames* (Paris: Musée de la Mode and du Costume, 1992), 16.

27. Ibid., 18–19.

28. Ibid., 35.

29. Ibid.

30. Piedade da Silveira, "Maison Popelin-Ducarre," in *Dessin de Mode: Jules David 1808–1892 et son temps* (Paris: Mairie du VIe Arrondissement, 1987), 17.

31. A selection of the clothing and headdresses worn by Mrs. Rotch are now in the Museum of Fine Arts, Boston.

32. Quoted in Nicola Shilliam, "The Sartorial Autobiography: Bostonians' Private Writings about Fashionable Dress, 1760s–1860s," in *Textile & Text* 13, no. 3 (1991): 21.

33. Both of these dresses are housed in the Museum of Fine Arts, Boston (their accession numbers are 46.207a–b and 46.209a–c).

34. Quoted in Lisa Kurzner, "A French Seamstress and Her Boston Clients: The Story of a 19th-Century Dress" (unpublished paper, Department of Textile and Fashion Arts files, Museum of Fine Arts, Boston, 1980).

35. Jean-Philippe Worth, *A Century of Fashion* (Boston: Little, Brown, 1928), 12. There are inconsistencies in the spelling of the name Roger/Rodger in the literature. The name is spelled Roger on the labels of the two dresses in the MFA's collection.

36. Françoise Tétart-Vittu, "The French-English Go-Between: 'Le Modèle de Paris' or the Beginning of the Designer, 1820–1880," *Costume*, no. 26 (1992): 43.

37. Now known as the Musée de la Mode et du Costume, the museum also has within its archive more than five hundred fashion designs and gouaches by Charles Pilatte, Etienne Leduc, Léon Sault, and others.

38. Tétart-Vittu, "The French-English Go-Between," 41.

39. The story of Worth's establishment of a dressmaking department appears in Worth, *A Century of Fashion*, 17. Subsequent authors have repeated the information: see Edith Saunders, *The Age of Worth: Couturier to the Empress Eugénie* (London: Longmans, Green, 1954), 27, and Diana de Marly, *Worth: Father of Haute Couture* (New York: Holmes and Meier, 1980), 24.

40. Tétart-Vittu and Silveira, *Au Paradis des Dames*, 41.

41. Ibid., 42.

42. Ibid., 43.

43. LaRousse, *Grand Dictionnaire Universel*, 4:112.

44. Tétart-Vittu and Silveira, *Au Paradis des Dames*, 43.

45. Elizabeth Ann Coleman, *The Opulent Era: Fashions of Worth, Doucet, and Pingat* (New York: Brooklyn Museum, 1989), 12–13.

46. Ibid., 16.

47. Ibid.

48. Lami, *Dictionnaire de L'Industrie*, 3:760.

49. Worth, *A Century of Fashion*, 21.

50. Coleman, *The Opulent Era*, 25.

51. Ibid., 25.

52. Tétart-Vittu and Silveira, *Au Paradis des Dames*, 37.

53. Whitaker Auction Catalog, http://www.whitakerauction.com/Session_2.pdf, November 19, 2005. Lot 827 was a two-piece black faille dress brocaded with polychrome silk. The petersham band was labeled "Olympe 154 Canal Street New Orleans."

54. See the essay "Paris to Providence: French Couture and the Tirocchi Shop" by Susan Hay, in *From Paris to Providence: Fashion, Art, and the Tirocchi Dressmakers' Shop, 1915–1947*, ed. Susan Hay (Providence: Museum of Art, Rhode Island School of Design, 2000), 133–71.

55. For early twentieth-century dressmaking techniques, see Pamela A. Parmal, "Line, Color, Detail, Distinction, Individuality: A. & L. Tirocchi, Providence, Dressmakers," in Hay, *From Paris to Providence*, 25–49.

56. The most important work on Madeleine Vionnet's innovative cuts has been done by Betty Kirke. See Betty Kirke, *Madeleine*

Vionnet (San Francisco: Chronicle, 1998).

57. "To Bring 100 Gowns: Mme. Poiret Will Wear in America Her Husband's Latest Creations," *New York Times*, September 7, 1913.

58. See Caroline Evans, "Multiple, Movement, Model, Mode," in *Fashion and Modernity*, ed. Christopher Breward and Caroline Evans (Oxford: Berg Publishers, 2005), 126.

59. See Madelyn Shaw, "American Fashion: The Tirocchi Sisters in Context," in Hay, *From Paris to Providence*, 105–30, for a discussion of the emerging American design industry during the early twentieth century.

60. Fédération Française de la Couture, du Prêt-à-Porter des Couturiers et des Créateurs de Mode, "Federation Activities," Mode à Paris, http://www.modeaparis.com/va/toutsavoir/index.html.

61. Bernadine Morris, "Passport to Paris Fashion," *New York Times*, November 29, 1981.

62. For a discussion of Paris and its acceptance of the Japanese designers, as well as those from other foreign countries, see Yuniya Kawamura, *The Japanese Revolution in Paris Fashion* (Oxford: Berg Publishers, 2004).

63. Ibid., 44.

HAUTE COUTURE AND READY-TO-WEAR: A RECENT HISTORY

1. Archives, Chambre Syndicale de la Couture Parisienne, Paris.

2. Guillaume Garnier, *Paris-Couture années 30* (Paris: Musée de la Mode et du Costume, 1987).

3. Author interview with Max Heilbronn, June 26, 1991.

4. The term "jockey" was used in this context to designate an elegant woman, preferably titled, who had an eye for highlighting a given house's new designs and getting them maximum publicity. Among the most famous "jockeys" were Catherine Deneuve for Saint Laurent and Inès de la Fressange for Chanel.

5. Cf. Yvonne Deslandres, *Le Costume, image de l'homme* (Paris: Albin Michel, 1976), 263: "It is difficult to describe the stylist's job, which is different from the draper's. The modeliste's draper's task is to translate a design sketch onto a full-scale fabric prototype and to draw the pattern. The term *stylist*, moreover, designates not only a designer of garments but also an inventor of forms that can be used in every field of the so-called 'decorative arts,' and in every sphere of daily life."

6. Author interview with Ghislaine de Polignac, October 22, 1992.

7. Author interviews with Christiane Bailly, January 14, 1991, and Emmanuelle Khanh, June 9, 1991.

8. Hebe Dorsey had taken over for Eugenia Sheppard at the *Herald Tribune* that same year. She was succeeded by Suzy Menkes in 1988.

9. Author interview with Melka Treanton, Dorsey's former assistant, November 14, 1991.

10. As early as 1897, to protect himself against Viennese counterfeiters who were ransacking the fashion industry, Raudnitz, from the house of Raudnitz & Cie., met with several of his colleagues (including Jacques Doucet, Madeleine Cheruit, and Jeanne Lanvin) to agree on a common release date, to be set as late as possible.

11. Dior appointed Christian Legrez as his first director of licensing in 1952.

12. Hebe Dorsey, "Conclusion: Prêt-à-Porter v Couture," in Ruth Lynam, ed., *Couture: An Illustrated History of the Great Paris Designers and Their Creations* (Garden City, NY: Doubleday, 1972), 253.

13. Emma-Christie lasted for only two seasons.

14. "L'idée simple qui va démoder le luxe," *Elle*, May 24, 1971.

15. British *Vogue*, June 1971.

16. Didier Grumbach, *Histoires de la Mode* (Paris: Editions du Seuil, 1993), 221.

17. French *Vogue*, November 1973; *Women's Wear Daily*, March 4 and April 3, 1974; Hebe Dorsey, "The Fashion Adventure in Paris," *International Herald Tribune*, October 23, 1973.

18. The evening ended with a memorable outdoor celebration on the Place du Marché Saint-Honoré, which was pictured on the cover of *Women's Wear Daily*, September 26, 1975.

19. Open letter from Robert Ricci, Nina Ricci Parfums, to the company's clientele, January 12, 1972.

20. Felicity Green, "Left Bank Couture: Yves Saint Laurent," in Lynam, *Couture: An Illustrated History*, 237.

21. Claude Berthod, "Piere Cardin le solitaire," *Elle*, June 3, 1972, 6.

22. Grumbach, *Histoires*, 233.

23. Nina Hyde in the *Washington Post*, April 30, 1978.

24. *Japan Times*, November 23, 1978.
25. Karl Lagerfeld, France Andrevie, Claude Montana, Kenzo, Angelo Tarlazzi, Thierry Mugler, Issey Miyake, Marithé and François Girbaud, Jean Paul Gaultier, and Tan Giudicelli.
26. Its members were Françoise Montenay (Chanel), François Baufumé (Christian Dior), Patrick Thomas (Hermès), Didier Grumbach (Thierry Mugler), and Jacques Mouclier (Fédération president).
27. Minutes of the board of directors' meeting, La Fédération Française de la Couture, du Prêt-à-Porter des Couturiers et des Créateurs de Mode, October 1, 1996.
28. The possibility of once again grouping the two skills in a single demonstration will ultimately put an end to the highly perverse and irrational practice of having the couture and ready-to-wear collections handled by two different stylists. Indeed, couture that has no industrial constraints and no true commercial potential merely devalues the ready-to-wear line underwriting it.

AZZEDINE ALAÏA

1. Jean Nouvel, as quoted in Pamela Golbin, *Fashion Designers* (New York: Watson-Guptill, 2001), 21.
2. Susannah Frankel, *Visionaries: Interviews with Fashion Designers* (London: V&A Publications, 2001), 54.
3. Claire Wilcox, "Alaïa, Azzedine," in *Encyclopedia of Clothing and Fashion*, ed. Valerie Steele (Detroit: Thomson Gale, 2005), 1:33.
4. Cathy Horyn, "Who is the Modern Man? What Will He Wear?" *New York Times*, February 2, 2006.

HUSSEIN CHALAYAN

1. Bradley Quinn, "A Note: Hussein Chalayan, Fashion and Technology," *Fashion Theory* 6, no. 4 (December 2002): 359.
2. Hussein Chalayan, as quoted in Frankel, *Visionaries*, 70.
3. Hussein Chalayan, as quoted in Quinn, "A Note: Hussein Chalayan," 363.

4. Ibid., 362.
5. Ibid.

CHANEL

1. *Vogue*, October 1, 1926, 69.
2. Coco Chanel, as quoted in Melissa Richards, *Chanel: Key Collections* (New York: Welcome Rain Publishers, 2000), 81.

CHRISTIAN DIOR

1. Christian Dior, as quoted in Brigid Keenan, *Dior in Vogue* (London: Octopus Books, 1981), 18.
2. John Galliano, as quoted in Armand Limnander, "Christian Dior runway review," Style.com, July 7, 2001, http://www.style.com/fashionshows/collections/F2001CTR/review/CDIOR.

CHRISTIAN LACROIX

1. Christian Lacroix, *Pieces of a Pattern: Lacroix by Lacroix* (London: Thames and Hudson, 1992), 183.
2. Bernadine Morris, "For Lacroix, a Triumph; For Couture, a Future," *New York Times*, July 27, 1987.
3. Christian Lacroix, as quoted in Kevin Almond, "Lacroix, Christian," in *Contemporary Fashion*, ed. Richard Martin (New York: St. James Press, 1995), 303.
4. Lacroix, *Pieces of a Pattern*, 53.
5. Ibid., 129.
6. Sarah Mower, "Christian Lacroix runway review," Style.com, July 8, 2003, http://www.style.com/fashionshows/collections/F2003CTR/review/CLACROIX.

MAISON MARTIN MARGIELA

1. Maison Martin Margiela, as quoted in Frankel, *Visionaries*, 34.
2. Valerie Steele, "Margiela, Martin," in Martin, *Contemporary Fashion*, 344.
3. *Monographie 2: Maison Martin Margiela ligne*

4 (Epernay: *Encens* magazine, 2004), 46 (unpaginated).

ROCHAS

1. Quoted in Richard Martin, "Marcel Rochas," in Martin, *Contemporary Fashion*, 340.
2. Caroline Rennolds Milbank, *Couture: The Great Designers* (New York: Stewart, Tabori, and Chang, 1985), 222.
3. Ibid.
4. Ibid.
5. Melinda Watt, "Belgian Fashion," in Steele, *Encyclopedia of Clothing and Fashion*, 1:143.
6. Olivier Theyskens, as quoted in Horacio Silva, "Style: This Old House," *New York Times*, November 23, 2003.
7. Olivier Theyskens, as quoted in "Marcel Rochas," *History of Fashion and Costume*, http://www.designerhistory.com/historyofashion/rochas.html.
8. Ginia Bellafante, "The Frenchwoman in All Her Moods," *New York Times*, March 5, 2004.
9. Sarah Mower, "Rochas runway review," Style.com, March 1, 2006, http://www.style.com/fashionshows/collections/F2006RTW/review/ROCHAS.
10. Olivier Theyskens, as quoted in Veerle Windels, *Young Belgian Fashion Design* (Gent: Ludion, 2001), 115.

VALENTINO

1. Valentino, as quoted in Bernadine Morris, "Valentino's Spring Breezes, Givenchy's Bouquets," *New York Times*, January 26, 1990.
2. Valentino, as quoted in Marie Paule Pellé and Patrick Mauriès, *Valentino's Magic* (New York: Abbeville Press, 1998), 22.
3. Aurora Fiorentini, "Valentino," in Steele, *Encyclopedia of Clothing and Fashion*, 3:389.
4. Patricia Peterson, "Valentino's Collection is Enthusiastically Greeted," *New York Times*, July 23, 1964.
5. Valentino, as quoted in Pellé and Mauriès, *Valentino's Magic*, 56.
6. Valentino, as quoted in Frankel, *Visionaries*, 83–84.

VIKTOR & ROLF

1. Viktor Horsting, as quoted in Román Alonso and Lisa Eisner, "Double Dutch," *New York Times Magazine*, December 8, 2002.
2. Elein Fleiss, "Passive Violent Clothes," *Purple Prose* 7 (Autumn 1994): 73, reprinted in *E magazine: Viktor & Rolf par Viktor et Rolf* (Amsterdam: Artimo, 2003), 24.
3. *Elle*, September 2001, reprinted in *E magazine*, 210.
4. Rolf Snoeren, as quoted in British *Vogue*, August 2000, 95, reprinted in *E magazine*, 146.

YOHJI YAMAMOTO

1. Yohji Yamamoto, as quoted in Golbin, *Fashion Designers*, 209.
2. Sandy Black, *Knitwear in Fashion* (New York: Thames and Hudson, 2002), 92.
3. Patricia Mears, "Yamamoto," in Steele, *Encyclopedia of Clothing and Fashion*, 3:454.
4. Quoted in Caroline Cox, "Yamamoto, Yohji," in Martin, *Contemporary Fashion*, 552.
5. Stephen Gan, *Visionaires: Fashion 2001* (New York: Rizzoli, 1999), 124.
6. Ibid.
7. Yohji Yamamoto, as quoted in Nicole Phelps, "Yohji Yamamoto runway review," Style.com, October 2, 2005, http://www.style.com/fashionshows/collections/S2006RTW/review/YJIYMOTO.
8. Ibid.

Suggested Readings

Baudot, François. *Alaïa*. New York: Universe, 1997.

———. *Chanel*. New York: Universe, 1996.

———. *Christian Lacroix*. New York: Universe, 1997.

———. *Fashion: The Twentieth Century*. New York: Universe, 1999.

Black, Sandy. *Knitwear in Fashion*. New York: Thames and Hudson, 2002.

Crowston, Clare Haru. *Fabricating Women: The Seamstresses of Old Regime France, 1675–1791*. Durham: Duke University Press, 2001.

de la Haye, Amy, and Shelly Tobin. *Chanel: The Couturiere at Work*. London: Victoria and Albert Museum, 1994.

de Marly, Diana. *Louis XIV and Versailles*. New York: Holmes and Meier, 1987.

E magazine: Viktor & Rolf par Viktor et Rolf. Amsterdam: Artimo, 2003.

Evans, Caroline, et al. *Hussein Chalayan*. Rotterdam: NAI Publishers, 2005.

Fox, Robert, and Anthony Turner, eds. *Luxury Trades and Consumerism in Ancien Régime Paris*. Aldershot, UK: Ashgate, 1998.

Frankel, Susannah. *Visionaries: Interviews with Fashion Designers*. London: V&A Publications, 2001.

Golbin, Pamela. *Fashion Designers*. New York: Watson-Guptill, 2001.

Grumbach, Didier. *Histoires de la Mode*. Paris: Editions du Seuil, 1993.

Hay, Susan, ed. *From Paris to Providence: Fashion, Art, and the Tirocchi Dressmakers' Shop, 1915–1947*. Providence: Museum of Art, Rhode Island School of Design, 2000.

Horsting, Viktor, and Rolf Snoeren. *Viktor & Rolf*. Amsterdam: Artimo, 2000.

Kawamura, Yuniya. *The Japanese Revolution in Paris Fashion*. Oxford: Berg, 2004.

Keenan, Brigid. *Dior in Vogue*. London: Octopus Books, 1981.

Koda, Harold. *Extreme Beauty: The Body Transformed*. New York: Metropolitan Museum of Art, 2001.

Koda, Harold, and Andrew Bolton. *Chanel*. New York: Metropolitan Museum of Art, 2005.

Lacroix, Christian. *Pieces of a Pattern: Lacroix by Lacroix*. London: Thames and Hudson, 1992.

Maison Martin Margiela. *Maison Martin Margiela Street Special Edition Volumes 1 and 2*. Tokyo: *Street* Magazine, 1999.

Martin, Richard, ed. *Contemporary Fashion*. New York: St. James Press, 1995.

———. *The St. James Fashion Encyclopedia: A Survey of Style from 1945 to the Present*. Detroit: Visible Ink Press, 1997.

Martin, Richard, and Harold Koda. *Christian Dior*. New York: Metropolitan Museum of Art, 1996.

McDowell, Colin. *Galliano*. London: Weidenfeld and Nicolson, 1997.

Mohrt, Françoise. *Marcel Rochas: 30 ans d'Elégance et Créations, 1925–1955*. Paris: J. Damase, 1983.

Monographie 2: Maison Martin Margiela ligne 4. Epernay: *Encens* magazine, 2004.

Morris, Bernardine. *Valentino*. New York: Universe, 1996.

Palais Galliera. Musée de la Mode et du Costume. *Au paradis des dames: Nouveautés, modes et confections 1810–1870*. Paris: Paris-Musées, 1992.

———. *Le dessin sous toutes ses coutures: Croquis, illustrations, modèles, 1760–1994*. Paris: Paris-Musées, 1995.

Palmer, Alexandra. *Couture and Commerce: The Transatlantic Fashion Trade in the 1950s*. Vancouver: University of British Columbia Press, in association with the Royal Ontario Museum, 2001.

Pelle, Marie Paule, and Patrick Mauriès. *Valentino's Magic*. New York: Abbeville Press, 1998.

Richards, Melissa. *Chanel: Key Collections*. New York: Welcome Rain Publishers, 2000.

Roche, Daniel. *The Culture of Clothing: Dress and Fashion in the Ancien Regime*. Translated by Jean Birrell. Cambridge: Cambridge University Press, 1996.

Roger-Milès, L. *Les Créateurs de la Mode*. Paris: Ch. Eggimann, 1910.

Seeling, Charlotte. *Fashion: The Century of the Designer, 1900–1999*. Cologne: Könemann, 2000.

Sozzani, Franca. *Valentino*. New York: Rizzoli, 2001.

Steele, Valerie, ed. *Encyclopedia of Clothing and Fashion*. 3 vols. Detroit: Thomson Gale, 2005.

Worth, Jean-Phillipe. *A Century of Fashion*. Boston: Little, Brown, 1928.

Yohji Yamamoto "Rewind/Forward": 238 Fashion Pictures, 1995–2000. Paris: Yohji Yamamoto, 2001.

Acknowledgments

Initiating an exhibition exploring contemporary Paris fashion entails taking a blind leap of faith. The process of choosing the houses and securing their participation, all before the clothing to be exhibited was actually designed, produced quite a bit of anxiety. I am grateful to the MFA's director Malcolm Rogers and the Museum's exhibition team for believing in the concept and encouraging us to proceed with the show. I also thank Didier Grumbach, president of the Fédération Française de la Couture, du Prêt-à-Porter des Couturiers et des Créateurs de Mode, for backing the project from the very beginning and for participating in countless ways. His influence with and support of the designers now showing in Paris contributed greatly to our success in enlisting the participation of such notable houses. I am also grateful to his assistant, Chantal Beauvois.

Above all, however, we could not have published this book or produced the accompanying exhibition without the collaboration of the ten houses that agreed to work with us on this project: Azzedine Alaïa, Hussein Chalayan, Chanel Haute Couture, Christian Dior Haute Couture, Christian Lacroix Haute Couture, Maison Martin Margiela, Rochas, Valentino Haute Couture, Viktor & Rolf, and Yohji Yamamoto. We are extremely grateful to the designers of these houses — Azzedine Alaïa, Hussein Chalayan, Karl Lagerfeld, John Galliano, Christian Lacroix, Martin Margiela, Olivier Theyskens, Valentino, Viktor Horsting, Rolf Snoeren, and Yohji Yamamoto — for sharing their work with us. Each designer has consistently shown beautifully designed and crafted clothing that has broadened our ideas regarding fashion's role in contemporary society. We are honored to have had the chance to work with ten of the finest fashion houses in the world.

Meeting and working with the representatives from each house has been one of the greatest pleasures and privileges of this project. I am grateful to them for their help with tasks too numerous to detail here. I would like to thank Caroline Fabre-Bazin, of Azzedine Alaïa; Milly Patrzalek and Leila Burstow, of Hussein Chalayan; Marika Genty, Cécile Godet-Dirles, and Arlette Thibeault, of Chanel; Philippe Le Moult, Soïzic Pfaff, and Alexandre Saunal, of Christian Dior; Elisabeth Bonnel and Bérengère Broman, of Christian Lacroix; Patrick Scallon, Emilie Thang, and Emanuela Pipan, of Maison Martin Margiela; Nicolas Frontière, of Rochas; Graziano de Boni, Carlos Souza, Olivia Eslami, and Jeannie Kim, of Valentino; Bram Claassen and Willemijn Sluijs, of Viktor & Rolf; and Coralie Gauthier and Carla Wachtveitl, of Yohji Yamamoto.

Several photographers have generously permitted us to use their work to illustrate this book, notably Anuschka Blommers and Niels Schumm, Nick Knight, Simon Procter, and Peter Stigter. Jun Kanai and Masako Omori, both of Issey Miyake Design Studio, provided the wonderful image of Issey Miyake's work from 1977. I am also grateful to the MFA's Photo Studios — especially Damon Beale, Michael Gould, Greg Heins, David Mathews, and John Woolf — for their outstanding photography of the objects in the Museum's collection.

The fashion industry's calendar moves at a different pace than that of a museum. While museum exhibitions might take seven to ten years from concept to installation, fashion designers show four to six collections a year, and trends evolve at a dizzying speed. Resetting our museum clocks to respond to fashion's frenzied pace has been a challenge for everyone, particularly in the publication of this book, for which writing deadlines actually occurred before the Fall–Winter 2006–7 ready-to-wear collections had even been shown. Susan Ward and Lauren Whitley, with contributions by Hillary Kidd, wrote the insightful house profiles on a very tight schedule, and Hillary Kidd, Susan Ward, and Alexandra Bennett Huff extended heroic efforts to gather together the photography. I thank Terry McAweeney, Mark Polizzotti, and Sarah McGaughey Tremblay, in MFA Publications, for their hard work and dedication in producing a book that matches the high standards set by the designers on the runway and provides a historical context for the exhibition. I would also like to acknowledge Susan Marsh, whose brilliant design has brought the past and present together in such a modern and beautiful way.

While this book is not, strictly speaking, a catalogue of the exhibition, I must recognize those from the MFA who have lent their talent, enthusiasm, and energy to the exhibition itself, including Jennifer Bose, former Director of Exhibitions and Design; Erika Field, Corporate Relations Manager; Kim French, Deputy Director, Communications; Katie Getchell, Deputy Director, Curatorial; Kelly Gifford, Public Relations Manager; Dawn Griffin, Director of Public Relations and Communications Strategy; Claudia Iannuccilli, Associate Conservator, Textiles; Paige Johnston, Exhibitions and Design Coordinator; Jill Kennedy-Kernohan, Registrar for Exhibitions; Lisa Krassner, Director of Member and Visitor Services; Jennifer Liston Munson, Exhibition Graphics Designer; Barbara Martin, Associate Director for Public Learning; Bill McAvoy, Director of Institutional Support; Patrick McMahon, Director of Exhibitions and Design; Meredith Montague, Head of Textile Conservation; Janet O'Donoghue, Director of Creative Service; Jaime Roark, Exhibition Designer; Lois Solomon, Manager of Adult Learning Programs; Joel Thompson, Assistant Conservator, Textiles; Tomoko Tomimaru, Exhibition Designer; John Vaporis, Manager, Media Services; and Benjamin Weiss, Manager of Adult Learning Resources.

In addition, I extend my gratitude to colleagues and friends outside the MFA who have given advice and support throughout this project, particularly Titi Halle; Mme Marie-Andrée Jouve; Harold Koda, Curator, Costume Institute, Metropolitan Museum of Art; Russell Nardozza, Geoffrey Beene, Inc.; Alexandra Palmer, Nora E. Vaughan Fashion Costume Curator, Royal Ontario Museum; Chris Paulocik, Conservator, Costume Institute, Metropolitan Museum of Art; and Françoise Tétart-Vittu, Curator, Musée de la Mode et du Costume. Finally, I would like to thank my husband, William Van Siclen, for the support, love, and understanding he has shown me throughout this exciting, but intense, project.

PAMELA A. PARMAL
David and Roberta Logie Curator
of Textile and Fashion Arts

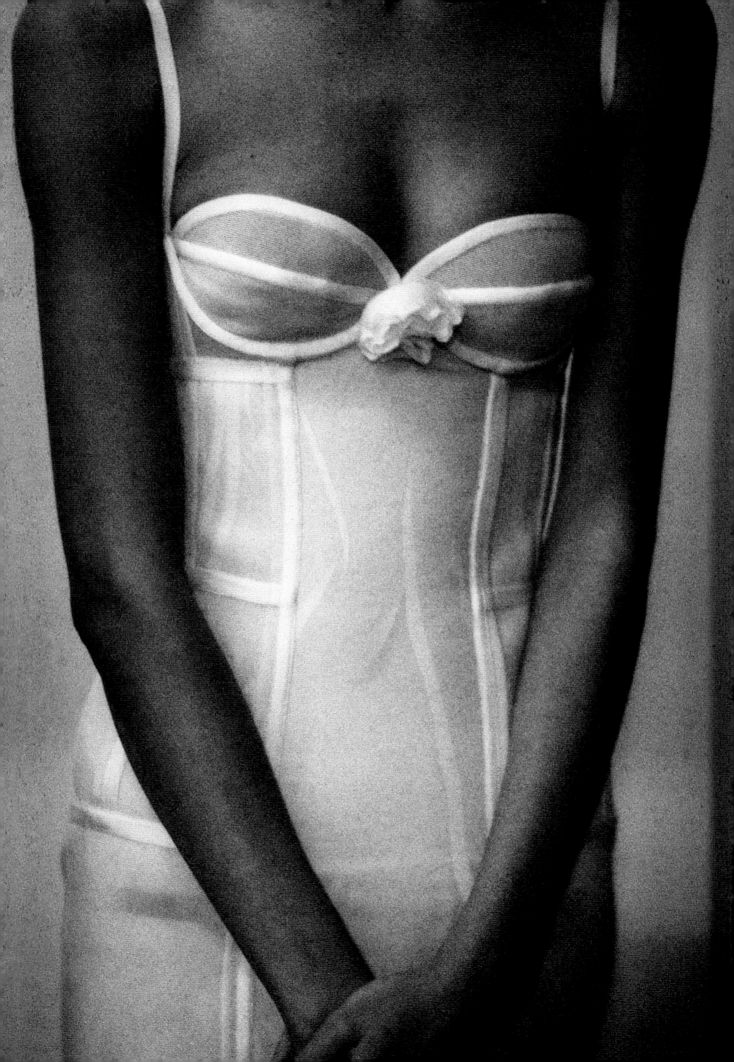

List of Illustrations

p. 178: Valentino, Spring–Summer 1969 haute couture. Photo courtesy of Valentino Haute Couture Archives

p. 179: Valentino, Spring–Summer 1968 haute couture. Photo courtesy of Valentino Haute Couture Archives

p. 180: Valentino, Spring–Summer 1967 haute couture. Photo by Henry Clarke © Condé Nast Archive / CORBIS

p. 182: Valentino, Spring–Summer 1982 haute couture. Photo © Vittoriano Rastelli / CORBIS

p. 183: Valentino, Spring–Summer 1981 haute couture. Photo courtesy of Valentino Haute Couture archives

p. 184: Valentino, Spring–Summer 1992 ready-to-wear. Photo © Julio Donoso / CORBIS SYGMA

p. 185: Valentino, Spring–Summer 2006 haute couture. Photo courtesy of Valentino Haute Couture Archives

p. 186: Viktor & Rolf, Fall–Winter 2006–7 collection. Photo © Peter Stigter

p. 188: Viktor & Rolf, Spring–Summer 2003 collection. Photo © Anuschka Blommers / Niels Schumm

p. 189: Viktor & Rolf, Fall–Winter 2003–4 collection. Photo © Peter Stigter

p. 190: Viktor & Rolf, Spring–Summer 2002 collection. Photo © Peter Stigter

p. 192: Viktor & Rolf, Fall–Winter 2000–2001 collection. Photo © Anuschka Blommers / Niels Schumm

p. 193: Viktor & Rolf, Fall–Winter 2001–2 *Black Hole* collection. Photo © Peter Stigter

p. 195: Viktor & Rolf, Fall–Winter 2002–3 *Long Live the Immaterial* collection. Photo by Pierre Verdy / AFP / Getty Images

p. 196: Yohji Yamamoto, Fall–Winter 2006–7 collection. Photo © Monica Feudi, courtesy of Yohji Yamamoto

p. 198: Yohji Yamamoto, Fall–Winter 1988–89 collection. Photo © Nick Knight, courtesy of Yohji Yamamoto

p. 200: Yohji Yamamoto, Fall–Winter 1998–99 collection. Photo © Monica Feudi, courtesy of Yohji Yamamoto

p. 201: Yohji Yamamoto, Fall–Winter 1986–87 collection. Photo © Nick Knight, courtesy of Yohji Yamamoto

p. 202: Yohji Yamamoto, Spring–Summer 2006 collection. Photo © Monica Feudi, courtesy of Yohji Yamamoto

p. 203: Yohji Yamamoto, Spring–Summer 1999 *Juste des vêtements* exhibition, Musée de la Mode et du Textile, Paris. Photo © Gael Amzalag, courtesy of Yohji Yamamoto

p. 205: Yohji Yamamoto, Fall–Winter 2006–7 collection. Photo © Monica Feudi, courtesy of Yohji Yamamoto

p. 206: Olivier Theyskens for Rochas, Backstage Fall–Winter 2005–6. Photo © Ali Mahdavi

p. 216: Olivier Theyskens for Rochas, Backstage Fall–Winter 2004–5. Photo © Ali Mahdavi

pp. 222–23: Detail of plate on p. 45

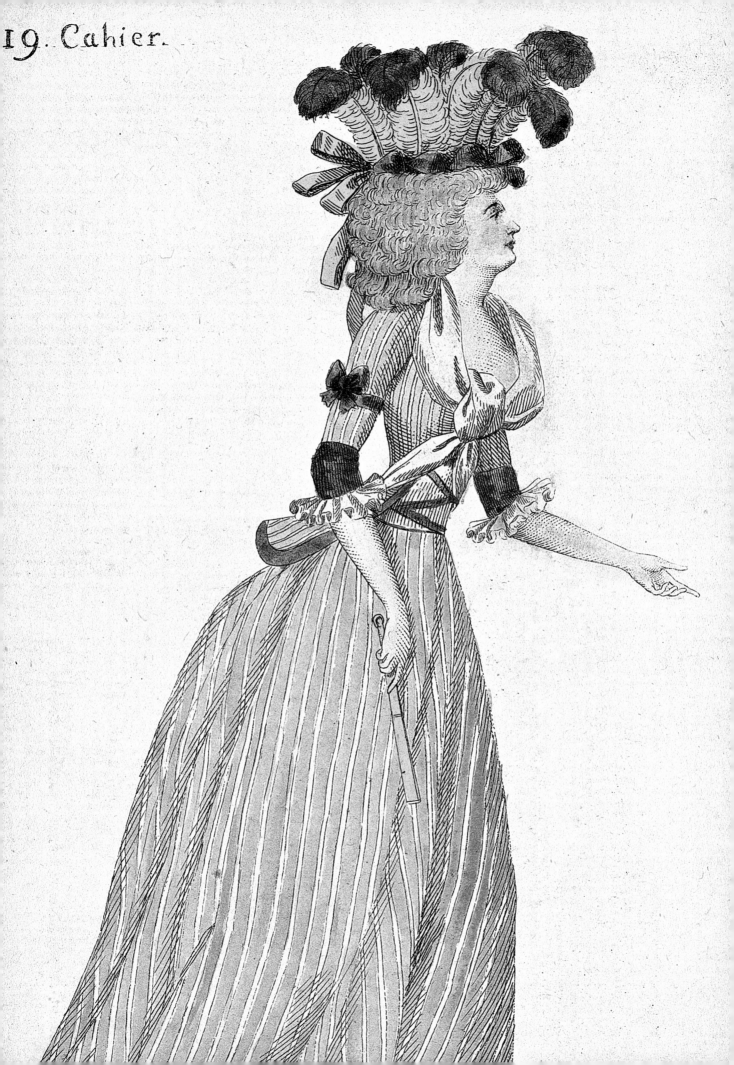

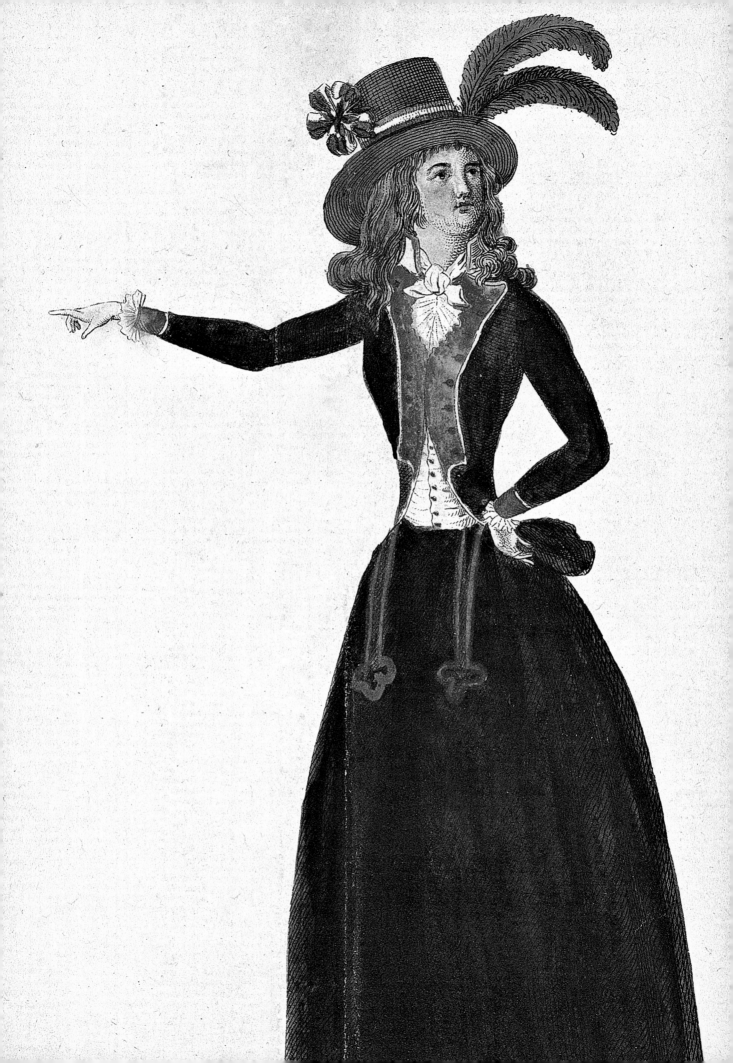

MFA Publications
a division of the Museum of Fine Arts, Boston
465 Huntington Avenue
Boston, Massachusetts 02115
www.mfa-publications.org

This book was published in conjunction with the exhibition "Fashion Show: Paris Collections 2006,"
organized by the Museum of Fine Arts, Boston, from November 12, 2006, to March 18, 2007.
The exhibition is sponsored by State Street Global Advisors.

STATE STREET GLOBAL ADVISORS | SS&A.

For a complete listing of MFA Publications, please contact the publisher at the above address,
or call 617 369 3438.

Cover: *Un Ange Passe*, Paris 2004, photo by Simon Procter
Additional photo credits are noted in the List of Illustrations.

Edited by Sarah McGaughey Tremblay and Mark Polizzotti
"Haute Couture and Ready-to-Wear" translated from the French by Mark Polizzotti
Produced by Theresa McAweeney
Designed by Susan Marsh
Printed and bound at Graphicom, Verona, Italy

Trade distribution:
Distributed Art Publishers / D.A.P.
155 Sixth Avenue, 2nd floor, New York, New York 10013
Tel. 212 627 1999 Fax 212 627 9484

FIRST EDITION

Printed in Italy
This book was printed on acid-free paper.